What Research Has to Say About Vocabulary Instruction

Alan E. Farstrup   S. Jay Samuels

Editors

INTERNATIONAL
Reading Association
800 BARKSDALE ROAD, PO BOX 8139
NEWARK, DE 19714-8139, USA
www.reading.org

The International Reading Association attempts, through its publications, to provide a forum for a wide spectrum of opinions on reading. This policy permits divergent viewpoints without implying the endorsement of the Association.

Executive Editor, Books   Corinne M. Mooney
Developmental Editor   Charlene M. Nichols
Developmental Editor   Tori Mello Bachman
Developmental Editor   Stacey Lynn Sharp
Editorial Production Manager   Shannon T. Fortner
Design and Composition Manager   Anette Schuetz
Project Editors   Tori Mello Bachman and Wesley Ford

Cover   Design, Linda Steere; Photograph, © iStockphoto.com/blackred

Library of Congress Cataloging-in-Publication Data
What research has to say about vocabulary instruction / Alan E. Farstrup, S. Jay Samuels, editors. -- 1st ed.
    p. cm.
Includes index.
ISBN 978-0-87207-698-3
1. English language--Grammar--Study and teaching (Elementary) 2. English language--Grammar--Study and teaching (Secondary) I. Farstrup, Alan E. II. Samuels, S. Jay.
LB1631.W376 2008
372.6'044--dc22
                                                                                    2008028566

Table of Contents

Note From the Editors

Promoting the acquisition of a broad and deep vocabulary has been a concern and a priority of educators and reading specialists for many years. The publication of the National Institute of Child Health and Human Development's *Report of the National Reading Panel, Teaching Children to Read* in April of 2000 sparked renewed and strong interest in this topic. Vocabulary instruction was examined among other key topics that included phonemic awareness, phonics, fluency, and comprehension. Significantly, the review of research related to vocabulary instruction was embedded within the broader topic of reading comprehension in the panel's report. Vocabulary was and is clearly understood to be a critical aspect of reading and language comprehension and of the overall and very complex process of reading for understanding and critical thinking.

In the International Reading Association's (IRA) highly successful volume *What Research Has to Say About Reading Instruction* (Farstrup & Samuels, 2000), vocabulary was addressed from a variety of developmental and instructional perspectives illustrating how deeply embedded it is within and throughout all aspects of the reading and learning-to-read processes. In IRA's *What Research Has to Say About Fluency Instruction* (Samuels & Farstrup, 2006), the topic of vocabulary development also appeared prominently and was cited as a crucial prerequisite element for the attainment of true reading fluency. Given this indication of the importance of vocabulary instruction, it is appropriate to devote a new book in this series to the topic.

In framing the content of this volume, we sought to address vocabulary instruction as it is informed by both solid research and classroom experience. We did not wish to take a formulaic approach that simply laid out past instructional tactics and outlines but rather to tap the combined wisdom of a wide range of researchers and practitioners to provide a rich variety of approaches and ideas. We also strongly believe that vocabulary instruction has relevance in a variety of situations and that there are multiple proven approaches available to teachers from which choices can be made that are appropriate to the contexts and needs of different students. Teachers need and deserve much more than narrowly scripted, inflexible instructional approaches or tactics. They need to be well informed about underlying theories and research evidence that forms a basis for effective instruction and that offers them alternatives to meet individual needs.

We asked our chapter authors to take such factors into account when composing their manuscripts for this book. We strongly believe that informed and well-prepared teachers, when presented with evidence-based approaches and alternatives, can and will make good decisions and choices that lead to appropriate, logical, and effective instruction in their classrooms. It has been our clear purpose here, as has been the case in our previous volumes, to gather leading scholars and practitioners so they can provide educators with the best possible information and insights that will help them to promote effective vocabulary development by using well-researched instruction in their classrooms.

Readers will find chapters in this book that deal with vocabulary development for content area instruction, strategies for fostering incidental word learning through word play, guidelines for teaching vocabulary in the middle grades, instruction appropriate for second-language learners, word-study strategies, and much more. We asked our authors to cite relevant research and also to provide specific instructional suggestions and alternatives based on their research and their experience. Readers will find that different chapters and authors take different perspectives on vocabulary instruction and that they don't always agree. This is what happens when strong scholars and practitioners are gathered to bring varying experiences and points of view to bear on the topic of vocabulary instruction.

We believe readers of this volume will gain new insights as they ponder the differing views and suggestions. Just as in the fields of medicine or engineering, opinions and research interpretations in education differ, as do the students we serve. By providing well-considered opinions and perspectives from our authors, we are confident readers are fully capable of drawing their own conclusions, making the best possible uses of the valuable information throughout this book.

Helping students in our schools gain strong oral and reading vocabularies is more important than ever. We believe that a strong and growing vocabulary is essential for overall reading success, so our primary audience for the book is classroom teachers and those who are being prepared to be teachers. Teacher educators will also find valuable information that will be useful in their work. Each chapter concludes with questions for discussion in the hope and expectation that they will provoke continued dialogue leading to further insights and reflection about the topic of vocabulary instruction. We hope that this book proves both stimulating and useful and that it sparks a deeper understanding of a wide range of practices that support good vocabulary instruction and of the research and theory that undergirds it.

AEF, SJS

REFERENCES

Farstrup, A.E., & Samuels, S.J. (Eds.). (2002). *What research has to say about reading instruction* (3rd ed.). Newark, DE: International Reading Association.

National Institute of Child Health and Human Development. (2000). *Report of the National Reading Panel. Teaching children to read: An evidence-based assessment of the scientific research literature on reading and its implications for reading instruction* (NIH Publication No. 00-4769). Washington, DC: U.S. Government Printing Office.

Samuels, S.J., & Farstrup, A.E. (Eds.). (2006). *What research has to say about fluency instruction*. Newark, DE: International Reading Association.

About the Editors

Alan E. Farstrup

 Alan E. Farstrup is Executive Director of the International Reading Association (IRA) in Newark, Delaware. He completed his Bachelor of Arts degree at the University of Iowa in 1965, earned his teaching credential from the University of California at Berkeley in 1967, and received his PhD in Reading Curriculum and Instruction from the University of Minnesota in 1977.

Alan has been a junior high reading and English teacher and a member of reading education faculties of the University of Texas at San Antonio and the University of Rhode Island. He has served as a reading specialist and consultant. He directed the Institute of Human Science and Services at Rhode Island. He was also a U.S. Peace Corps volunteer in Afghanistan in 1965 and 1966.

Alan was IRA's director of research before assuming the post of Executive Director in 1992. His responsibilities include administrative leadership, supporting the IRA Board of Directors, and representing the Association on issues of reading research, policy, and classroom practice. He is a member of the United Nations Educational, Scientific, and Cultural Organization's International Literacy Prize Jury; has extensive experience in the development of educational standards and assessments; and is IRA liaison to numerous organizations and agencies worldwide.

Alan is coeditor with S. Jay Samuels of *What Research Has to Say About Reading Instruction* (Second and Third Editions) and *What Research Has to Say About Fluency Instruction*.

S. Jay Samuels

S. Jay Samuels started teaching elementary school shortly after the end of World War II. At that time, the schools were crowded and teachers were in short supply. Los Angeles needed teachers, so recruiters came to the New York area. Jay took a job offered by a recruiter because he knew that Muscle Beach, the Mecca for bodybuilding, would be conveniently located to where he would be teaching. He entered the University of California, Los Angeles, doctoral program, where he received a doctorate in educational psychology.

Jay later joined the Educational Psychology Department at the University of Minnesota and has been there for over 40 years. Through Psychology Professor David LaBerge, Jay developed an interest in reading fluency. At the university, Jay received a Distinguished Teaching Award for his large teacher training lecture class on learning, cognition, and assessment. The National Reading Conference and the International Reading Association also have recognized Jay with research awards for reading. Jay was inducted into the Reading Hall of Fame in 1990. Jay is also a member of the National Reading Panel.

Jay met Alan Farstrup when Alan was a doctoral student at the University of Minnesota. Over the years Alan and Jay have worked together to produce books that they trust will provide teachers with the latest in research and pedagogy from the leaders in the reading field.

Contributors

Camille L.Z. Blachowicz
National-Louis University
Chicago, Illinois, USA

Marco A. Bravo
Santa Clara University
Santa Clara, California, USA

Gina N. Cervetti
University of California, Berkeley
Berkeley, California, USA

Peter Fisher
National-Louis University
Chicago, Illinois, USA

Susan Leigh Flinspach
University of California,
    Santa Cruz
Santa Cruz, California, USA

Michael F. Graves
University of Minnesota
Minneapolis, Minnesota, USA

Janis M. Harmon
University of Texas at San Antonio
San Antonio, Texas, USA

Wanda B. Hedrick
University of North Florida
Jacksonville, Florida, USA

Lori Helman
University of Minnesota
Minneapolis, Minnesota, USA

Elfrieda H. Hiebert
University of California, Berkeley
Berkeley, California, USA

Shira Lubliner
California State University,
    East Bay
Haywood, California, USA

Anthony V. Manzo
University of Missouri,
    Kansas City
Kansas City, Missouri, USA

Ula C. Manzo
California State University,
    Fullerton
Fullerton, California, USA

William E. Nagy
Seattle Pacific University
Seattle, Washington, USA

Evangeline Newton
University of Akron
Akron, Ohio, USA

Rick M. Newton
Kent State University
Kent, Ohio, USA

Nancy Padak
University of Akron
Akron, Ohio, USA

Timothy Rasinski
Kent State University
Kent, Ohio, USA

Judith A. Scott
University of California,
   Santa Cruz
Santa Cruz, California, USA

Karen D. Wood
University of North Carolina
   at Charlotte
Charlotte, North Carolina, USA

Introduction

Vocabulary Instruction: A Critical Component for Skillful Reading

Alan E. Farstrup and S. Jay Samuels

A rapidly expanding vocabulary is a signal feature in the development of oral language in young children. It is a critical factor in the advancement of powerful reading and critical thinking abilities among adolescents, young adults, and adults. In short, a strong and continually growing oral and reading vocabulary is a fundamental component for the development and expansion of reading ability and sophistication at all levels. This volume, *What Research Has to Say About Vocabulary Instruction*, details the theory and research underlying vocabulary development and effective instruction while providing valuable and practical instructional guidance. It addresses the importance of a solid and growing vocabulary for expanding reading success in the total and complex context of the full extent of reading and learning processes.

We have asked our chapter authors to provide their insights into effective vocabulary instruction from a variety of perspectives. We have deliberately structured this volume for the purpose of providing a range of credible research perspectives and a broad sampling of instructional strategies. The extent of topics addressed is wide, encompassing, for example, word derivations, direct and incidental strategies for vocabulary learning, academic settings and vocabularies, subject-specific vocabularies, vocabulary building in middle and secondary school classrooms, and the power and potential of a growing vocabulary for second-language learners.

This book is aimed at an audience of teachers and of students preparing to become teachers. It is also intended to be a useful resource for teacher educators, reading specialists, and literacy coaches who can use this volume not only in preparatory college and university courses but also in the context of professional development programs and workshops at the school district and building levels. National, state, and provincial leaders and officials will also find the information and insights included here to be helpful both in setting policy and in providing support for

What Research Has to Say About Vocabulary Instruction, edited by Alan E. Farstrup and S. Jay Samuels.
© 2008 by the International Reading Association.

ongoing professional development programs. The need is great as is the important recognition that vocabulary building is an essential element in the complex process of building excellence in reading for the students and communities we all serve.

Nancy Padak, Evangeline Newton, Timothy Rasinski, and Rick M. Newton address the traditional and very important topic of word study and etymology in their chapter, "Getting to the Root of Word Study: Teaching Latin and Greek Word Roots in Elementary and Middle Grades." Here they take into account that more than half of all words in the English language have their origins in Latin or Greek roots, and they provide an approach based on the meanings of these roots by which students can learn words of high semantic utility and strategies that expand their awareness and understanding of how these words function in the English language. Concrete suggestions and alternatives for instruction are provided.

In "Attentional Vocabulary Instruction: Read-Alouds, Word Play, and Other Motivating Strategies for Fostering Informal Word Learning," authors Camille L.Z. Blachowicz and Peter Fisher explore and explain a variety of research- and experience-based approaches to vocabulary learning where teachers set up rich literacy environments that motivate students to explore and learn new words and meanings informally while at the same time functioning in a formal teaching and learning context. The authors set forth research bases for two specific ways of fostering informal vocabulary learning, and they give detailed guidance for implementing them in the classroom.

There is no single, most effective method of teaching reading or vocabulary. Research findings are important: They can and should be used to provide insight and direction. Good teachers use a variety of proven approaches chosen based on the specific needs of their students. Michael F. Graves explicates his views on vocabulary instruction in light of these important realities in his chapter, "Instruction on Individual Words: One Size Does Not Fit All." Graves explores the importance, extent, and complexity of vocabulary instruction and describes several multifaceted, research-based programs of vocabulary instruction. A variety of approaches and procedures are presented for teachers to consider and adapt to their own classroom situations.

Ula C. Manzo and Anthony V. Manzo designed their chapter, "Teaching Vocabulary-Learning Strategies: Word Consciousness, Word Connection, and Word Prediction," to be very practically oriented to the needs and concerns of classroom teachers. This chapter suggests three important types of strategies for vocabulary instruction and situates them in the context of what we know about language acquisition with a strong focus on the efficiencies that can be gained by directly teaching these strategies. The three main components—word consciousness, intentional teaching of selected words, and word analysis for meaning—and how to implement them in the classroom are described in detail.

"The Nature, Learning, and Instruction of General Academic Vocabulary," a chapter authored by Elfrieda H. Hiebert and Shira Lubliner, addresses the reality that many students have difficulty functioning in a formally academic setting. School texts often use a particular type of vocabulary and syntax referred to here as academic language. Students need to learn how to recognize and deal with the special academic language found in most school textbooks. This is especially true for content-specific subject matter in which the expository language used is much more complex and formal than everyday English. This important chapter sets forth both examples of academic language and specific instructional suggestions for helping students to understand and use general academic vocabulary effectively.

Marco A. Bravo and Gina N. Cervetti take on the subject of content area vocabulary instruction in their chapter, "Teaching Vocabulary Through Text and Experience in Content Areas." They too recognize that the more formal and specialized vocabulary found in content areas such as science, social studies, history, or mathematics presents unique and different challenges to students accustomed to less formal and vernacular uses of language. This chapter explores the links between word knowledge and comprehension of complicated content area materials. It provides a solid review of relevant research as well as a rich variety of instructional suggestions aimed at providing high quality content area vocabulary instruction.

Content area vocabulary instruction is also the focus of the chapter "Vocabulary Instruction in Middle and Secondary Content Classrooms: Understandings and Direction From Research," authored by Janis M. Harmon, Karen D. Wood, and Wanda B. Hedrick. While recognizing the importance of prior knowledge and experience within specific content areas, the authors deal with the importance of issues such as knowledge of specialized grammar and of less familiar language structures encountered by students in the much more formal contexts of content area reading materials. In this chapter Harmon, Wood, and Hedrick express their goal of having students able to "read like a scientist or a mathematician or a historian" as they gain independent skill in reading specialized content texts. They cite relevant research and describe evidence-based instructional strategies that will be useful in content area classrooms.

Schools and classrooms are increasingly diverse in their composition. They bring together students from many cultural, ethnic, national, and linguistics backgrounds. In "More Than Merely Words: Redefining Vocabulary Learning in a Culturally and Linguistically Diverse Society," Judith A. Scott, William E. Nagy, and Susan Leigh Flinspach address the importance and complexity of providing appropriate yet challenging vocabulary instruction in schools and classrooms in which diversity of linguistic experience and skill are hallmarks. They review an extensive research literature to support their contention that the challenges faced in classrooms of diversity are too great for educators to limit themselves to single or narrow methodologies. The chapter sets forth sociological theory as well as cognitive and linguistic understandings to buttress the argument that a multiplicity of approaches is essential if we are to meet the needs of these students. In making their case for a balanced approach, the authors detail a number of very practical instructional techniques.

"English Words Needed: Creating Research-Based Vocabulary Instruction for English Learners," by Lori Helman, provides additional insights and guidance for teachers working with English learners. Large numbers of students come to school with a home oral language other than English, and teachers need advice and concrete suggestions for effective teaching practices so they can meet the needs of these learners. The needs are extensive: In 2008 it was estimated that nearly 10 million young people came from a home language environment other than English and that, of those struggling with the English language, nearly three-quarters spoke Spanish as a primary language. Helman underlines the importance of oral language ability as a critical basis for success in the use of English, especially in grasping word meanings and using academic language more effectively. Several instructional techniques and strategies are described and discussed, and the need for additional research in this area is emphasized.

Questions for Discussion are included in each chapter. These questions are intended to spark lively debate and reflection about the information and ideas presented by this collection of experienced and insightful authors. Readers of *What Research Has to Say About Vocabulary Instruction* will experience a variety of perspectives on how best to promote rich and growing vocabularies. The needs of students in many different settings are addressed. There is a strong emphasis on the role of oral language development and its links to vocabulary growth and overall reading success. Vocabulary instruction is situated as but one important element of many comprising the overall learning-to-read process. The importance of having access to and using multiple proven approaches and techniques according to the specific needs of individuals and groups is a feature common to all of the chapters presented in this volume. The research and instructional techniques presented in this volume are intended to be useful to educators in a variety of settings and are not limited to a North American context. We believe the information in this book has international utility and look forward to its widespread consideration and use.

SUGGESTED READING

Farstrup, A.E., & Samuels, S.J. (Eds.). (2002). *What research has to say about reading instruction* (3rd ed.). Newark, DE: International Reading Association.

Graves, M.F. (2006). *The vocabulary book: Learning and instruction.* New York: Teachers College Press.

National Institute of Child Health and Human Development. (2000). *Report of the National Reading Panel. Teaching children to read: An evidence-based assessment of the scientific research literature on reading and its implications for reading instruction. Reports of the subgroups.* Washington, DC: U.S. Government Printing Office. Retrieved June 16, 2008, from www.nichd.nih.gov/publications/nrp/upload/report_pdf.pdf

Chapter 1

Getting to the Root of Word Study: Teaching Latin and Greek Word Roots in Elementary and Middle Grades

Nancy Padak, Evangeline Newton, Timothy Rasinski, and Rick M. Newton

Each Monday morning, Joanna Newton introduces her grade 2 students to a new word root. After a short discussion about the root, she tapes a sheet of butcher block paper to a counter, writes the root at the top, and places a bowl of markers next to it. Her students spend the next few days on the lookout for words that use the root. They know words from the root can appear when they read, listen, or talk to each other. They also know how to explore for new words in dictionaries and on the Internet. Each time they discover a word that fits, Joanna's students write it on the chart paper, always initialing the entry. On Friday morning, Joanna's class assembles to review the collected words. Each student explains where he or she found the word, what it means, and how the root "gives you a clue." Classmates listen carefully to these explanations, because they must decide whether the word is "real" or if they need more information to make sure.

This week the root is *tri-*. After *triplets* and *tripod*, one student, Niko (all names are pseudonyms), shares *tricentipede*. He explains that since a centipede is a bug with 100 legs, a tricentipede must be a bug with 300 legs! After considerable discussion, his classmates decide they need more evidence. They ask Niko to look for pictures of a tricentipede to prove whether or not one exists. He agrees to report back at the end of the day.

Well over half of English words—nearly 75% according to some estimates—are derived from Greek or Latin roots. Because Latin and Greek prefixes, bases, and suffixes have distinctive semantic features and consistent orthographic patterns, students who have cultivated an awareness of them can become adept at linking the pronunciation, spelling,

What Research Has to Say About Vocabulary Instruction, edited by Alan E. Farstrup and S. Jay Samuels.
© 2008 by the International Reading Association.

and meaning of many challenging words (Bear, Invernizzi, Templeton, & Johnston, 2000; Rasinski & Padak, 2008). They are thus able to coordinate sound and sense when they encounter new words.

The study of word origins and derivatives helps students grasp an essential linguistic principle: English words have a discernible logic because their meanings are historically grounded. This knowledge, used in conjunction with word analysis skills, empowers them as learners. Although no single approach to vocabulary development has conclusively been found more successful than another, researchers agree that a focus on Greek and Latin derivatives offers a powerful tool for teachers to nurture students' vocabulary development (Blachowicz & Fisher, 2000; Newton & Newton, 2005; Stahl, 1999). We believe this approach is also a powerful way to provide instruction that meets diverse student needs. English-language learners, for example, have been identified as the largest growing population in American schools (Flynn & Hill, 2005). Because so many of these children speak first languages semantically embedded in the Latin lexicon (e.g., Spanish), enhancing this linguistic connection can accelerate students' vocabulary growth (Blachowicz, Fisher, Ogle, & Watts-Taffe, 2006). Similarly, research in content area vocabulary has demonstrated the effectiveness of teaching Greek and Latin word roots, especially for struggling readers (Harmon, Hedrick, & Wood, 2005).

Moreover, as students move across grade levels, they face an "increased load of new words, new concepts, and multiple meanings" in school texts of increasing difficulty (Blachowicz & Fisher, 2000, p. 511). Nagy and Anderson (1984) estimated that in grade 5, students meet 10,000 new words in their reading alone and that school texts used in grades 3–9 contain approximately 88,500 distinct word families. Most of the new words they encounter in these texts will be of Greek and Latin origin.

Recently Blachowicz et al. (2006) called for a "comprehensive, integrated, schoolwide" approach to vocabulary instruction, one that encompasses more than a "list of words to teach at the beginning of the week" (p. 526). They urged teachers to make vocabulary a "core consideration" across grade levels and subjects, one that is based on a "common philosophy and shared practices" (p. 527). Salient components of such a program focused on fostering "word consciousness," the "intentional teaching of selected words," and teaching "generative elements of words and word-learning strategies to build independence" (p. 527). Blachowicz et al. (2006) emphasized the critical need for students to make "semantic connections among words," connections students can verbalize. They further noted that research that focuses on teaching structural analysis or morphology has found this approach "generative in learning new words" (p. 530).

In this chapter, we present a systematic, strategy-based approach to vocabulary development based on the exploration of Greek and Latin roots as semantic units. While this approach is most effective when implemented across a school or district (Rasinski, Padak, Newton, & Newton, 2007), we present word roots and activities that individual teachers can easily use as the foundation for their classroom vocabulary instructional plan.

Vocabulary for "School" Literacy

Academic texts in general have a disproportionate number of words from Latin and Greek roots because words associated with scholarly, scientific, and technical advances are most often of Greek or Latin origin. Consequently, as students progress through school, they encounter more and more words of classical, rather than Anglo-Saxon, origin. Moreover new technologies have brought us new words that expand the presence of Greek and Latin roots in the English lexicon (e.g., Internet, megabyte).

The context in which words are used provides another layer of complexity in "school" literacy. We use oral vocabulary to listen and speak, print vocabulary to read and write. Speech is contextualized language; "precision of word choice is seldom crucial in everyday conversation" (Nagy & Scott, 2000, p. 279). Written texts, on the other hand, tend to be decontextualized, so precision of word choice "is the primary communicative tool of the writer" (p. 279). Decontextualized language contains "richer vocabulary" (p. 279) and more unfamiliar words than spoken language (Cunningham, 2005). In school, most of the new vocabulary words children meet will be in decontextualized written texts, much of it in content area textbooks, so "exposure to such language is important for children's vocabulary growth" (Nagy & Scott, 2000, p. 279).

Because learning new words in content area subjects often requires learning new concepts as well, students face additional challenges. Most content area words, for example, are "low-frequency" and "do not appear in other contexts" (Harmon et al., 2005, p. 263). Furthermore the same words may represent dissimilar concepts in different content areas: consider a "revolution" in history or in science. In addition, key content area vocabulary is often a building block for more advanced conceptual knowledge. Unlike primary-level students who can use context to determine the general meaning of a word, older students must learn new conceptual vocabulary with enough precision to scaffold other concepts.

Although teaching and learning vocabulary for school success is a daunting prospect, decades of research have identified general principles that can guide instructional planning. In the next section, we discuss curricular issues and answers provided by research.

Research-Based Guidelines for Planning Instruction

Blachowicz and Fisher (2000) found that two decades of research has determined that vocabulary acquisition depends on active student engagement that (a) fosters an "understanding of words and ways to learn them," (b) personalizes word learning, (c) immerses students in words, and (d) provides them with "repeated exposures" to new words through "multiple sources of information" (p. 504).

Researchers also agree that teachers need to employ a variety of methods that enhance the depth and breadth of students' word knowledge (Blachowicz et al., 2006; Lehr, Osborn, & Hiebert, 2004), but they offer less clear-cut guidance regarding the specific words or word parts that would make up an effective vocabulary program. Most agree, for example, that some direct instruction of key words is important, but generating a widely accepted list of specific grade-level words to teach has proven elusive (Kamil & Hiebert, 2005).

Several vocabulary lists have been developed based on the frequency with which words appear in grade-level text. Marzano, Kendall, and Paynter (2005) pointed out that, although "vocabulary words are commonly thought of in terms of grade levels, there is little agreement as to what a grade-level designation signifies and how to assign grade levels to words" (p. 129). Some have called for a list of basic words that are morphologically connected to other words. Morphological analysis is an important strategy because it allows students to make connections among semantically related words or word families (Nagy, Anderson, Schommer, Scott, & Stallman, 1989; Nagy & Scott, 2000). Biemiller (2005) argued that even different student populations learn words "largely in the same order" (p. 225) and called for teaching a corpus of common root word meanings, even in primary grades.

Rather than focus on specific vocabulary words, we identify specific Greek and Latin roots that can be taught as core semantic units. These roots can be presented using the same four instructional principles highlighted above. Currently many teachers do present roots as a meaningful strategy for vocabulary instruction; we expand its presence in the curriculum by recommending selected roots of high utility.

Our approach includes teaching generative elements of words and word-learning strategies in ways that give students the ability to learn new words independently. By separating and analyzing the meaning of a prefix, suffix, or other word root, children can often unlock the meaning of an unknown word. If we teach students that the word *tri-* means *three*, for example, they can use that information to figure out *tricycle*, *trio*, and *triplets*. When introducing the concept of *photosynthesis*, we can easily point out its roots: *photo* means *light* and *syn* means *with*. As children grapple with the complex process of how light (*photo*) is combined with (*syn*) carbon dioxide and water to make sugar, knowledge of these word roots will support their efforts.

Knowing that words can be broken down into meaning units is a powerful strategy for vocabulary development. Until recently, teaching word roots was a strategy reserved for upper grade or content area classrooms. But a growing body of research tells us that this strategy should be introduced early. In fact, by the second grade, students should be adept at using word roots as a vocabulary strategy (Biemiller, 2005).

In the next section, we share design principles that can be used to select, evaluate, or create effective vocabulary instruction. We also recommend instructional routines based on "gradual release of responsibility" (Weaver, 2002), which begins with teacher-led discussion that scaffolds increasingly independent learning. The routines were developed for a comprehensive vocabulary program, "Building Vocabulary from Word Roots," aimed at fostering word awareness, metalinguistic knowledge, and ultimately, students filled with curiosity and joy about words (Rasinski et al., 2007).

Guidelines for Planning Instruction

First, instruction should include planned teaching of selected word roots with multiple kinds of information provided (e.g., semantic, structural) (Blachowicz et al., 2006). Research tells us that children can only learn 8–10 new words each week through direct instruction (Stahl & Fairbanks, 1986) because learning requires repetition and multiple exposures. Yet as Graves (2005) noted, just because there are many more words than we can teach doesn't mean that we shouldn't teach any of them. Some direct instruction is useful. Learning key word parts enables students to master new words that are semantically connected. In this way instruction becomes efficient—by learning one word part, students have clues to meaning for all the words that contain it. So, we recommend that teachers begin the week by inviting students to "meet a root" like Joanna did with her second graders: Select a root to introduce and discuss through direct instruction. (See p. 17, this chapter, for specific instructions for this activity.)

Because word learning is a matter of knowing "how" (procedural) rather than knowing "that" (declarative), students need strategies for determining word meaning that will help them become metacognitively and metalinguistically aware; they must understand and know how to manipulate structural features of language (Nagy & Scott, 2000). Classroom-based studies of elementary students have demonstrated the effectiveness of focused instruction in the strategies of word parts and context clues (Baumann, Font, Edwards, & Boland, 2005). Thus the second stage of the instructional cycle is to design many opportunities for students to combine and create new words from the roots they meet.

Using context clues, for example, is a frequently used reading strategy for determining the meaning of an unknown word. Although context in reading has many dimensions, it most often refers to figuring out the meaning of an unknown word by getting help from the words, phrases, sentences, or illustrations surrounding it (Harris & Hodges, 1995). Assistance from context may be semantic, based on the meaning of the preceding or following passages, or structural, based on grammatical or syntactic markers within a word or sentence. Using context clues is an especially important strategy for vocabulary development because, as we noted earlier, many English words have multiple meanings. Identifying which meaning is the best fit depends entirely on context. Learning how to use the surrounding semantic context, whether grammatical, structural or oral, helps children expand vocabulary. Most vocabulary-related school tasks assume that students already have this kind of knowledge, but that is frequently not true. It is important to teach students to read and reason the meaning of new words through the use of context clues.

Students should be immersed in words and given frequent opportunities to use new words in diverse oral and print contexts to learn them on a deep level (Blachowicz & Fisher, 2000, 2006). Discussion, reading, writing, and listening are thus important components of a vocabulary program. Related to this principle is another: the importance of wide reading. The more students read, the better.

Vocabulary instruction must foster word consciousness, an awareness of and interest in words (Graves & Watts-Taffe, 2002). Words themselves are interesting, and our ultimate goal is to create lifelong word lovers. Activities like word exploration (etymology) and word play (puns, riddles) are central to vocabulary development. Crossword puzzles, word scrambles, riddles, and tongue twisters are fun, but they are also good vocabulary practice. Time during which students play and explore word games on their own or with others is time well spent. The final step in the instructional model is to extend and enrich students' vocabulary by encouraging them to become word sleuths, a habit that they may well carry with them throughout (and beyond) their school years.

Don't forget that teachers can also stimulate such habits by sharing their own love of words. Each of us has favorite texts that we turn to because the words move us to laughter or tears. Reading these aloud to students and talking about the power of words is an effective practice. Teachers can also whet students' appetites by sharing interesting word histories and then showing students how to explore the origin of lots of words themselves. Posted lists of websites or print resources for students to investigate themselves can help make word learning and word play a priority in the classroom as well.

Dictionaries and other reference works can add interest to a vocabulary program. Although most students begin to learn about reference tools in the primary grades, they may not know the enormous variety of electronic and print dictionaries now available. They may know the concept of synonym and antonym, but they may not know how to use a thesaurus. (Some of the electronic ones available are really fun to use!) Practice with reference tools will help students learn to use them automatically.

In the next section, we suggest a list of specific roots to use as a foundation on which to build your vocabulary program.

What Roots Are Worth Teaching?

Tables 1.1 to 1.3 present the most useful word roots aligned with language arts and content area vocabulary for primary, intermediate, and middle school students. We recommend that this three-level sequence form the focus of instruction in Greek and Latin word parts. This instructional sequence teaches selected roots while also cultivating metalinguistic awareness. It is based on three principles: (1) words have an internal semantic logic, (2) words are made of units that contain meaning, and a semantic (meaning) relationship exists between units, (3) a word's meaning can be unlocked through analysis of its semantic units.

Table 1.1. Level 1 roots for primary/elementary students

Building words from familiar vocabulary

Prefixes

co-, con-	with, together
de-	own, off of
ex-	out
in-	not (*"negative"*)
pre-	before
re-	back, again
sub-	under, below
un-	not (*"negative"*)

Bases

audi-, audit-	hear, listen
graph-, gram-	write, draw
mov-, mot-, mobil-	move
port-	carry
vid-, vis-	see

Numerical bases

bi-	two
tri-	three

Suffixes

-able, -ible	can, able to be done
-er	more
-est	most
-ful	full of
-less	without

The roots recommended in Tables 1.1 to 1.3 are neither mandatory nor exhaustive. They were drawn from a broader sequence developed for a comprehensive vocabulary program based on Greek and Latin word roots (Rasinski et al., 2007). That sequence was generated by (a) identifying those Latin and Greek roots that appear most frequently in the English lexicon, (b) determining which roots have most utility at primary, upper elementary, and middle school levels, and (c) identifying what metalinguistic information is essential and when it should be taught. In addition, six teachers, grades 2–8, have been working with us in the development of the lists and the teaching strategies that are described in the next section of the chapter. Each reports that students are successful with and enjoy the activities.

The level 1 roots can be introduced in the primary grades. This list emphasizes familiar Latin prefixes and suffixes with only a handful of

Table 1.2. Level 2 roots for upper elementary students

Building school vocabulary

Prefixes

a-, ab-, abs-	away, from
di-, dif-, dis-	apart, in different directions, not
pro-	forward, ahead
tra-, tran-, trans-	across, change

Assimilating prefixes

ad-	to, toward, add to
con-, com-, col-	with, together
in-, im-, il-	in, on, into (directional)
in-, im-, il-	not (negative)

Parallel Latin and Greek prefixes

Latin Greek

contra-, contro-, counter-, anti-	against
circu-, circum-, peri-	around
multi-, poly-	many
super-, sur-, hyper-	over
sub-, hypo-	under, below

Bases

cred-, credit-	believe
cur-, curs-, cours-	run, go
dict-	say, tell, speak
duc-, duct-	lead
mis-, mit-	to send
pon-, pos-, posit-	put, place
scrib-, script-	write
terr-	earth
fac-, fic-, fact-, fect-	do, make

Parallel Latin and Greek bases

Latin Greek

aqua-, hydro-	water
ped-, pod-	foot, feet

Suffixes

-arium, -orium	place for, container for
-ify	to make
-or, -er	one who does
-ose, -ous, -eous, -ious	full of

Latin bases. As students move into the upper elementary grades, the level 2 list presents more bases, particularly those that students will encounter in science. Some of these bases have parallel Greek and Latin roots for

Table 1.3. Level 3 roots for middle school students

Expanding word flexibility

Prefixes

auto-	self
inter-	between, among
post-	after
ob-	(assimilates) up against, in the way
per-	through, thorough
tele-	from afar

Bases

solv-, solut-	free, loosen
sent-, sens-	think, feel
tend-, tens-, tenu-	stretch, thin
trac-, tract-	pull, draw, drag
ven-, vent-	come
volu-, volut-, volv-	roll

Parallel Latin and Greek bases

Latin Greek

am(a)-, amat-, phil(o)-	love
fort-, forc-, dynamo-	power, strong
lumen-, luc-, luc photo-	light
nat-, natur-, gen-, gener-	be born, give birth, produce
nov-, neo-	new
omni-, pant-	all, every
spec-, spect scop-	look at, watch
viv-, vit bi(o)-	live, life
voc-, vok-, voice phon-	voice, call

"Flexing" suffixes

-ate	do
-ation	state or condition
-ant, -ent	in the process, having the characteristics of
-ance, -ancy, -ence, -ency	state or quality
-crat	ruler
-cracy	one who believes in rule by
-ologist	one who studies
-olgy	study of
-phobe	one who fears
-phobia	fear

the same concept. The Latin *aqua* and the Greek *hydro*, for example, both mean *water*; students can easily grasp them simultaneously. As they move into middle school, students encounter bases that represent more complex concepts they will be meeting in mathematics and science. In addition, the concept of flexibility when approaching word roots, which we call "flexing," is addressed. Level 3 presents a list of these roots. (See Figure 1.1 for metalinguistic concepts emphasized at each level.)

Begin the study of Greek and Latin roots by using compound words to introduce children to the notion of roots as semantic units that have meaning. Word dissection activities, which we call divide and conquer when working with students, are designed to help students identify semantic units and build a connection that unlocks a word's meaning (Newton & Newton, 2005). The logic of this activity is mathematical: Just as 1 + 3 = 4, *pre* + *view* = *preview* or look beforehand.

Once students have understood how to dissect familiar compound words, they learn about prefixes that attach to whole words; eventually they also learn about assimilated prefixes, or those that change spelling

Figure 1.1. Metalinguistic concepts

Level 1: Primary/elementary

Building words from familiar vocabulary

- Teach the three kinds of "roots": prefixes (directional, negative), bases (core meaning), and suffixes (word ending).
- Teach the strategy of word dissection (divide and conquer) to build awareness of word parts as semantic units that generate meaning.
- Emphasize familiar prefixes and suffixes; introduce bases in words students already know.
- Heighten awareness that the divided units contain both meaning and sound. This shifts students from a phonological to a semantic unit approach.

Level 2: Upper elementary

Building school vocabulary

- Teach the concept of assimilation of prefixes.
- Emphasize Greek and Latin prefixes and bases with parallel meanings.
- Heighten awareness of Latin-based content vocabulary in literature, history, social studies, and of Greek-based words in science and technology.

Level 3: Middle school

Expanding word flexibility

- Teach suffixes that add flexibility to a base (e.g., create, creation; democracy, democratic; biology, biologist).
- Emphasize bases, especially Greek and Latin bases with parallel meanings representing concepts important in content area vocabulary.
- Heighten awareness of long words that begin with two or more prefixes (independent; unconventional) and of the use of cognates as a strategy for deducing the meaning of a new word.

when attached to certain bases. Students also develop concepts about bases and suffixes, including ways in which suffixes affect the meaning of base roots. All this is accomplished using grade-level appropriate vocabulary. Teaching activities scaffold students to understand and then use word parts to identify unfamiliar vocabulary.

To go beyond surface or "passive" understanding of word parts, students need instructional routines based on a variety of activities (Rasinski et al., 2007). Fifteen or 20 minutes of concentrated word work several times each week should suffice. At the end of this sequence of instruction, students will have amassed an impressive number of words that are appropriate for their grade levels in school. As important, they will have mastered a number of strategies for additional vocabulary building that they can apply as lifelong word learners.

Instructional Activities

The activities described below, several of which are adapted from Newton, Padak, and Rasinski (2008), help students learn to take words apart (word dissection) and to generate new vocabulary using word parts (word composition). In addition, we describe several word games that provide active and enjoyable practice. Independent reading, writing, and discussion opportunities complement the vocabulary curriculum.

Divide and Conquer Chart

Teachers may want to introduce and practice this routine (Rasinski et al., 2007) with familiar compound words or prefixes. Once students become comfortable with the procedure, they can apply it as they explore new words in a variety of learning contexts.

Purpose
To help students understand that words are often made up of recognizable "root" parts that can help them unlock the meaning of an unfamiliar word

Materials
- A list of about 10 familiar compound words or a list of words that carry the same prefix or root
- A divide and conquer template that has been prepared in advance and duplicated for each student (a four-column chart with blanks to correspond to word parts of focus; see Figure 1.2)

Figure 1.2. Divide and conquer template example

Whole word	First word	+	Second word	=	Whole word means
playground	play	+	ground	=	ground where we play
bedroom	bed	+	room	=	room where a bed is
sunlight	sun	+	light	=	light from the sun

Procedure

1. Review the concept of "compound words" or prefixes by asking students to explain what they are (a single word that contains two or more complete words; a unit added to the front of a word that affects its meaning).

2. Write the word *birthday* on the board. Ask someone to explain what *birthday* means. Now ask another student to identify what two words are in *birthday*. Ask how each of those words contributes to the meaning of the word *birthday* (e.g., a *birthday* is the day of your birth.)

3. Show students the list of words. Read the list of words together orally. Now ask students to choose a word on the list and to tell what two words it contains and what it means. As students offer explanations, reinforce that the meaning of each compound word is built from the semantic relationship between the two units. (Here is a tip: The second word in a compound word usually describes the main idea. The first word gives a detail about the main idea.)

4. When all words on the list have been discussed, tell students that they have just used a strategy called divide and conquer. Explain that words are made up of word parts or meaning units called roots. Tell students that they can often figure out an unknown word by "dividing and conquering" its parts or roots.

5. Write these three compound words that use the word *book: bookcase, bookshelf, bookmark*. Ask students to divide and conquer each of these words. (A bookcase is a "case for books"; bookshelf is a "shelf for books"; bookmark "marks the book" where the reader left off). As students offer explanations, note how the word *book* always has the same meaning. Remind students that the new word can be figured out by connecting the meaning of each word's root.

6. Distribute the divide and conquer template with the list of words with the same prefix or other compound words. Students will have a list of 10 words that can be used for a variety of extension activities that use art, drama, or writing.

Word Spokes

This strategy (Rasinski et al., 2007) works well as a follow-up to divide and conquer and can be done individually or as a group or partner activity.

Purpose

To develop students' word analysis skills by manipulating word roots

Materials

- An age-appropriate list of familiar prefixes or word roots
- A word spokes template (a circle with several spokes attached to it, much like a bicycle tire; see Figure 1.3 for an example) that has been prepared in advance and duplicated

Procedure

1. Begin by reviewing the concept that sometimes words are made up of recognizable root parts that provide clues to word meaning. Write the prefix *re-*, or choose another familiar prefix. Tell students that *re-* almost always means *back* or *again*, and that they can figure out the meaning of lots of *re-* words by keeping that in mind. Tell them that they are going to build many *re-* words in an activity called word spokes.

2. Put a blank word spokes template on an overhead transparency. Write the prefix *re-* in the center circle, and tell students that they must "spoke" out five or more different words that have the prefix *re-*.

3. As students call out words, write a different *re-* word in each spoke. Emphasize the *back* or *again* aspect of the words students provide.

4. Students can then do their own word spokes with roots they choose or you can assign roots. If students work on the same root, point out the variety of words and ways in which the root can be used. If students work on different roots, ask why they chose their words, how the words mean *back* or *again*, and so forth. Talking about the words directly and using the words in classroom conversation are good ways to give students practice using them.

Figure 1.3. Word spokes: *Phil/philo*

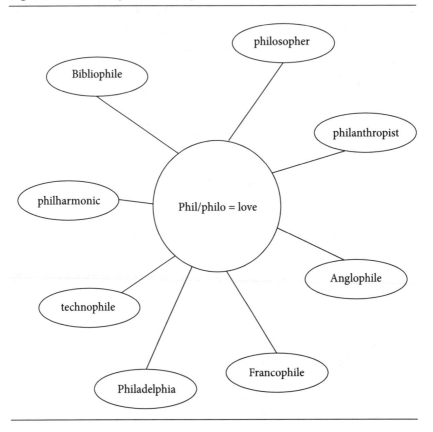

The Figure 1.3 provides an example of word spokes using the Greek root for love—*phil/philo.*

Odd Word Out

One way to make the meaning of a word clear is to compare how it is similar to or different from other words. Word composition activities such as this are particularly important because research indicates students are often able to recognize more words (passive vocabulary) than they generate (active vocabulary) through oral and written communication (see Nagy & Anderson, 1984). This quick teacher-constructed activity, odd word out (Rasinski et al., 2007), asks students to choose which word does not fit and then to explain why. This can be used as a small-group discussion activity; whole-group conversation should follow.

Purpose

To help students learn to manipulate root parts and generate new vocabulary

Materials

- Several sets of three words that share a word part
- Sets can be written on the chalkboard or chart paper. Alternatively, a worksheet such as the one presented in Figure 1.4 can be developed

Procedure

1. Select three or four words, two or three of which share some characteristic. Words could be related semantically or syntactically. Words could also be related by the presence or absence of word parts. Consider this example:

   Cat   Dog

   Ant   Tiger

   The odd word could be *ant*, because an ant is not a mammal, because it has more than four feet, or because the word *ant* begins with a vowel. The odd word could also be *tiger* because it's not a three-letter word or because it has two syllables. The groups of words you select for odd word out will often have multiple answers, which promotes children's thinking about the many ways in which words can be related to one another.

2. Present one set of words. Ask students to talk with partners to determine which word in the set could be the odd word out. Encourage them to generate as many ways as possible to eliminate one word.

3. Invite students to share their ideas. Praise the diversity in thinking.

Figure 1.4. Odd word out template example

Look at the four words. Write the one that doesn't belong on the line. Then write how the other words are the same.

precook   preheat
premixed   pretest

The word that doesn't belong is _____*pretest*_____. The other words are the same because ___they have to do with cooking___.

4. The remaining sets of words can be addressed in a whole group or with students working in pairs.

Be the Bard

William Shakespeare was one of the greatest wordsmiths in history. He invented words, including an estimated 8% of all the words he used in his writings. Many of the words he invented, such as *bedroom, skim milk, besmirch, exposure, hornbook, fairyland, unquestioned, madcap, noiseless,* and *marketable* were simply the combination of already existing words and word roots.

Shakespeare is surely a good model for any student of English words. If Shakespeare had permission to invent words, students can be given, from time to time, license to do the same. Students we have worked with in the past have invented words such as *matermand* (a mother's order), *teleterra* (a distant land), *terraphile* (someone who loves the earth; an ecologist).

One student came to class one day with a new word that he couched in the form of a riddle for this classmates. He posed his invented word *autophile* and asked his fellow class members what they most likely have in their pockets or purses if they were an autophile; the choices were a wad of money, a set of car keys, or a mirror. Most of the class immediately called out "a set of car keys" (a lover of cars or automobiles) to which this student responded "Wrong!" The correct answer was a mirror. Since the root auto refers to self, an autophile is someone who is in love with him or herself, a narcissist. Such a person would love to spend time looking at his or her reflection in a mirror. The class was surprised and delighted by the answer, but also posed the question, why are cars often called autos or automobiles? The discussion that followed was rich and engaging.

Purpose

To build or reinforce conceptual knowledge by inventing and defining new words and concepts using word roots already learned

Materials

- A list of at least 10 roots that have been previously taught

Procedure

1. Give students the task of inventing new words by combining previously taught words and then devising definitions for the words.
2. Provide a list of word roots previously taught. Review them with the students.

3. Show students how to invent a new word, like Shakespeare did, by combining two or more of the roots already taught. Share a word or two that you have made and explore the definition of the word with students.

4. Ask students to work alone or with a partner to invent two or three words and be ready to provide a definition for the word.

5. Allow time for discussion of words.

Word Theater

This versatile strategy (Hoyt, 1999), based on the popular game charades, uses pantomime and oral language to make word meanings concrete. It works especially well as a partner or small group activity.

Purpose

To build or reinforce conceptual knowledge by acting out the meaning of a new or familiar vocabulary word

Materials

- A list of at least 10 words containing the word part of focus that can be dramatized easily

Procedures

1. List the words on the chalkboard or on chart paper so that everyone can see them. Tell students that they will pick one word and then work with a partner to act out its meaning, but without speaking.

2. Ask students to find a partner. Each child should read the list of words to his or her partner. When both partners have read the list to each other, they should choose a word. Tell them they have two minutes to decide how to get the word's meaning across by acting it out.

3. Ask each team to act out its word while other students try to guess which word they have chosen. Make sure the list of words is visible, so that students can keep reading and rereading the words as they try to figure out which one is being pantomimed. As students look for connections between the acting and the word list, they will better understand the concepts each word represents.

Variation

The word skits (Rasinski et al., 2007) game works well with students who are both experienced in pantomiming words and comfortable working in small teams (3–4 students per team). Each team chooses one word and writes its definition on an index card. Working together, they create a skit or situation that shows the meaning of the word. The skit is performed without words. Classmates try to guess the word being shown. Once the word is correctly identified, the definition is read out loud.

Individual and Collaborative Activities

Individual and collaborative activities that use words in creative ways, including word games, are another important component of vocabulary instruction. Although they focus on practice, they are fun, which promotes interest in words. Moreover students need to encounter new words or word parts in multiple ways to learn them.

Root of the Week

This activity is a great way to get students to pay attention to words in their daily reading, writing, speaking, and listening.

Purpose
To focus attention on words that share a prefix or root word

Materials text
- Teacher-selected root (prefix, suffix, or base)
- Chart paper and markers

Procedure
1. Ask students to be on the lookout for words they encounter that contain the specific root of the week.
2. Post a chart with the root in bold letters at the top. Number each line.
3. Tell students that whenever they discover a word with that root, they should add it to the list. Tell them to (a) write the word, (b) circle the word part, and (c) write where the word was found.
4. At the end of the week, review the list. Students love hunting for these words, so you may find your class filling more than one sheet each week. Find a spot in the room to collect all the charts. As the weeks pass, you will have many lists of words you can use for different purposes.

Wordo

A vocabulary version of bingo, Wordo (Rasinski et al., 2007) is a wonderful way for students to play with new words they are learning.

Purpose

To experience an age-appropriate group of words through simultaneous use of oral and written language

Materials

- A list of 12–16 words
- A Wordo card for each child (a 3 × 3 or 4 × 4 matrix; make sure boxes are large enough for students to write in)

Procedure

1. Write the words you have chosen on the board.
2. Pass out a Wordo card to each student. Ask each student to choose a free box and mark it. Then have them write one of the words in each of the remaining boxes. Students choose whatever box they wish for each word.
3. Call a clue for each word. The clue can be the definition for the word, a synonym, an antonym, or a sentence with the target word deleted. (For very young children, or those playing for the first time, you may want to simplify the process by saying the word and then asking them to mark it.)
4. Students need to figure out the correct target word, then put an *X* through it. (If you want to clear the sheets and play again, use small scraps of paper or other items to mark the squares.)
5. When a student has four *X*'s or markers in a row, column, diagonal, or four corners he or she can call out "Wordo!"
6. Check their words and, if correct, declare that student the winner. Then have students clear their sheets and play another round of Wordo. The winner of the first game can be the one to call out clues.

Variation

Word bank Wordo uses students' personal word banks on which individual words are written, one per card, which simply changes how the Wordo cards are developed.

From their word bank of word cards previously or currently being taught, have students select any group of 9, 16, or 25 cards. Have the students arrange their cards into a 3 × 3, 4 × 4, or 5 × 5 matrix, face up, in front of them. That matrix becomes the Wordo card. From here the procedure follows the same routine in steps 3–6 of the previously described Wordo game. When a student finds a word that is called or that is a correct answer to a clue given by the teacher, they simply turn the word over, leaving the blank side of the card face up. A complete row, column, diagonal, or four corners of blank cards results in a Wordo win.

To play another game, students simply turn all their word cards face up again and, if so desired, rearrange their order to form a new Wordo game card. No matter how it is played, Wordo is an engaging game that allows all students to practice the words and word roots they need to know. Wordo can also be used as a review activity with words from other subject areas such as spelling, social studies, science, and math.

Card Games

Card games such as Memory or Concentration or Go Fish are engaging independent activities that also work well with word bank cards.

Purpose

To provide reinforcement in a fun atmosphere

Materials

- A set of word cards—these can be duplicates of the same words, words and definitions, or pairs of related words (e.g., *look, looks, looking, looked*; *return, rewind, rethink, refund*)

Procedure

1. If necessary, remind students how to play the games. Memory, for example, begins with students shuffling the word cards and then placing them face down into a grid.
2. One student selects two cards, turns them over, and says each word. If they match, the student keeps them and takes another turn.
3. If they do not match, the student turns them back over, and the second student takes a turn.
4. The game continues until players have matched all the words in the grid.

Twenty Questions

The vocabulary version of this popular game (Newton, Padak, & Rasinski, 2008) uses oral language and personal connections to deepen conceptual knowledge. If you want to build a little competitive spirit, divide the class into two teams for this activity.

Purpose

To ask questions that will help students figure out a "mystery" word

Materials

- A list of words containing a word root of focus, or a paper bag with at least a dozen words on slips of paper

Procedure

1. If students have never played twenty questions, review the following rules for them: Indicate the list of words. Tell students that one of them will get to be "It." That student will choose a word that classmates will try to guess by asking yes-or-no questions. If no one can figure out the word after 20 questions have been asked, then the student who is It reveals the word.

2. Remind students that the person who is It can only give a yes or no answer to the questions. You may want to scaffold this by taking the first turn as It yourself. Otherwise, invite someone to begin. Then let students take over, asking questions until someone has guessed the correct word.

3. If someone guesses the correct word, that person becomes It and gets to choose the next word.

4. Repeat the process. This game can take as much or as little time as you choose. It's a quick filler or Friday afternoon wind-down activity.

Root Word Riddles

Who doesn't enjoy the brain-teasing process trying of solving a riddle? This strategy (Rasinski et al., 2007) invites students to create and guess riddles with words from the same root. Students get to think creatively as they try to guess a word by connecting semantic clues. This works well as a partner or team activity.

Purpose

To broaden students' knowledge of vocabulary words from the same root

Materials

- A list of 6–10 words from the targeted root or word part
- Chart paper
- Paper and a pencil for all students

Procedure

1. Begin by reviewing the meaning of the root. Read the list of words together. Ask students to explain what each word means. Make sure their explanation includes the meaning of the root.

2. If students have not created riddles before, share some riddles with them; there are many good books of riddles to choose from. Spend some time not only solving riddles, but talking about how riddles are constructed. Ask students what types of clues seem particularly helpful.

3. Pick a word from the list and tell students you will create a riddle for them to guess. Tell them you are going to give them three clues. Write out the first clue. Make sure to begin it with the words "I mean...." Then write out a second and third clue. (Example of clues for the word "invisible" might include the following: I mean something you cannot see. My opposite is "visible." I have four syllables. What am I?)

4. Ask students to pick a word from the list and make their own riddle to share with others.

5. Spend some time swapping riddles. When students have written riddles about the same word, point out the variety of clues and ways in which the word can be described. Note how each of the words shares a certain meaning based on its common root.

Conclusions

Primary grade teachers find that rimes, phonograms, or word families (e.g., *-at, -it, -ock, -um*) are superb vehicles for teaching word decoding or phonics. Word study and phonics scholars almost universally endorse the use of word families as an effective method for teaching phonics. Knowledge of one word family can help a reader decode many words.

For example, knowledge of the -am word family can help a reader sound out many one syllable words such as *ham, jam, slam, ram,* and *cram.* The same word family can also help a reader sound out more sophisticated multisyllabic words such as *Alabama, hamster, ambulance, camera,* and many more.

In a sense, Latin and Greek roots are like the next level of word families, with one major exception: Knowledge of Latin and Greek roots not only helps readers sound out words, it also provides readers with critical cues for determining the meaning of words containing the roots (e.g., knowing that the prefix *sur-* means "more of something, or beyond," the meaning of words such as *surtax* and *surreal* becomes much more accessible and transparent).

Reading and language scholars are increasingly recognizing the importance of Latin and Greek roots in teaching reading. The challenges for teachers are to identify appropriate roots to be taught to children at various ages and to develop and implement engaging instructional activities that will not only help students learn the roots and important English words, but also take delight in the meaningful connections of words in our wonderful language and get a sense of how so many words in English were formed. We hope that in this chapter we have made some initial steps in this direction and have whetted your appetite for making Latin and Greek word roots a regular part of your instructional routines in reading and language arts. Fin!

Questions for Discussion

1. How do you currently teach vocabulary to your students? What principles or guidelines do you follow? Are you satisfied with your approach? Are students learning the vocabulary that you present deeply and fully? How do you know? Do your students find vocabulary learning engaging and enjoyable?

2. Should an effective vocabulary program focus on general vocabulary, content area vocabulary, or both? Why?

3. One of the keys to effective vocabulary instruction is to provide students with multiple opportunities to see, say, write, and hear new words. List several authentic ways to accomplish this.

4. How might you use the principles outlined in this chapter to differentiate instruction for students with advanced vocabularies?

For students with seemingly small vocabularies? For students learning English?

5. How can you elicit support for your vocabulary program from parents and others in the child's home environment?

REFERENCES

Baumann, J.F., Font, G., Edwards, E.C., & Boland, E.M. (2005). Strategies for teaching middle-grade students to use word-part and context clues to expand reading vocabulary. In E.H. Hiebert & M.L. Kamil (Eds.), *Teaching and learning vocabulary: Bringing research to practice* (pp. 179–205). Mahwah, NJ: Erlbaum.

Bear, D.R., Invernizzi, M., Templeton, S., & Johnston, F. (2000). *Words their way* (2nd ed.). Upper Saddle River, NJ: Prentice Hall.

Biemiller, A. (2005). Size and sequence in vocabulary development: Implications or choosing words for primary grade vocabulary. In E.H. Hiebert & M.L. Kamil (Eds.), *Teaching and learning vocabulary: Bringing research to practice* (pp. 223–242). Mahwah, NJ: Erlbaum.

Blachowicz, C.L.Z., & Fisher, P. (2000). Vocabulary instruction. In M.L. Kamil, P.B. Mosenthal, P.D. Pearson, & R. Barr (Eds.), *Handbook of reading research* (Vol. 3, pp. 503–524). Mahwah, NJ: Erlbaum.

Blachowicz, C.L.Z., & Fisher, P. (2006). *Teaching vocabulary in all classrooms* (3rd ed.). Upper Saddle River, NJ: Prentice Hall.

Blachowicz, C.L.Z., Fisher, P., Ogle, D., & Watts-Taffe, S.M. (2006). Vocabulary: Questions from the classroom. *Reading Research Quarterly, 41*(4), 524–539.

Cunningham, A.E. (2005). Vocabulary growth through independent reading and reading aloud to children. In E.H. Hiebert & M.L. Kamil (Eds.), *Teaching and learning vocabulary: Bringing research to practice* (pp. 45–68). Mahwah, NJ: Erlbaum.

Flynn, K., & Hill, J. (2005, December). *English-language learners: A growing population.* Mid-continent Research for Education and Learning (MCREL policy brief). Retrieved April 3, 2007, from www.mcrel.org/PDF/PolicyBriefs/5052PI_PBEnglishLanguageLearners.pdf

Graves, M.F. (2005). *The vocabulary book: Learning and instruction.* New York: Teachers College Press.

Graves, M.F., & Watts-Taffe, S.M. (2002). The place of word consciousness in a research-based vocabulary program. In A.E. Farstrup & S.J. Samuels (Eds.), *What research has to say about reading instruction* (3rd ed., pp. 140–165). Newark, DE: International Reading Association.

Harmon, J.M., Hedrick, W.B., & Wood, K.D. (2005). Research on vocabulary instruction in the content areas: Implications for struggling readers. *Reading & Writing Quarterly, 21*(3), 261–280.

Harris, T.L., & Hodges, R.E., (Eds.). (1995). *The literacy dictionary: The vocabulary of reading and writing.* Newark, DE: International Reading Association.

Hoyt, L. (1999). *Revisit, reflect, retell: Strategies for improving reading comprehension.* Portsmouth, NH: Heinemann.

Kamil, M.L., & Hiebert, E.H. (2005). Teaching and learning vocabulary: Perspectives and persistent issues. In E.H. Hiebert & M.L. Kamil (Eds.), *Teaching and learning vocabulary: Bringing research to practice* (pp. 1–23). Mahwah, NJ: Erlbaum.

Lehr, F., Osborn, J., & Hiebert, E.H. (2004). *Research-based practices in early reading series: A focus on vocabulary.* Retrieved January 15, 2007, from www.prel.org/products/re_/ES0419.htm

Marzano, R.J., Kendall, J.S., & Paynter, D.E. (2005). A list of essential words by grade level. In D.E. Paynter, E. Bodrova, & J.K. Doty (Eds.), *For the love of words: Vocabulary instruction that works* (pp. 127–202). San Francisco: Jossey-Bass.

Nagy, W.E., & Anderson, R.C. (1984). How many words are there in printed school English? *Reading Research Quarterly, 19*(3), 304–330.

Nagy, W.E., Anderson, R.C., Schommer, M., Scott, J.A., & Stallman, A. (1989). Morphological families in the internal lexicon. *Reading Research Quarterly, 24*(3), 262–282.

Nagy, W.E., & Scott, J.A. (2000). Vocabulary processes. In M.L. Kamil, P.B. Mosenthal, P.D. Pearson, & R. Barr (Eds.), *Handbook of reading research* (Vol. 3, pp. 269–284). Mahwah, NJ: Erlbaum.

Newton, E., Padak, N., & Rasinski, T. (2008). *Evidence-based instruction in reading: A professional development guide to vocabulary.* Boston: Allyn & Bacon.

Newton, R.M., & Newton, E. (2005). A little Latin and...a lot of English. *Adolescent Literacy in Perspective*, June, 2–7. Retrieved December 15, 2006, from www.ohiorc.org/adlit/ip_content.aspx?recID=159&parentID=158

Rasinski, T., & Padak, N. (2008). *From phonics to fluency: Effective teaching of decoding and reading fluency in the elementary school* (2nd ed.). New York: Longman.

Rasinski, T., Padak, N., Newton, R.M., & Newton, E. (2007). *Building vocabulary from word roots.* Huntington Beach, CA: Teacher Created Materials.

Stahl, S.A. (1999). *Vocabulary development.* Cambridge, MA: Brookline Press.

Stahl, S.A., & Fairbanks, M.M. (1986). The effects of vocabulary instruction: A model-based meta-analysis. *Review of Educational Research, 56*(1), 72–110.

Weaver, C. (2002). *Reading process and practice* (3rd ed.). Portsmouth, NH: Heinemann.

Chapter 2

Attentional Vocabulary Instruction: Read-Alouds, Word Play, and Other Motivating Strategies for Fostering Informal Word Learning

Camille L.Z. Blachowicz and Peter Fisher

Ever since Isabel Beck discovered that a 79-cent piece of poster board she later called "word wizard" could increase students' incidental word learning, the issue of motivating students to learn through indirect means as well as through explicit instruction has captivated teachers and researchers alike. In Beck's highly controlled study of vocabulary learning in the middle grades (Beck, Perfetti, & McKeown, 1982), a curious phenomenon surfaced. Out of all the classrooms involved in the research project, students in one classroom learned more incidental vocabulary—words no one was attempting to teach. When trying to locate the source of this learning, the researchers were unable to come up with any instruction or materials that could account for the difference.

Then one researcher noted a poster of interesting words in the classroom. When the teacher was asked about it, she noted that it was the "word wall"—a place where students could write new words they encountered in reading, in conversation, on TV, or in their daily experiences. If they could write the word, talk about where they heard or saw it, and use it, they received points in a class contest. Very little expense, instructional time, or effort was involved, but the students became "tuned in" to learning new words in a way that positively affected their learning. They actively watched and listened for new words and shared them with their peers. They were motivated word learners and had learned because of school settings or activities which did not reflect traditional, teacher-led vocabulary instruction.

In this chapter, we examine the research bases for two specific modes of encouraging what we will call informal word learning in the

What Research Has to Say About Vocabulary Instruction, edited by Alan E. Farstrup and S. Jay Samuels.
© 2008 by the International Reading Association.

elementary grades: read-alouds and word play. We use the term *informal word learning* to include what is typically called incidental word learning as well as other forms of teacher planned exposures and activities which would not be considered explicit or direct instruction. In our classes and professional development work, we have often referred to this as *attentional* instruction in which teachers look for opportunities to infuse learning into the school day in many and varied ways. Attentional instruction consists of planned experiences with words, which take teacher forethought and follow-through but do not constitute formal, explicit instruction. Swanborn and de Glopper (1999), in their meta-analysis of incidental word learning, argued that "*incidental* implies that the purpose for reading does not specifically provoke learning or directing attention to the meaning of unknown words" (p. 262). The research base for this form of incidental word learning—learning from auditory and visual sources in noninstructional settings—is wide, historical, and varied (Nagy, Herman, & Anderson, 1985; Swanborn & de Glopper, 1999). We also recognize that there is a broad research base for the effectiveness of teaching contextual word learning (Fukkink, Blok, & de Glopper, 2001). Further there is a strong base of research on forms of intentional and explicit instruction that affects the growth of vocabulary knowledge in school age children (Baumann & Kame'enui, 1991; Blachowicz & Fisher, 2000; Blachowicz, Fisher, Ogle, & Watts-Taffe, 2006). Yet, it is clear from all this research that the incredible growth in word knowledge of students across the school years cannot be accounted for by intentional, explicit instruction alone (Cunningham, 2005; Nagy, 1988). Wide reading, talk, media, first hand and vicarious experiences, and other experiences must all be factored in to the learning that we call vocabulary development.

This growth becomes increasingly important when considering the significant body of research that suggests that wide differences in concept and vocabulary knowledge exacerbate the achievement gap that is seen in so many schools, especially schools with large numbers of children of poverty (Hart & Risley, 1995). Educators sometimes talk about the Matthew Effect, the sad reality that having a well-developed vocabulary allows you to learn new words more easily than classmates with a smaller fund of word knowledge (Stanovich, 1986). This is especially significant in the content areas—not knowing what *circle* means makes it more difficult for a student to understand and learn new terms like *diameter*, *radius*, and *circumference*. Learners need anchor concepts and vocabulary to learn new words which are then connected to the concepts they already know.

In this chapter, we consider the research bases for two areas of school experience that we believe can play a major part in the vocabulary growth of school age children: reading aloud to students and engaging them in word play and word games. There is a well-established body of research that provides guidelines and caveats for using read-alouds. To discuss word play and word games, we link the processes involved to what we know from other areas of literacy research. In each case, these are widely used examples of "attentional" instruction.

Read-Alouds and Vocabulary Development

There has been considerable research into the value of storybook reading in facilitating the development of language and literacy in young children (e.g., Blachowicz & Obrochta, 2007; Dickinson & Keebler, 1989). Studies investigating the approaches teachers adopt while reading storybooks to students have noted that variations in reading styles have influenced the communicative contributions that occurred during the storybook reading activity (Cochran-Smith, 1984; Dickinson & Keebler, 1989; Martinez & Teale, 1989).

In particular, reading aloud to students has been examined as an important curricular practice that positively affects concept and vocabulary learning. Sometimes referred to as shared storybook reading, read-alouds are productive means for giving students opportunities to develop new meaning vocabulary. A recent survey of teacher practices (Fisher, Flood, Lapp, & Frey, 2004) concluded that reading aloud to students is a common and well-regarded practice in early elementary classrooms. Over 93% of primary teachers surveyed indicated they used read-alouds, and 91% of them recommended the practice to parents. Because children's books present more advanced, less familiar vocabulary than everyday speech (Cunningham & Stanovich, 1998), listening to books being read helps students go beyond their existing oral vocabularies by presenting them with advanced concepts and vocabulary. Discussion after read-alouds also gives students opportunities to use new vocabulary in the more decontextualized setting of a book discussion (Snow, 1991).

Numerous studies have documented that young students can learn word meanings both incidentally and purposefully from read-aloud experiences (Eller, Pappas, & Brown, 1988; Elley, 1988; Hargrave & Sénéchal, 2000; Robbins & Ehri, 1994). Research suggests this holds true across various grade levels, with different types of text, and with various populations of students (Brabham & Lynch-Brown, 2002; Brett,

Rothlein, & Hurley, 1996; Stahl, Brozo, Smith, & Commander, 1991). Involving students in discussions during and after listening to a book has also produced significant word learning, especially when the teacher scaffolded this learning by asking questions, adding information, or prompting students to describe what they heard. Whitehurst and his associates (Whitehurst et al., 1994, 1999) have called this process dialogic reading.

Research also suggests that this scaffolding may be more essential to those students who are less likely to learn new vocabulary easily. Children with less rich initial vocabularies are less likely to learn new vocabulary incidentally and need a thoughtful, well-designed, scaffolded approach to maximize learning from shared storybook reading (Robbins & Ehri, 1994; Sénéchal, Thomas, & Monker, 1995). So the research points to read-alouds with teacher scaffolding as a positive way to develop the oral vocabularies of young learners.

Active Participation in Read-Alouds

Besides the impact of teacher scaffolding, the role of active learning in vocabulary development has been well established. Students who engage with words by hearing them, using them, manipulating them semantically, and playing with them are more likely to learn and retain new vocabulary (Beck, McKeown, & Kucan, 2002; Blachowicz & Fisher, 2001; Stahl & Fairbanks, 1986). Further relating new words to what is already known creates elaborated schemata and links between concepts that provide for enduring learning (Anderson & Nagy, 1991).

A series of studies by Sénéchal and her colleagues (Hargrave & Sénéchal, 2000; Sénéchal & Cornell, 1993; Sénéchal et al., 1995) found that preschool children's engagement and *active* participation in storybook reading was more productive for vocabulary learning in storybook read-alouds than passive listening even to the most dramatic "performance" of book reading. This has been confirmed by a growing number of recent studies that have scaffolded young students' learning by focusing their attention on target words and engaging students in interactive discussion about books using specific vocabulary before, during, and after reading (Brett et al., 1996; Ewers & Brownson, 1999; Penno, Wilkinson, & Moore, 2002; Wasik & Bond, 2001). The activity of the learners is an important component of learning from read-alouds.

Use of the senses, particularly of visualization, is an important activity for both engagement and for focusing attention in learning. Sensory representation helps learners connect with new information and provides alternative codes for understanding and retention (Paivio, 1971; Sadoski, Kealy, Goetz, & Paivio, 1997). Classic, seminal work on concept mapping (Johnson, Toms-Bronowski, & Pittelman, 1982) has been extended to current strategies such as concept muraling (Farris & Downey, 2004), which represents words and their relations to a topic in a semantically organized graphic. All of these studies attest to the enduring power of visualization in word learning.

How then does this apply to instruction? We will describe three research-based methods of scaffolding read-alouds in relation to vocabulary learning: dialogic reading, text talk, and vocabulary visits.

Dialogic Reading

Whitehurst and his colleagues constructed a process for adult read-alouds with preschoolers that he called dialogic reading (Whitehurst et al., 1994). In this process, the teacher or parent helps the child become the interpreter of the story by acting as audience, questioner, and support. In the basic reading technique, termed PEER, the adult

- **P**rompts the child to say something about a specific word or concept in the book
- **E**valuates the child's response
- **E**laborates the child's response by reformulating, adding information or other extensions
- **R**epeats the prompt so the child can restate an elaborated response

After a first reading, the PEER process occurs on every page. For example, looking at a book with a police car on it, the adult might point to the police car and prompt, "What is this?" After the child says, "car," the adult would say, "Yes[evaluation], that's a police car[expansion]. Can you say police car[request for repetition]?" As the book is reread, the child becomes responsible for more and more of the words.

Many different kinds of prompts can be used. Some basic prompts include

- Cloze prompts work well with predictable and patterned books and rhymes such as "Hickory, dickory, dock, the mouse ran up the _____," letting the student fill in the correct word as they proceed through the poem or story. These prompts emphasize language patterns as well as word meaning.

- *WH* prompts, which ask what, where, when, why, and how questions. These can use pictures as well as text.
- Recall prompts that ask students to retell part of the story
- Connection prompts ask students to relate pictures, words, or ideas in the book to some experiences outside the book. For example, you might want to connect the police car book to a visit to the local police station.
- Open-ended prompts might simply ask students to tell what is going on in the book or story, or they might be more complex such as "What if…?" "What do you think?" "I wonder how…" and so forth. These can be the hardest for students to respond to and may need to be connected to another type of prompt.

Dialogic reading has proved to be an effective language and vocabulary development strategy for preschoolers, and many of the concepts of PEER have been adapted to classroom questioning with read-alouds.

Text Talk

In an observation study of early literacy classrooms, Dickinson and his colleagues were struck by the infrequency of read-aloud experiences (Dickinson, McCabe, Anastasopoulos, Peisner-Feinberg, & Poe, 2003). In 169 days of observation, there was no reading aloud observed on 69 of the observational days. Further, reading aloud was typically a large-group experience, with only about one third of the classrooms demonstrating small-group read-aloud experiences. Beck and McKeown (2001) proposed a process they called text talk, which encourages student-to-student interaction with the concepts, vocabulary, and ideas of the test.

Text talk interactions are based on open-ended questions that the teacher first poses during the read-aloud that ask children to consider ideas about the story. As the text talk continues, students are encouraged to pose their own questions and student-to-student conversations are encouraged. Text talks have six components:

1. Selected texts that have some complex events to help children build meaning
2. Interspersed open-ended questions that require students to explain and describe text ideas
3. Follow-up questions that encourage elaboration of initial ideas

4. Pictures, which are presented after students have responded to the text

5. Background knowledge, which is used to support meaning building and support or disprove assertions

6. Vocabulary word identification, which engages students in direct discussion after the story is completed

There are three objectives for the students:

1. Respond to open-ended questions using support from language in the text.

2. Interpret story elements based on textual language.

3. Use context clues to help define story vocabulary.

Specific to vocabulary, words are displayed after the first reading of the story and their meaning is discussed. Then, students are asked to decontextualize each word by giving examples of other situations in which it might be used. The teacher can use specific probes. For example, for the use of the word *insulting* in Henkes's *Lilly's Purple Plastic Purse* (1996), a text talk might look like this:

"She pinched his tail and she yelled insulting comments into his crib."

• What do we know about how Lilly feels about Julius?

• If she is yelling the comments, what kind of things do you think she is saying?

• What might *insulting* mean?

• Can you think of a time when someone might say something insulting?

For assessment, anecdotal records or direct questions can help assess student learning. Beck, et al. (2002) offer some guiding questions such as the following:

• Are students using the language of the story to make interpretations?

• Are students going beyond the immediate events of the story to make deductions and draw conclusions?

- Are students building meaning based on the text rather than relying too much on their prior knowledge?
- Were students able to use context clues to interpret the meaning of text vocabulary?

Vocabulary Visits

Studies have shown that peers provide a strong influence on student communications (Cazden, 1988; Newkirk & McLure, 1992; Peterson & Eeds, 1990). Vygotsky (1978) argued that problem solving in collaboration with peers enabled children to expand their understanding and learning. The mentor leads the child through scaffolded information to reach a level of increased understanding. This also occurs in peer interactions when a more experienced child leads peers to consider other perspectives and include prior knowledge to arrive at new interpretations of an event.

One study has reported that most elementary teachers in the U.S. read to their students several times a week. To work with teachers on tweaking the read-aloud practices already used in most classrooms, Blachowicz and Obrochta (2007) developed a process they called vocabulary visits, which used field trips as a metaphor for the enhanced read-aloud process after teachers observed that students came back from these educational excursions with many new concepts and vocabulary words. Blachowicz and Obrochta analyzed the field trips with teachers and deduced that the vocabulary visits were good vehicles for vocabulary learning because

- Field trips have a content focus. Good field trips connect to the curriculum and its content, which provides an integrated context for learning and a relational set of concepts and terms.
- Field trips engage the senses. Students are seeing, hearing, smelling, feeling, and sometimes tasting as they encounter new concepts and vocabulary.
- Field trips are preceded by preparation that helps "plow the soil" for planting the seeds of new learning. Students know what they are going to encounter, and often teachers do a read-aloud to get them ready.
- Field trips involve the mediation and scaffolding of an adult. A docent, teacher, parent, or other chaperone is there to help explain, clarify, focus, or point out interesting things.

- Field trips involve exploration, talking, reading, and writing by the students.
- Field trips involve follow-up of new concepts and terms.

The ultimate goal of vocabulary visits, then, is to structure read-aloud book experiences as virtual field trips for the classroom using the characteristics of preparation, mediation and scaffolding, exploration, and follow-up; vocabulary visits use scaffolded book read-alouds and active learning using visuals and appeals to the other senses to develop new concepts and vocabulary.

Vocabulary visits use informational literature, a rich source of new vocabulary and concepts. Nonfiction books not only present students with new vocabulary that will be essential for further learning, they provide familiarity with text structures that proliferate in the later grades. Furthermore, read-alouds of informational books stimulate thinking and discussion that help develop higher order comprehension strategies. Lastly, when combined in thematic informational text sets, these books provide the necessary repetition and use in multiple contexts that results in durable word learning.

Despite all the potential benefit of using nonfiction books, only a small part (12%–14%) of the texts frequently used for classroom instruction are informational texts (Hoffman et al., 1994; Moss & Newton, 2002). Surveys found that less than 7% of materials selected by literacy educators for instruction are informational. Similarly, less than 15% of materials used by teachers for read-alouds were of an informational variety (Yopp & Yopp, 2006). All of these lines of research suggest that increasing informational read-alouds of thematically connected texts may have a beneficial effect on vocabulary learning.

Table 2.1 compares the vocabulary visits procedure with the standard read-aloud process for first-grade students (Blachowicz & Obrochta, 2007). The vocabulary visits model fine-tunes the read-aloud process in several ways. First, informational texts are selected in sets to provide for repetition of vocabulary and concepts. In the preparation stage, 10–15 vocabulary words are selected for emphasis. In the standard read-aloud model, previewing and purpose setting typically happens with a picture walk. However, in vocabulary visits, students are presented with the topic of the text set and asked to write an individual list of words they already know about the topic before the reading begins. This is their "first write."

Table 2.1. Means and standard deviations on pretest, posttest, and gains on content vocabulary for read-aloud and vocabulary visits treatments

Class/Model	Story	Measure	Pretest	Posttest	Gain
1 RA	Plants	Mean	8.5833	13.9167	5.3333
		N	12	12	12
		SD	4.56186	5.61586	3.31205
1 VV	Environ.	Mean	6.8333	17.2500	10.4167
		N	12	12	12
		SD	3.27062	7.30037	5.10718
2 RA	Environ.	Mean	8.5714	15.2857	6.7143
		N	14	14	14
		SD	2.92770	6.24412	4.56456
2 VV	Plants	Mean	10.7143	22.4286	11.7143
		N	14	14	14
		SD	5.41264	9.07841	5.79693
3 RA	Environ.	Mean	8.9375	16.5625	7.6250
		N	16	16	16
		SD	4.86441	7.81425	4.41022
3 VV	Plants	Mean	13.4667	24.0000	10.5333
		N	15	15	15
		SD	8.50938	12.51285	5.86596
4 RA	Plants	Mean	8.3000	13.7000	5.4000
		N	10	10	10
		SD	4.90011	6.18331	3.53396
4 VV	Environ.	Mean	6.8333	17.2500	10.4167
		N	12	12	12
		SD	3.27062	7.30037	5.10718

Note. RA = standard read-aloud model. VV = vocabulary visits model. SD = standard deviation. From Blachowicz, C.L.Z., & Obrochta, C. (2007). "Tweaking practice": Modifying read-alouds to enhance content vocabulary learning in grade 1. In D.W. Rowe, R.T. Jimenez, D.L. Compton, D.K. Dickinson, Y. Kim, K.M. Leander, et al. (Eds.), *56th yearbook of the National Reading Conference* (pp. 111–121). Oak Creek, WI: National Reading Conference. Reprinted with permission.

The read-aloud model then uses an uninterrupted, fluently read text following the picture walk. Vocabulary visits, instead, begin with group talk. Students meet on the rug and the teacher uses the poster along with the first question, What do you see in this picture? As students contribute words related to what they see or think, the teacher records their contributions by putting sticky notes on the poster.

The teacher's job is to scaffold and mediate as needed by supporting student learning. Scaffolding occurs when a teacher or other adult provides support for students' learning by asking them to think more deeply about the word and to express their thinking. Some examples of scaffolding might include requesting physical response ("Touch your skull."), asking specific definitional questions ("What is a skull?"), asking for functional explanations ("A skull protects your brain."), and asking for an extension of word meaning ("Do you know any other words related to skull?" e.g., *cranium*). After each response the teacher restates or proves further. Other senses are called into play as well. For example, in a vocabulary visit about weather, the teacher asked, "What do you hear in a storm?" and "What are some words for how you feel in rain?" After 5–10 minutes, there are usually quite a number of words on the chart that the students have now heard, seen, discussed, and sometimes acted out.

Students are called upon to make physical responses during the reading of the book in a vocabulary visit. We use the "thumbs up" procedure to encourage active listening; students put their thumbs up when they hear one of the new words. Sometimes the teacher stops or rereads a sentence when no thumbs go up for a critical term, but the goal is to have a fairly normal reading experience, not one with constant interruptions.

In both the read-aloud and vocabulary visit models students discuss what they learned after the reading; however, during a vocabulary visit, they add a few new words to the chart. As a follow-up to either model, books are put in a central location for reading during independent reading time, and students are asked to read at least one of the books each week and record it in their reading logs. Students are encouraged to write about what they read in their writing journals as well.

A semantic sorting activity is also included as a follow-up to a vocabulary visit. These are simple sorts working from the posted words to categorize words in some meaningful way. For example, for the weather unit, one sort was types of storms, what you might see in a storm, and what you might hear in a storm. At the end of the entire five-book sequence, all students prepare a final list of all the words they know that are related to the topic. This is called the "final write" in the vocabulary visit process and serves as a post-assessment. No charts are visible during this process. Comparisons of student vocabulary learning in six first-grade classrooms showed that students using both models learned new words. However, there was a significant effect for condition favoring the vocabulary visits group ($F (3,101) = 21.932$, $p < .0001$) with no significant effect or interaction for either topic or class.

Others have suggested similar forms of scaffolded read-alouds (for example, Coyne, Simmons, & Kame'enui, 2004; De Temple & Snow, 1996;

Juel & Deffes, 2004), but space prevents reviewing them all here. In general, research strongly supports the idea of providing a scaffold for word learning during read-alouds, although some learning of words will occur in any form of interactive learning. A different form of scaffolding occurs when teachers encourage students to manipulate and play with words for fun.

Word Play and Vocabulary Development

Most of us have enjoyed watching word play in young children. They may explore the humor in words through alliteration, puns, and riddles. We have also watched children enjoy more formal word games, both with and without manipulatives, such as Boggle or I-Spy. Playing with words encourages students to develop forms of metalinguistic awareness that are vital to learning word meanings (Nagy & Scott, 2000). In the remainder of this chapter, we use the term *"word play"* to encompass both aspects of playing with words verbally or with gamelike manipulatives.

Unlike the research on read-alouds, the research on word play is more indirect as there have been few studies of quality carried out in this area. Smagorinsky (1991) described a program that used six games to develop vocabulary. Other studies have shown positive effects for using games with second-language learners (Yip & Kwan, 2006) and computer games with adult learners (Benne & Baxter, 1998). Though these are a small number of studies, we believe the evidence base from other research in literacy and learning supports using word play in the classroom (Blachowicz & Fisher, 2004). Our belief relates to these four research-grounded statements about word play:

1. Word play is motivating and an important component of the word-rich classroom. The motivated learner is the engaged learner who has a personal sense of self-confidence in participating in learning activities (Au, 1997), participates in a knowledgeable and strategic fashion, and is socially interactive (Guthrie & Wigfield, 1997). This engagement and enjoyment is highly correlated with achievement in all areas of literacy (Campbell, Voelkl, & Donahue, 1997), including vocabulary learning.

2. Word play calls on students to reflect metacognitively on words, word parts, and context. A current approach is to consider vocabulary instruction as metalinguistic development (Nagy & Scott, 2000). The ability to reflect on, manipulate, combine, and

recombine the components of words is an important part of vocabulary learning (Tunmer, Herriman, & Nesdale, 1988). Phonemic awareness (being able to segment phonemes, such as the *am* in *ambulance*), morphological awareness (the awareness of word-part meanings), and syntactic awareness (how a word functions in language) all play important parts in word learning (Carlisle, 1995, 2000). There is also evidence that this type of metalinguistic learning is developmental over the school years (Anglin, 1993; Roth, Speece, Cooper, & De La Paz, 1996).

3. Word play requires students to be active learners and capitalizes on possibilities for the social construction of meaning. Many studies have shown the efficacy of putting word meaning into graphic form such as a map or web, a semantic feature chart, or advanced organizer (Johnson, Toms-Bronowski, & Pittelman, 1982). It is critical to note, however, that mere construction of such graphics without discussion is not effective (Stahl & Vancil, 1986). Other approaches that stress actively relating words to one another are clustering strategies that call for students to group words into related sets. These include brainstorming, grouping, and labeling (Marzano & Marzano, 1988), designing concept hierarchies (Wixson, 1986) or constructing definition maps related to concept hierarchies (Bannon, Fisher, Pozzi, & Wessel, 1990; Schwartz & Raphael, 1985), and mapping words according to their relation to story structure categories (Blachowicz, 1986). All these approaches involve student construction of maps, graphs, charts, webs, or clusters that represent the semantic relatedness of words under study to other words and concepts.

4. Word play develops domains of word meaning and relatedness as it engages students in practice and rehearsal of words. Besides the obvious active learning involved, word play also provides a vehicle for use and rehearsal, a creation of a personal record including visualization in graphics and drawing (Pressley & Woloshyn, 1995), and kinesthetic representations in drama (Duffelmeyer, 1980). Discussion, sharing, and use of the words are necessary components of active involvement as is feedback and scaffolding on the part of the teacher.

It is a great surprise that there is not more research on using word games and puzzles in vocabulary development given their universality both historically and currently. Elsewhere (Blachowicz & Fisher, 2004), we have suggested a variety of games and playful activities for developing vocabulary. These can be generative or receptive and focus on different aspects of word learning, but they generally relate to spelling and meaning. In the sections that follow, we detail three types of word play that enhance vocabulary development: (1) word games, (2) puzzles, and (3) riddles, jokes, and puns.

Word Games

Games are often competitive, but the enjoyment can also come simply from the successful completion of a task. Some card games may emphasize semantic relationships by working on the pairing principle. For example, a pair is made when you match a word with a synonym, a definition, an antonym, a cloze sentence in which it makes sense, a picture symbolizing its meaning, or an English translation. In others, cards can be used to develop memory and reinforce learning, such as Concentration.

Other memory games may use a scoring method to motivate learning. Word fluency (Readence & Searfoss, 1980), for example, encourages students to use categorization to learn vocabulary. It is especially useful in a tutoring or small group situation; we have found it promotes self-esteem by demonstrating how many words a struggling reader may already know. The goal is to name as many words as possible in one minute. The teacher or student chosen to be monitor tallies the words as the student says them. If the student hesitates for 10 seconds or more, the teacher suggests looking around the room or to think about an activity they recently completed. After the student's initial effort, the teacher models naming words in categories, which is much easier and faster than choosing random words. The rules for scoring are (a) no repetitions, no number words, no sentences, (b) one point is earned for each word, and (c) one point is earned for each category of four words or more. Students see this as a challenge and enjoy it. They want to try to beat their own scores. Once a student is familiar with the activity, the teacher can provide categories from topics that have been studied recently, such as animals, science, or families, for example. The student must only name words that could be in these categories.

Board games may be teacher-made or adaptations of commercial games such as Candyland or Boggle. One advantage of using these is that students may already be familiar with the rules. In addition, many of these games can now be played on a computer; no more trouble with lost pieces. (See also Chapter 1, this volume, for specific suggestions for word games.)

Word Puzzles

Involvement in creating and doing puzzles can build a lifelong interest in words for students. A perusal of any newsstand or bookstore shows the popularity of word puzzles, especially crossword puzzles . One thing for teachers to note is that, although crossword puzzles are familiar to most adults, the process is not familiar to most children. Take the time to work through a crossword puzzle with your students until they get the general idea of how they are completed. Keeping blank grids in your classroom for creating crossword puzzles is also a wonderful way to stimulate thinking about words and definitions.

Jumbles call for readers to unscramble words and letters to match a clue, which is sometimes presented in cartoon form. Most newspapers run a daily jumble that can provide good classroom material—as well as an incentive to browse the paper each day. This can be a good starter in middle school or high school advisory or homeroom periods.

Elementary students love secret codes. Decoding a word, phrase, or sentence demands a substantial use of context and inference. Many books of coded and encrypted messages can be purchased in bookstores and supermarkets and at newsstands.

One of our favorite word puzzles is an alphabet-antonym table (Powell, 1986), which is very easy to construct (see Table 2.2) It is an alphabetic-generative activity that requires students to use their vocabulary knowledge and, if necessary, a dictionary, thesaurus, or synonym/antonym dictionary. A teacher might select *fail, forbid, forget, fraction*, and *front* as target words. She then presents the antonyms to the students without the target words—in this example, *succeed, allow, remember, whole*, and *back* (see Figure 2.1). The students have to guess the target words, knowing that they all begin with the letter *f*. Once students have the idea, the teacher may not clue them as to the beginning letter. An alphabet-synonym table can be constructed in a similar manner. Once students have the idea, they can work in groups or individually to construct one for their peers. If students have trouble finding a synonym or antonym, they can use a reference book. We find a thesaurus is most effective.

Riddles, Puns, and Jokes

Mike Thaler (1988), a prolific author and conference speaker, has collected many ideas for riddle and joke making. One way to make word riddles that are questions with pun-like responses is to choose a subject and generate a list of related terms. For example, if your subject is *pig*

Table 2.2. Constructing an alphabet-antonym table

Instructions	Example
1. Write down five or six words that all begin with the same letter.	Whole White Wicked Winter Wakeful Washed
2. Next to each one write the antonym.	Whole—Part White—Black Wicked—Good Winter—Summer Wakeful—Sleepy Washed—Dirty
3. Now present just the second list to the class (or fellow students) and ask them to fill in the correct antonyms, all of which must start with the same letter.	Part Black Good Summer Sleepy Dirty

Figure 2.1. Alphabet-antonym table for words beginning with *f*

Succeed	
Allow	
Remember	
Whole	
Back	

your list might contain *ham, pork, pen, grunt, hog,* and *oink.* You take the first letters off one of the words and make a list of words that begin with that letter pattern. For example, if you chose *ham,* you would make a list that began with *am* such as *ambulance, amnesia, amphibian,*

and *America*. Then you put back the missing letter and get *hambulance,
hamnesia, hamphibian*, and *hamerica*. Then you would make up riddles
for the words.

> Riddle: How do you take a pig to a hospital?
> Answer: In a hambulance!

> Riddle: What do you call it when a pig loses its memory?
> Answer: Hamnesia!

Taking students through five steps—(1) shared experience, (2) think-
aloud through the riddle, (3) group creation, (4) independent scaffolded creation, and (5) independent practice—ensures the process is
transparent to the students. Students can be further supported by having many books of jokes, riddles, and puns that give pleasurable practice as they become "riddlers." (See Chapter 1, this volume, for more
riddle ideas.)

Name riddles. Thaler (1988) also suggested name riddles in which you
must look for names with the related word part.

> Riddle: What pig discovered the theory of relativity?
> Answer: Albert Swinestein!

Hink pink. A hink pink is a pair of rhyming words that match a defining
phrase. Each word in the pair is the same number of syllables. The person who creates the phrase clues the guesser with the term hink pink
(two 1-syllable words), hinky pinky (two 2-syllable words), hinkety
pinkety (two 3-syllable words), and so forth:

> Clue: hink pink—an angry father
> Answer: mad dad

> Clue: hinkety pinkety—an evil clergyman
> Answer: sinister minister

Hink pinks are fun, and often students can come up with more than
one answer for a clue. Any meaningful answer is acceptable. The trick
to understanding hink pinks is to learn to write them. Start with the
answer, which is usually an adjective paired with a noun. These words
must share the same number of syllables and rhyme, for example, *mad
dad* from above. To write the question, brainstorm synonyms for each

word (e.g., possible synonyms for the word *mad* include *angry, irritated, upset*; synonyms for *dad* include *father, pop, pater*). Pick one from each set to make their riddle (e.g., What's an angry father, an irritated pater, or an upset pop?).

Helpful Resources

There are many books and resources online to assist teachers in adding read-alouds and word play to the classroom. Trelease's *The Read-Aloud Handbook* (2001) is a standard for teachers. For older students, Richardson's *Read It Aloud! Using Literature in the Secondary Content Classroom* (2000) is a valuable book.

Word games for vocabulary are well illustrated in books and articles by Johnson (2000) and Blachowicz and Fisher (2004, 2006). In addition, there are sites on the Internet that teachers and students can consult:

www.vocabulary.com—This website can be used by both teachers and students in middle school or above.

www.wordsmith.org/awad—A.Word.A.Day (AWAD) has a theme of the week, such as words of German origin or words related to Halloween.

www.randomhouse.com/features/rhwebsters/game.html—The game on this website is called "Beat the Dictionary," and it is basically a version of online "hangman."

rhyme.lycos.com—This website contains a rhyming dictionary and thesaurus program.

www.wordexplorations.com—This site describes itself as an advanced English vocabulary site that will expand visitors' vocabulary by focusing on Latin and Greek elements used in English.

Conclusions

It is indisputable that we learn the meaning of most of the words we know from repeated exposures within the context of listening and reading. Based on their analysis of 20 studies of incidental word learning, Swanborn and de Glopper (1999) suggested that we may learn 15 of every 100 unfamiliar words we see in text. Clearly this number must vary with grade level, ability, and the nature of the text, but it is confirmation of what we know from common sense—informal word learning occurs in a variety of settings and a variety of ways. However some students may need more help than others to develop good vocabularies. This chapter has cited research showing that especially with young children, words can be taught effectively within the act of reading aloud—a common classroom procedure. This is one type of informal learning.

Playing with words can also be informal learning. Others have argued persuasively that there are core words in the curriculum that can and should be directly taught to ensure academic success (Biemiller, 2001; Marzano, 2004). We do not dispute this. However, our concern is that such instruction may be seen by some as the whole vocabulary curriculum, replacing what can be rich and diverse vocabulary instruction such as that described and advocated by Beck, McKeown, and Kucan (2002). Learning should be fun at least part of the time and engaging all of the time. Games and word play can provide a context in which students can enjoy word learning and develop word consciousness (Graves & Watts-Taffe, 2002). Perhaps in the past there has not been enough emphasis on direct or formal vocabulary instruction, and there has been too much reliance on incidental word learning. We believe, however, that there is a place for both formal and informal vocabulary instruction in all classrooms and that reading aloud to students as well as engaging in word play can provide important and motivating avenues for developing interest in words as well as word knowledge.

Questions for Discussion

1. What is the most important idea from this chapter for the work you will be/are doing in the schools? Why?

2. How would you explain the importance of and research base for incidental learning in the classroom to a colleague? To a parent?

3. You have been named "Ruler of the School." How would you implement read-alouds across the grades?

4. Which idea, research area, or researcher in this chapter would you like to read more about? Why?

NOTE

This work was supported in part by The Shaw Fund for Literacy.

REFERENCES

Anderson, R.C., & Nagy, W.E. (1991). Word meanings. In R. Barr, M.L. Kamil, P.B. Mosenthal, & P.D. Pearson (Eds.), *Handbook of reading research* (Vol. 2, pp. 690–724). White Plains, NY: Longman.

Anglin, J.M. (1993). Vocabulary development: A morphological analysis. *Monographs of the Society for Research on Child Development, 58*(10, Serial No. 238).

Au, K.H. (1997). Ownership, literacy achievement and students of diverse cultural backgrounds. In J.T. Guthrie & A. Wigfield (Eds.), *Reading engagement: Motivating readers through integrated instruction* (pp. 168–182). Newark, DE: International Reading Association.

Bannon, E., Fisher, P.J., Pozzi, L., & Wessel, D. (1990). Effective definitions for word learning. *Journal of Reading, 34*(2), 301–302.

Baumann, J.F., & Kame'enui, E.J. (1991). Research on vocabulary instruction: Ode to Voltaire. In J. Flood, J.M. Jensen, D. Lapp, & J.R. Squire (Eds.), *Handbook of research on teaching the English language arts* (pp. 602–632). New York: Macmillan.

Beck, I.L., & McKeown, M.G. (2001). Text talk: Capturing the benefits of read-aloud experiences for young children. *The Reading Teacher, 55*(1), 10–20.

Beck, I.L., McKeown, M.G., & Kucan, L. (2002). *Bringing words to life: Robust vocabulary instruction.* New York: Guilford.

Beck, I.L., Perfetti, C.A., & McKeown, M.G. (1982). Effects of long-term vocabulary instruction on lexical access and reading comprehension. *Journal of Educational Psychology, 74*(4), 506–521.

Benne, M.R., & Baxter, K.K. (1998). An assessment of two computerized vocabulary games reveals that players improve as a result of review. *Journal of Educational Computing Research, 18*(3), 245–258.

Biemiller, A. (2001). Teaching vocabulary: Early, direct, and sequential. *American Educator, 25*(1), 24–28, 47.

Blachowicz, C.L.Z. (1986). Making connections: Alternatives to the vocabulary notebook. *Journal of Reading, 29*(7), 643–649.

Blachowicz, C.L.Z., Fisher, P., Ogle, D., & Watts-Taffe, S.M. (2006). Vocabulary: Questions from the classroom. *Reading Research Quarterly, 41*(4), 524–539.

Blachowicz, C.L.Z., & Fisher, P. (2000). Vocabulary instruction. In M.L. Kamil, P.B. Mosenthal, P.D. Pearson, & R. Barr (Eds.), *Handbook of reading research* (Vol. 3, pp. 503–523). Mahwah, NJ: Erlbaum.

Blachowicz, C.L.Z., & Fisher, P. (2004). Keep the "fun" in fundamental: Encouraging word awareness and incidental word learning in the classroom through word play. In J.F. Baumann & E.J. Kame'enui (Eds.), *Vocabulary instruction: Research to practice* (pp. 218–237). New York: Guilford.

Blachowicz, C.L.Z., & Fisher, P. (2006). *Teaching vocabulary in all classrooms* (3rd ed.). Upper Saddle River, NJ: Merrill/Prentice Hall.

Blachowicz, C.L.Z., & Obrochta, C. (2007). "Tweaking practice": Modifying read-alouds to enhance content vocabulary learning in grade 1. In D.W. Rowe, R.T. Jimenez, D.L. Compton, D.K. Dickinson, Y. Kim, K.M. Leander, & et al. (Eds.), *56th yearbook of the National Reading Conference* (pp. 111–121). Oak Creek, WI: National Reading Conference.

Brabham, E.G., & Lynch-Brown, C. (2002). Effects of teachers' reading aloud-styles on vocabulary acquisition and comprehension of students in the early elementary grades. *Journal of Educational Psychology, 94*(3), 465–473.

Brett, A., Rothlein, L., & Hurley, M. (1996). Vocabulary acquisition from listening to stories and explanations of target words. *The Elementary School Journal, 96*(4), 415–422.

Campbell, J.R., Voelkl, K.E., & Donahue, P.L. (1997). *NAEP 1996 trends in academic progress* (NCES Publication No. 97–985). Washington, DC: US. Department of Education.

Carlisle, J.F. (1995). Morphological awareness and early reading achievement. In L. Feldman (Ed.), *Morphological aspects of language processing* (pp. 189–209). Hillsdale, NJ: Erlbaum.

Carlisle, J.F. (2000). Awareness of the structure and meaning of morphologically complex words: Impact on reading. *Reading and Writing: An Interdisciplinary Journal, 12*(3–4), 169–190.

Cazden, C.B. (1988). *Classroom discourse: The language of teaching and learning.* Portsmouth, NH: Heinemann.

Cochran-Smith, M. (1984). *The making of a reader.* Norwood, NJ: Ablex.

Coyne, M.D., Simmons, D.C., & Kame'enui, E.J. (2004). Vocabulary instruction for young children at risk of experiencing reading difficulties: Teaching word meanings during shared storybook reading. In J.F. Baumann & E.J. Kame'enui (Eds.), *Vocabulary instruction: Research to practice* (pp. 41–58). New York: Guilford.

Cunningham, A.E. (2005). Vocabulary growth through independent reading and reading aloud to children. In E.H. Hiebert & M.L. Kamil (Eds.), *Teaching and learning vocabulary: Bringing research to practice* (pp. 45–68). Mahwah, NJ: Erlbaum.

Cunningham, A.E., & Stanovich, K.E. (1998). What reading does for the mind. *American Educator, 22*(1–2), 8–15.

De Temple, J.M., & Snow, C.E. (1996). Styles of parent-child book reading as related to mothers' views of literacy and children's literacy outcomes. In J. Shimron (Ed.), *Literacy and education: Essays in memory of Dina Feitelson* (pp. 49–68). Cresskill, NJ: Hampton Press.

Dickinson, D.K., & Keebler, R. (1989). Variation in preschool teachers' styles of reading books. *Discourse Processes, 12*(3), 353–375.

Dickinson, D.K., McCabe, A., Anastasopoulos, L., Peisner-Feinberg, E., & Poe, M. (2003). The comprehensive language approach to early literacy: The interrelationships among vocabulary, phonological sensitivity, and print knowledge among preschool-aged children. *Journal of Educational Psychology, 95*(3), 465–481.

Duffelmeyer, F.A. (1980). The influence of experience-based vocabulary instruction on learning word meanings. *Journal of Reading, 24*(1), 35–40.

Eller, G., Pappas, C.C., & Brown, E. (1988). The lexical development of kindergartners: Learning from written context. *Journal of Reading Behavior, 20*(1), 5–24.

Elley, W.B. (1988). Vocabulary acquisition from listening to stories. *Reading Research Quarterly, 24*(2), 174–187.

Ewers, C.A., & Brownson, S.M. (1999). Kindergarteners' vocabulary acquisition as a function of active vs. passive storybook reading, prior vocabulary, and working memory. *Reading Psychology, 20*(1), 11–20.

Farris, P.J., & Downey, P.M. (2004). Concept muraling: Dropping visual crumbs along the instructional trail. *The Reading Teacher, 58*(4), 376–384.

Fisher, D., Flood, J., Lapp, D., & Frey, N. (2004). Interactive read-alouds: Is there a common set of implementation practices? *The Reading Teacher, 58*(1), 8–17.

Fukkink, R.G., Blok, H., & de Glopper, K. (2001). Deriving word meaning from written context: A multicomponential skill. *Language Learning, 51*(3), 477–496.

Graves, M.F., & Watts-Taffe, S.M. (2002). The place of word consciousness in a research-based vocabulary program. In A.E. Farstrup & S.J. Samuels (Eds.), *What research has to say about reading instruction* (3rd ed., pp. 140–165). Newark, DE: International Reading Association.

Guthrie, J.T., & Wigfield, A., (Eds.). (1997). *Reading engagement: Motivating readers through integrated instruction.* Newark, DE: International Reading Association.

Hargrave, A.C., & Sénéchal, M. (2000). A book reading intervention with preschool children who have limited vocabularies: The benefits of regular reading and dialogic reading. *Early Childhood Research Quarterly, 15*(1), 75–95.

Hart, B., & Risley, T.R. (1995). *Meaningful differences in the everyday experience of young American children.* Baltimore: Paul H. Brookes.

Hoffman, J.V., McCarthy, S.J., Abbott, J., Christian, C., Corman, L., Curry, C., et al. (1994). So what's new in the new basals? A focus on first grade. *Journal of Reading Behavior, 26*(1), 47–73.

Johnson, D.D. (2000). *Vocabulary in the elementary and middle school.* Boston: Allyn & Bacon.

Johnson, D.D., Pittelman, S.D., Toms-Bronowski, S., & Levin, K.M. (1984). *An investigation of the effects of prior knowledge and vocabulary acquisition on passage comprehension* (Program Rep. No. 84-5). Madison: Wisconsin Center for Education Research, University of Wisconsin.

Johnson, D.D., Toms-Bronowski, S., & Pittelman, S.D. (1982). *An investigation of the effectiveness of semantic mapping and semantic feature analysis with intermediate grade level students* (Program Rep. No. 83-3). Madison: Wisconsin Center for Education Research, University of Wisconsin.

Juel, C., & Deffes, R. (2004). Making words stick. *Educational Leadership, 61*(6), 30–34.

Martinez, M.G., & Teale, W.H. (1989). Classroom storybook reading: The creation of texts and learning opportunities. *Theory Into Practice, 28*(2), 126–135.

Marzano, R.J. (2004) *Building background knowledge for academic achievement.* Alexandria, VA: Association for Supervision and Curriculum Development.

Marzano, R.J., & Marzano, J.S. (1988). *A cluster approach to elementary vocabulary instruction.* Newark, DE: International Reading Association.

Moss, B., & Newton, E. (2002). An examination of the informational text genre in basal readers. *Reading Psychology, 23*(1), 1–13.

Nagy, W.E., & Scott, J. (2000). Vocabulary processes. In M.L. Kamil, P.B. Mosenthal, P.D. Pearson, & R. Barr (Eds.), *Handbook of reading research* (Vol. 3, pp. 269–283). Mahwah, NJ: Erlbaum.

Nagy, W.E. (1988). *Teaching vocabulary to improve reading comprehension.* Newark, DE: International Reading Association.

Nagy, W.E., Herman, P.A., & Anderson, R.C. (1985). Learning words from context. *Reading Research Quarterly, 20*(2), 233–253.

Newkirk, T., & McLure, P. (1992). *Listening in: Children talk about books (and other things)*. Portsmouth, NH: Heinemann.

Paivio, A. (1971). *Imagery and verbal processes*. New York: Holt, Rinehart and Winston.

Penno, J.F., Wilkinson, I.A.G., & Moore, D.W. (2002). Vocabulary acquisition from teacher explanation and repeated listening to stories: Do they overcome the Matthew effect? *Journal of Educational Psychology, 94*(1), 23–33.

Peterson, R., & Eeds, M. (1990). *Grand conversations: Literature groups in action*. Richmond Hill, Ontario: Scholastic.

Powell, W.R. (1986). Teaching vocabulary through opposition. *Journal of Reading, 29*(7), 617–621.

Pressley, M., & Woloshyn, V. (1995). *Cognitive strategies instructions that really improves children's academic performance* (2nd ed.). Cambridge, MA: Brookline Books.

Readence, J.E., & Searfoss, L.W. (1980). Teaching strategies for vocabulary development. *English Journal, 69*(7), 43–46.

Richardson, J. (2000). *Read it aloud! Using literature in the secondary content classroom*. Newark, DE: International Reading Association.

Robbins, C., & Ehri, L.C. (1994). Reading storybooks to kindergarteners helps them learn new vocabulary words. *Journal of Educational Psychology, 86*(1), 54–64.

Roth, F., Speece, D., Cooper, D.H., & De La Paz, S. (1996). Unresolved mysteries: How do metalinguistic and narrative skills connect with early reading? *The Journal of Special Education, 30*(3), 257–277.

Sadoski, M., Kealy, W.A., Goetz, E.T., & Paivio, A. (1997). Concreteness and imagery effects in the written composition of definitions. *Journal of Educational Psychology, 89*(3), 518–526.

Schwartz, R., & Raphael, T. (1985). Concept of definition: A key to improving students' vocabulary. *The Reading Teacher, 39*(2), 198–205.

Sénéchal, M., & Cornell, E.H. (1993). Vocabulary acquisition through shared reading experiences. *Reading Research Quarterly, 28*(4), 360–374.

Sénéchal, M., Thomas, E., & Monker, J. (1995). Individual differences in 4-year-old children's acquisition of vocabulary during storybook reading. *Journal of Educational Psychology, 87*(2), 218–229.

Smagorinsky, P. (1991). *Expressions: Multiple intelligences in the English class*. Urbana, IL: National Council of Teachers of English.

Snow, C.E. (1991). The theoretical basis for relationships between language and literacy development. *Journal of Research in Childhood Education, 6*(1), 5–10.

Stahl, N.A., Brozo, W.G., Smith, B.D., & Commander, N. (1991). Effects of teaching generative vocabulary strategies in the college developmental reading program. *Journal of Research and Development in Education, 24*(4), 24–32.

Stahl, S.A., & Fairbanks, M. (1986). The effects of vocabulary instruction: A model-based meta-analysis. *Review of Educational Research, 56*(1), 72–110.

Stahl, S.A., & Vancil, S.J. (1986). Discussion is what makes semantic maps work in vocabulary instruction. *The Reading Teacher, 40*(1), 62–67.

Stanovich, K.E. (1986). Matthew effects in reading: Some consequences of individual differences in the acquisition of literacy. *Reading Research Quarterly, 21*(4), 360–407.

Swanborn, M.S.L., & de Glopper, K. (1999). Incidental word learning while reading: A meta-analysis. *Review of Educational Research, 69*(3), 261–285.

Thaler, M. (1988). Reading, writing, and riddling. *Learning, 17*(6), 58–59.

Trelease, J. (2001). *The read-aloud handbook*. Boston: Houghton Mifflin.

Tunmer, W.E., Herriman, M.L., & Nesdale, A.R. (1988). Metalinguistic abilities and beginning reading. *Reading Research Quarterly, 23*(2), 134–158.

Vygotsky, L.S. (1978). *Mind in society: The development of higher psychological processes* (M. Cole, V. John-Steiner, S. Scribner, & E. Souberman, Eds. & Trans.). Cambridge, MA: Harvard University Press.

Wasik, B.A., & Bond, M.A. (2001). Beyond the pages of a book: Interactive book reading and language development in preschool classrooms. *Journal of Experimental Psychology, 93*(2), 243–250.

Whitehurst, G.J., Epstein, J.N., Angell, A.L., Payne, A.C., Crone, D.A., & Fischel, J.E. (1994). Outcomes of an emergent literacy intervention in Head Start. *Journal of Educational Psychology, 86*(4), 542–555.

Whitehurst, G.J., Zevenbergen, A.A., Crone, D.A., Schultz, M.D., Velting, O.N., & Fischel, J.E. (1999). Outcomes of an emergent literacy intervention from Head Start through second grade. *Journal of Educational Psychology, 91*(2), 261–272.

Wixson, K.K. (1986). Vocabulary instruction and children's comprehension of basal stories. *Reading Research Quarterly, 21*(3), 317–329.

Yip, F.W.M., & Kwan, A.C.M. (2006). Online vocabulary games as a tool for teaching and learning English vocabulary. *Educational Media International, 43*(3), 233–249.

Yopp, R.H., & Yopp, H.K. (2006). Informational texts as read-alouds at school and home. *Journal of Literacy Research, 38*(1), 37–51.

LITERATURE CITED

Henkes, K. (1996). *Lilly's purple plastic purse*. New York: Scholastic.

Chapter 3

Instruction on Individual Words: One Size Does Not Fit All

Michael F. Graves

Today the importance of vocabulary is widely and firmly recognized. This current interest is due to a number of factors, among the most important of which are (1) Hart and Risley's *Meaningful Differences in the Everyday Experiences of Young American Children* (1995), which revealed the huge vocabulary deficit faced by many children of poverty, (2) a growing numbers of English-language learners in U.S. classrooms, who require assistance in developing their English vocabularies (American Educational Research Association, 2004), (3) the Report of the National Reading Panel (National Institute of Child Health and Human Development, 2000), which identified vocabulary as one of the five central components of reading instruction, (4) the report of the RAND Reading Study Group (2002), which identified vocabulary as crucial to reading comprehension, and (5) the No Child Left Behind legislation, which identified vocabulary instruction as one of the five required components of Reading First programs.

A great deal of evidence can be found that shows the current interest in vocabulary. Fifty percent of the respondents to *Reading Today's* most recent pole of What's Hot and What's Not in reading (Cassidy & Cassidy, 2008) agreed that vocabulary is a "hot" topic. At least five significant books on vocabulary instruction have been published in the past two years—Hiebert and Kamil's *Teaching and Learning Vocabulary* (2006), Stahl and Nagy's *Teaching Word Meanings* (2006), my own *The Vocabulary Book: Learning and Instruction* (Graves, 2006), Wagner, Muse, and Tannenbaum's *Vocabulary Acquisition: Implications for Reading Comprehension* (2007), and the present volume. Furthermore, one current PBS series (Martha Speaks, produced by WGBH television in Boston) focuses exclusively on building students' vocabularies, while another (a new version of *The Electric Company*, produced by Children's Television Workshop) includes vocabulary development as a major goal.

What Research Has to Say About Vocabulary Instruction, edited by Alan E. Farstrup and S. Jay Samuels.
© 2008 by the International Reading Association.

In this chapter, I first discuss the importance of vocabulary, the number of words students need to learn, and the vocabulary deficit faced by some children. Next, I discuss the multifaceted and long-term vocabulary program described in *The Vocabulary Book* (Graves, 2006). In my formulation, the program includes four parts: (1) providing rich and varied language experiences, (2) teaching individual words, (3) teaching word-learning strategies, and (4) fostering word consciousness. Very similar multifaceted programs have been described by Baumann and Kame'enui (2004), Stahl and Nagy (2006), and Blachowicz, Fisher, Ogle, and Watts-Taffe (2006).

Following this introductory material comes the central part of this chapter, a more detailed look at a number of different procedures for teaching individual words. By presenting a number of different procedures, I illustrate the central themes of this chapter—that there are many different ways to teach individual words, that different approaches serve different purposes, and that there is no single best approach.

The Importance of Vocabulary

This current interest in vocabulary is extremely fortunate because, as Petty, Harold, and Stoll (1967) pointed out some years ago, vocabulary is tremendously important to students' success:

> The importance of vocabulary is daily demonstrated in schools and out. In the classroom, the achieving students possess the most adequate vocabularies. Because of the verbal nature of most classroom activities, knowledge of words and ability to use language are essential to success in these activities. After schooling has ended, adequacy of vocabulary is almost equally essential for achievement in vocations and in society. (p. 7)

Petty and his colleagues' testimonial is well supported by research. The findings of over 100 years of vocabulary research include the following:

- Vocabulary knowledge is one of the best indicators of verbal ability (Sternberg, 1987; Terman, 1916).
- Vocabulary knowledge contributes to young children's phonological awareness, which in turn contributes to their word recognition (Goswami, 2001; Nagy, 2005).
- Vocabulary knowledge in kindergarten and first grade is a significant predictor of reading comprehension in the middle and secondary grades (Cunningham & Stanovich, 1997; Scarborough, 1998).

- Vocabulary difficulty strongly influences the readability of text (Chall & Dale, 1995; Klare, 1984).

- Teaching vocabulary can improve reading comprehension for both native English speakers (Beck, Perfetti, & McKeown, 1982) and English learners (Carlo et al., 2004).

- Growing up in poverty can seriously restrict the vocabulary children learn before beginning school and make attaining an adequate vocabulary a challenging task (Coyne, Simmons, & Kame'enui, 2004; Hart & Risley, 1995).

- Less advantaged students are likely to have substantially smaller vocabularies than their more advantaged classmates (Templin, 1957; White, Graves, & Slater, 1990).

- Learning English vocabulary is one of the most crucial tasks for English learners (Folse, 2004; Nation, 2001).

- Lack of vocabulary can be a crucial factor underlying the school failure of disadvantaged students (Becker, 1977; Biemiller, 1999).

How Many Words Do Students Learn?

The vocabulary learning task is enormous! Estimates of vocabulary size vary greatly, but a reasonable estimate based on the work of Anderson and Nagy (1992), Anglin (1993), Miller and Wakefield (2000), Nagy and Anderson (1984), Nagy and Herman (1987), Stahl and Nagy (2006), and White, Graves, and Slater (1990) is this: The books and other reading materials used by school children include over 180,000 different words. The average child enters school with a very small reading vocabulary, typically consisting largely of environmental print. Once in school, however, a child's reading vocabulary is likely to soar at a rate of 3,000–4,000 words a year, leading to a reading vocabulary of something like 25,000 words by the time he or she is in eighth grade, and a reading vocabulary of something like 50,000 words by the end of high school.

The Vocabulary Deficit of Some Children

I have already noted that some children of poverty have a serious vocabulary deficit, but this important finding deserves elaboration. The most compelling evidence came from Hart and Risley's (1995; see also 2003) longitudinal study of the vocabularies of 1- to 3-year-old children of professional, working class, and welfare children. Hart and Risley's results indicated that welfare children had vocabularies about half the size of their middle-class counterparts and that similar differences persisted into the school years. There is also evidence that having a small vocabulary is a very serious detriment to success in reading (Becker, 1977; Biemiller, 1999; Chall & Jacobs, 2003). These two facts make it especially important to find ways to bolster the oral and reading vocabularies of students who enter school with small stores of words. For similar reasons, bolstering the English vocabularies of English learners is critically important (American Educational Research Association, 2004; Folse, 2004; Nation, 2001).

A Multifaceted and Long-Term Vocabulary Program

The importance of vocabulary, the number of words that children need to learn, and the vocabulary deficit faced by some children are reasons for creating robust and comprehensive vocabulary programs, programs that are multifaceted and long term and can assist all students—children who enter school with relatively small vocabularies, English learners with small English vocabularies, children who possess adequate but not exceptional vocabularies, and children who already have rich and powerful vocabularies and are prepared for the challenge of developing still more sophisticated and useful vocabularies—in developing the vocabularies they need to succeed in school and beyond. Over the past 20 years, I have developed such a program (see, for example, Graves, 1984, 1992, 2000), and I recently described it in some detail in *The Vocabulary Book* (Graves, 2006). The program has received a good deal of support. It was reviewed favorably in the report of the RAND Reading Study Group (2002), used by Baumann and Kame'enui (2004) as a framework for their vocabulary book, endorsed by Blachowicz et al. (2006), used in a slightly modified form by Stahl and Nagy (2006) in their vocabulary book, and validated in a recent study by Baumann, Ware, and Edwards (2007). The program has four components: (1) providing rich and varied language experiences, (2) teaching individual words, (3) teaching word-learning strategies, and (4) fostering word consciousness. In the next several paragraphs, I briefly discuss each component and the rationale behind it. (See also Chapter 7, this volume, for discussion of how these four components can be used to teach content area vocabulary.)

Providing Rich and Varied Language Experiences

One way to build students' vocabularies is to immerse them in a rich array of language experiences so that they learn words through listening, speaking, reading, and writing. In kindergarten and the primary grades, listening and speaking are particularly important for promoting vocabulary growth. Most children enter kindergarten with substantial oral vocabularies and very small reading vocabularies. Appropriately most of the words in materials young children read are words that are in their oral vocabularies (Biemiller, in press). For this reason, young children will not learn many new words from reading. Where they will learn them is from discussion, from being read to, and from having their attention directly focused on words. In the intermediate grades and secondary schools, listening and speaking continue to be important. Students of all ages and English learners as well as native English speakers need to engage frequently in authentic discussions—give and take conversations in which they are given the opportunity to thoughtfully discuss meaningful topics.

Increasingly from the intermediate grades on, reading becomes the principle language experience for increasing students' vocabularies. If we can substantially increase the reading students do, we can substantially increase the words they learn. Thus one way to help students increase their vocabularies is to increase the amount of reading they do. Some researchers believe that such an increase is the most powerful thing we can do to improve students' vocabularies, and this may well be the case. Anyone interested in increasing students' vocabularies should do everything possible to see that they read as much and as widely as possible.

Teaching Individual Words

Another way to help students increase their vocabularies, and the one that will be the major focus of this chapter, is to teach them individual words. To be sure, the size of the vocabulary that students will eventually attain means that we cannot teach all of the words they need to learn. However, this does not mean that we cannot and should not teach some of these words. Fortunately research has revealed a good deal about effective— and ineffective—approaches to teaching individual words. Vocabulary instruction is most effective when it is rich, deep, and extended; however, because there are so many words to teach, there is not always enough time. Thus, there is a need for rich, deep, and extended instruction on some words and less robust, introductory instruction on others.

Teaching Word-Learning Strategies

A third approach to help students increase their vocabularies is to teach word-learning strategies. The most widely recommended strategy is that of using context. Recent reviews of research indicate that the strategy can be taught. And several studies (Baumann, Edwards, Boland, Olejnik, & Kame'enui, 2003; Baumann et al., 2002; Blachowicz & Zabroske, 1990; Buikema & Graves, 1993) describe research-based ways of doing so.

Using word parts to unlock the meanings of unknown words is another widely recommended strategy, and doing so is well supported by research (Anglin, 1993; Baumann, Font, Edwards, & Boland, 2005; White, Power, & White, 1989). I (Graves, 2004) described research-based procedures for teaching prefixes. White, Sowell, and Yanagihara (1989) discussed research-based procedures for teaching suffixes. And Edwards, Font, Baumann, and Boland (2005) discussed research-based procedures for teaching prefixes, suffixes, and roots. (See also Chapter 1, this volume, for further discussion of teaching roots.)

Using the dictionary is still another recommended approach students can use to learn word meanings themselves (Blachowicz & Fisher, 1996; Graves, Juel, & Graves, 2007), and the same authors who recommend teaching students to use the dictionary have suggested what needs to be taught and learned in order for them to do so.

Fostering Word Consciousness

The last component of the four-part program is fostering word consciousness. The term *word consciousness* refers to an awareness of and interest in words and their meanings. Word consciousness involves both a cognitive and an affective stance toward words, and it integrates metacognition about words, motivation to learn words, and deep and lasting interest in words (Graves & Walts-Taffe, in press).

Students who are word conscious are aware of the words around them—those they read and hear and those they write and speak. This awareness involves an appreciation of the power of words, an understanding of why certain words are used instead of others, and a sense of the words that could be used in place of those selected by a writer or speaker. It also involves, as Scott and Nagy (2004) emphasized, recognition of the communicative power of words, of the differences between spoken and written language, and of the particular importance of word choice in written language. And it involves an interest in learning and using new words and becoming more skillful and precise in word usage.

With something like 50,000 words to learn and with most of this word learning taking place incidentally as students are reading and listening, a positive disposition toward words is crucial. Word consciousness exists at many levels of complexity and sophistication and can and should be fostered among preschoolers as well as among students in and beyond high school.

While each of these four parts is crucial to building a comprehensive vocabulary program, a single chapter cannot deal with the whole of such a program. In the remainder of this chapter, I concentrate on teaching individual words—emphasizing, as I have noted, that many different types of instruction in individual words are necessary. Here, I will group these under three broad categories: (1) building students' oral vocabularies, (2) rich and powerful vocabulary instruction, and (3) introductory vocabulary instruction.

Building Students' Oral Vocabularies

Some children (especially some children of poverty and English-language learners) come to school with very small listening vocabularies, vocabularies that do not serve them well in school. This is an extremely important fact to recognize because reading instruction generally begins by assuming that children have a relatively large listening vocabulary and that the major initial task is to teach them to read the words they already have in their oral vocabulary. If, of course, children have a very small oral vocabulary, this doesn't work.

Fortunately over the past decade or so, there have been a number of studies in which researchers, teachers, parents, and aides used an oral reading procedure, shared book reading, with the goal of building students' vocabularies. Shared book reading performance was quite similar across these studies and repeatedly produced positive results. Among these studies is work by Whitehurst and his colleagues referred to as dialogic reading (Whitehurst et al., 1988; Whitehurst et al., 1994; Zevenbergen & Whitehurst, 2004), work by Beck and McKeown termed text talk (Beck & McKeown, 2001, 2007), work by Jules and Deffes called anchored reading (Juel & Deffes, 2004), and work by Biemiller, which I call direct and systematic instruction (Biemiller, 2001, 2004; Biemiller & Boote, 2006). Each of these is described in some detail in *The Vocabulary Book* (Graves, 2006). (See also Chapter 2, this volume, for further discussion of text talk and dialogic reading.) In the following sections, I first describe the general characteristics of these procedures and then give some specifics of one of them, Biemiller's direct and systematic instruction.

General Characteristics of Effective Shared Book Reading

The general characteristics of these procedures as synthesized by De Temple and Snow (2003) and Graves (2006) are as follows.

Effective shared book reading is interactive. That is, both the reader and the children play active roles. The reader frequently pauses, prompts children to respond, and follows up those responses with answers and perhaps more prompts. Children respond to the prompts or questions, elaborate on some of their responses, and perhaps ask questions of their own. Additionally, the reader scaffolds children's efforts to understand the words and the text.

Effective shared book reading usually involves reading the book several times. This allows the children and the reader to revisit the same topic and the same words several times, and it allows the children to begin actively using some of the words they have heard and perhaps had explained in previous readings.

Effective shared book reading directly focuses children's attention on a relatively small number of words. In some cases, the word work comes during the first reading, in some cases during subsequent readings, and in some cases after the book has been read.

Effective shared book reading requires the adult readers to read fluently, with appropriate intonation, and with expression. Skilled adult readers effectively engage children with their animated and lively reading style.

Effective shared book reading requires carefully selected books. The books need to be interesting and enjoyable for children, and they need to stretch children's thinking a bit. Of course, the books also need to include some challenging words that are worth studying and will enhance children's vocabularies.

Biemiller's Direct and Systematic Instruction

Direct and systematic instruction (Biemiller, 2001, 2004; Biemiller & Boote, 2006) is an interactive oral reading technique intended for kindergarten through second-grade children. As the name suggests, the procedure includes some very direct instruction, more direct than that provided in some of the other approaches. Also, direct and systematic instruction differs from some of the other programs in that vocabulary development is the sole concern. The procedure is directly motivated by the fact that the vocabularies of disadvantaged children lag well behind those of their more advantaged peers and that the instruction needed to make up that gap needs to be "early, direct, and sequential" (Biemiller, 2001, p. 24).

The first step is to select books. The program uses one book per week, and to teach the number of words necessary to markedly increase disadvantaged students' vocabularies the program should be used for at least one year and preferably for three years. About 30 books are needed for each year. As it has usually been implemented, the approach uses narratives. Typical of books appropriate for kindergarten are Norman Bridwell's *Clifford at the Circus* (1977) and Phoebe Gillman's *Jillian Jiggs* (1997). Typical of those appropriate for grade 1 are Alice Schertle's *Down the Road* (1995) and Dayal Khalsa's *Julian* (1989). And typical of those appropriate for grade 2 are Leo Lionni's *Alexander and the Wind-Up Mouse* (1969) and Stephanie McLellan's *The Chicken Cat* (2000).

The next step, and one that is given more attention in Biemiller's approach than in other interactive oral reading approaches, is selecting words. Unfortunately in this program as in the others, selecting words remains an art, not a science (Biemiller & Boote, 2006). Words are selected based on the teacher's intuition that they are (a) known by some but not all children at the grade level at which he or she is working and (b) are not rare or obscure and thus are likely to be useful to children as they progress into the upper elementary grades. Biemiller and his colleagues are currently working on establishing lists of words to teach at various grade levels. Some samples of words that have been used with the procedure and the percentages of students Biemiller and Boote (2006) reported as knowing the words prior to instruction are shown in Table 3.1.

Select about 24 words from each book. Students will not remember all the words that are taught, but Biemiller estimated that if this number of words were taught each week over a school year, children might learn 400 words. While such learning will not result in children with the smallest vocabularies catching up with those with larger vocabularies, it is a significant improvement over what they would know without instruction.

The third step is to implement the procedure, as follows:

1. Read the book through once; include some comprehension questions after reading it, but do not interrupt the reading with

Table 3.1. Sample of words used with direct and systematic instruction and percentages of students knowing them prior to instruction

Kindergarten	First grade	Second grade
slip (8%)	snag (4%)	envy (3%)
obey (16%)	chance (11%)	scowl (12%)
coop (22%)	certainly (29%)	glance (26%)
parade (34%)	realize (45%)	restless (40%)
fairy (57%)	pile (72%)	appetite (50%)

vocabulary instruction. (Experience has shown that children may object to interrupting the first reading of the book with vocabulary instruction.)

2. Reread the book on a second day, teaching about 8 words. When you come to a sentence containing a target word, stop and reread the sentence. After rereading the word, give a brief explanation. For example, after reading the sentence "It seemed like a good solution" in a second grade book, pose the question "What does solution mean?" Then, answer your question with something like "A solution is the answer to a problem." Remember to keep the definitions simple, direct, and focused on the meaning of the word as it was used in the story. At the end of the day's instruction, review the words taught by rereading the sentence in which they appeared and the definition you gave.

3. Reread the story two more times on subsequent days, teaching about 8 new words each time. Briefly define the words as you come to them and review all of the words learned that day at the end of the reading.

4. At the end of the week, review all of the words taught during that week, this time using a new context sentence to provide some variety but giving the same definition.

Used in this way, the procedure will require about half an hour a day and will result in students learning a significant number of words over the course of a year. Of course, if the procedure is used from kindergarten through second grade—this was Biemiller's goal—students will learn an even more significant number of words.

Rich and Powerful Vocabulary Instruction

As I explain in some detail in *The Vocabulary Book* (Graves, 2006), we know a great deal about what constitutes truly powerful vocabulary instruction. Instruction that involves activating prior knowledge, comparing and contrasting word meanings, making inferences, other forms of active learning, and frequent encounters is likely to be more effective than less active and briefer instruction (Baumann et al., 2003; Beck & McKeown, 1991; Beck, McKeown, & Kucan, 2002; Graves, 2006; Nagy, 2005; Stahl & Nagy, 2006). It is important to recognize that powerful vocabulary instruction comes at a cost: It takes time. Here are five powerful procedures; all of them take a significant amount of time, although those presented earlier take less time.

Semantic Mapping

Semantic mapping (Heimlich & Pittelman, 1986) is one of the best known and most widely used forms of powerful vocabulary instruction—and it should be. Because semantic mapping involves students in thinking about the relationship between the target word and related concepts, it is particularly suited to improving comprehension of a selection:

1. Put a word representing a central concept on the chalkboard.
2. Ask students to work in groups, listing as many words related to the central concept as they can.
3. Write students' words on the chalkboard grouped in broad categories.
4. Have students name the categories and perhaps suggest additional ones.
5. Discuss with students the central concept, the other words, the categories, and their interrelationships.

Figure 3.1 shows a semantic map for the word *tenement* that students might create before or after reading a social studies chapter on urban housing.

Semantic Feature Analysis

Semantic feature analysis (Pittelman, Heimlich, Berglund, & French, 1991) is another widely used powerful strategy. Because it requires students to distinguish between words with closely related meanings, it is particularly suited to refining word meanings. Implementing the approach is straightforward:

Figure 3.1. Semantic map for the word *tenement*

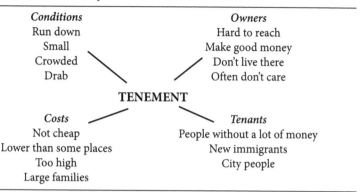

Conditions	Owners
Run down	Hard to reach
Small	Make good money
Crowded	Don't live there
Drab	Often don't care

TENEMENT

Costs	Tenants
Not cheap	People without a lot of money
Lower than some places	New immigrants
Too high	City people
Large families	

Note. From Graves, M.F. (2006). *The vocabulary book: Learning and instruction*. New York: Teachers College Press. Reprinted with permission.

1. Present students with a grid that contains a set of related words on one axis and a list of features that each of the words may or may not have on the other axis. Figure 3.2 shows a grid for *road* and *pathways*.

2. In the first work with semantic feature analysis, show students a completed grid, and discuss how the checks and pluses indicate whether or not a particular feature applies to each word.

3. In later work with the procedure, show students grids with the terms and attributes filled in but without the pluses and minuses, and ask students to insert them.

4. Later still, show grids with some terms and some attributes, and ask students to add to both the list of related words and the list of attributes, and then to fill in the pluses and minuses.

5. Finally, after students are proficient in working with partially completed grids you supply, they can create their own grids for sets of related words they suggest.

As with many techniques for vocabulary instruction, as part of semantic feature analysis there should be a good deal of discussion, for much of the power of the procedure lies in the discussion. With the grid shown in Figure 3.2, for example, discussion of the fact that *boulevards*, *freeways*, and *turnpikes* share the same features should lead to a discussion of whether additional attributes should be added to distinguish

Figure 3.2. Semantic feature analysis grid for *roads* and *walkways*

Roads and *Walkways*	Typical characteristics					
	narrow	wide	paved	unpaved	for walking	for driving
path	+	−	−	+	+	−
trail	+	−	−	+	+	−
road	+	+	+	+	−	+
lane	+	−	+	+	+	+
boulevard	−	+	+	−	−	+
freeway	−	+	+	−	−	+
turnpike	−	+	+	−	−	+

Note. From Graves, M.F. (2006). *The vocabulary book: Learning and instruction.* New York: Teachers College Press. Reprinted with permission.

among these. Alternately, you and your students might conclude that these three terms are synonyms.

Robust Vocabulary Instruction

Robust Vocabulary Instruction, developed by Beck and McKeown and their colleagues (Beck et al., 1982; Beck et al., 2002; Beck & McKeown, 2007) is probably the best known approach to powerful vocabulary instruction. The procedure has taken several forms and often is used to teach a set of words, but in the interest of space, this example shows a fairly simple version that deals with a single word—*ambitious*:

1. Begin with a student-friendly definition.

   ambitious—really wanting to succeed at something

2. Arrange for students to work with the word more than once. One encounter with a word is very unlikely to leave students with a rich and lasting understanding of its meaning. Two is a minimum, but more are desirable.

3. Provide the word in more than one context so that students' understanding is not limited to one situation. The several contexts need not come at the same time.

   Susan's *ambition* to become an Olympic high jumper was so strong that she was willing to practice six hours a day.

Rupert had never been an *ambitious* person, and after his accident he did little other than watch television.

4. Engage students in activities in which they need to deal with various facets of the word's meaning and investigate relationships between the target word and other words.

Would you like to have a really *ambitious* person as a friend? Why or why not?

Which of the following better demonstrates *ambition*? (1) A stock broker gets up every day and goes to work. (2) A stock broker stays late at work every day, trying to close as many deals as possible before leaving.

How likely is it that an *ambitious* person would be *lethargic*? How likely is it that an *ambitious* person would be *energetic*? Explain your answers.

5. Have students create uses for the words.

Tell me about a friend that you see as very *ambitious*. What are some of the things she does that show how *ambitious* she is?

6. Encourage students to use the word outside of class.

Come to class tomorrow prepared to talk about someone who appears to be *ambitious*. This could be a stranger you happen to notice outside of class, someone in your family, someone you read about, or someone you see on TV.

Quite obviously, robust vocabulary instruction will create deep and lasting understanding of words. Equally obviously, robust vocabulary instruction takes a great deal of time, certainly more time than you can spend on most words you teach. Additionally the procedure works best with interesting and provocative words that encourage the types of activities illustrated in the example. You will need to decide just when to use it.

The Frayer Method

The Frayer method, originally developed by Frayer, Frederick, and Klausmeier (1969), is a very powerful method of teaching new and potentially challenging concepts and represents the basic approach to concept development. The major steps of the method are presented here using the word/concept *globe*:

1. Define the new concept, giving its necessary attributes. When feasible, it is also helpful to show a picture illustrating the concept.

   A *globe* is a spherical (ball-like) representation of a planet.

2. Distinguish between the new concept and similar but different concepts with which it might be mistaken. In doing so it may be appropriate to identify some accidental attributes that might falsely be considered necessary attributes of the new concept.

   A *globe* is different from a *map* because a map is flat. A *globe* is different from a *contour map*, a map in which mountains and other high points are raised above the general level of the map, because a contour map is not spherical.

3. Give examples of the concept and explain why they are examples.

   The most common *globe* is a globe of the earth. Globes of the earth are spherical and come in various sizes and colors.

   A much less common *globe* is a globe of another planet. A museum might have a spherical representation of Saturn.

4. Give nonexamples of the concept.

   A map of California

   A map of how to get to a friend's house

5. Present students with examples and nonexamples, and ask them to distinguish between the two.

   An aerial photograph of New York (nonexample)

   A red sphere representing Mars (example)

   A walking map of St. Louis (nonexample)

   A ball-shaped model of the moon (example)

6. Have students present examples and nonexamples of the concept, have them explain why they are examples or nonexamples, and give them feedback on their examples and explanations.

Although the Frayer method is definitely time consuming, it is also very powerful, and provides a good illustration of what it takes to teach challenging concepts. When unknown words represent new ideas and are not simply new labels for known concepts, the Frayer method is worth serious consideration.

Introductory Vocabulary Instruction

As is the case with rich and powerful vocabulary instruction, we know a lot about less powerful and less time consuming instruction (see, for example, Blachowicz et al., 2006; Graves, 2006; Stahl & Nagy, 2006). We have a good answer to the question "How brief can vocabulary instruction be and still be effective?" As documented by Stahl and Fairbanks (1986), effective vocabulary instruction should include both a definition of the word and the word in context. Thus, I recommend neither instruction that presents a word in context with no definition nor instruction that gives a definition of a word but no context. Here are four procedures that contain these two crucial elements yet are not particularly time consuming. They will not serve to provide students with deep and rich word meanings, but they can serve the purpose of helping students understand a word when it appears in a text they are reading rather than stumbling over it.

Glossaries

Probably the least time consuming and least interruptive way of teaching words is to provide students with glossaries of the potentially challenging words in a text they are reading. Students see the words in the context of the selection and then have student-friendly definitions available. As Beck et al. (2002) have explained, dictionary definitions are often not very student friendly. They are brief; they are often abstract; and they often define relatively simple words using more difficult words. A student-friendly definition you create for a glossary, on the other hand, should explain the word as it is used in the selection, use everyday language, and be long enough to be helpful. The following are some slightly modified student-friendly definitions given by Beck et al.:

- *illusion*—something that looks like one thing but is really something else
- *morbid*—showing great interest in horrible details, especially about death
- *covert*—describes something that is done in a hidden or secret way

Definitions Plus Pictures

Sometimes the old adage that a picture is worth a thousand words is true. In fact, when defining concrete objects, this is frequently the case. Think, for example, of the challenge of defining *kangaroo* solely with words as opposed to defining it with words and showing a picture or two. Searching Google Images for *kangaroo* yielded 561,000 images. Not all of these actually pictured kangaroos, but many did. Or think of the word *tsunami* and the power of a verbal definition alone; a verbal definition plus some still pictures; or a verbal definition, some still pictures, and a video showing the devastation and power of a tsunami as it hits land. Searching Google Images for *tsunami* yielded over two million images. Searching YouTube produced some truly terrifying videos, ones that you would certainly want to screen for suitability, but ones that would clearly cement the concept in students' minds.

Context-Dictionary-Discussion Procedure

The next two methods are similar in that they provide fairly strong introductory instruction. They differ, however, in the amount of time they require from you and your students. The first method, the context-dictionary-discussion procedure (Graves, 2006), doesn't take much preparation time on your part, but it takes a fair amount of class time. It will provide students with a basic understanding of a word's meaning and give them practice in using the dictionary. As shown below, it consists of three steps:

1. Give students the word in context.

   excel—To get into the Olympics, a person must really *excel* at some Olympic sport.

2. Ask them to look it up in the dictionary.

3. Discuss the definitions they come up with.

What is particularly key with this method, as with much vocabulary instruction, is the discussion. Students need the opportunity to put forth their definitions, see if other students understand them and have similar interpretations, and get feedback from you. You definitely do not want students to internalize an incorrect definition for a word.

Context-Relationship Procedure

The last method I describe here, the context-relationship procedure (Graves, 2006), takes quite a bit of preparation time on your part. However, presenting words in this way takes only about a minute of class time per word, and I have repeatedly found that students remember the meanings for words taught in this fashion well:

1. Create a brief paragraph that uses the target word three or four times and in doing so gives the meaning of the word.

   Conveying—The luncheon speaker was successful in *conveying* his main ideas to the audience. They all understood what he said, and most agreed with him. *Conveying* has a more specific meaning than *talking*. *Conveying* indicates that a person is getting his or her ideas across accurately.

2. Follow the paragraph with a multiple-choice item that checks students' understanding of the word.

   Conveying means

   A. putting parts together.

   B. communicating a message.

   C. hiding important information.

3. Show the paragraph (on an overhead or LCD projector), read it aloud, and read the multiple-choice options.

4. Pause to give students a moment to answer the multiple-choice item, give them the correct answer, and discuss the word and any questions they have.

Of course, there are scores of other techniques for introductory vocabulary instruction. Many of them are described in Graves (2006, in press) and Stahl and Nagy (2006).

Conclusions

I began this chapter by noting the current interest in vocabulary, describing the importance of vocabulary, considering the large number of words that students need to learn, and stressing that some students have very small vocabularies and must substantially increase their store of words to succeed in school. Next, I stated the central theme of the chapter, that there are many different ways to teach individual words—that one size vocabulary instruction does not fit all. After that, I briefly described the four parts of a comprehensive program—Teaching Individual Words, Teaching Word-Learning Strategies, and Fostering Word Consciousness—explaining that while a comprehensive program consists of all four of these components, in this chapter I deal only with Teaching Individual Words. Finally, I described three purposes for teaching individual words: (1) building students' oral vocabularies, (2) providing rich and powerful instruction, and (3) providing introductory instruction. In these three sections, I described 11 different teaching procedures, illustrating that there is no single approach to teaching individual words that is appropriate in all situations, but that instead it takes many types of instruction to effectively assist students in learning the many words they need to learn to succeed in school and beyond. Of course, there are many other methods that can and should be used (see Graves, in press), but the 11 in this chapter provide a good sampling of the many methods available and illustrate how varied teaching individual words can and should be.

In closing, I want to briefly comment on how much time should be devoted to teaching individual words. There are two situations to consider here: (1) instruction for students who are making typical progress in vocabulary and (2) instruction for students with markedly small vocabularies. In neither case is it appropriate for teaching individual words to take up unreasonable amounts of time, but for students with markedly small vocabularies it will take considerable time. For students with typical vocabularies, I suspect that most school days and most reading selections will include some teaching of individual words, but that instruction will be brief, perhaps 5–10 minutes teaching potentially challenging words from selections students are reading. For students with very small vocabularies, however, instruction that can successfully bridge the gap will take more time. Instruction on words for individual selections may require 10–15 minutes per day, while another 30 minutes a day should probably be devoted to shared book reading to build these students' oral vocabularies. Admittedly, this means that children with small vocabularies are getting a lot of vocabulary instruction—but they need and deserve a lot of it.

Questions for Discussion

1. Suppose you were in the teachers' lounge and one of your colleagues announced that he or she did not do vocabulary instruction because it is simply too time consuming, and he or she had more important ways to spend class time. How would you respond to that colleague?

2. Suppose that you were teaching in the primary grades and had some students in your class you suspected of having very small vocabularies. How would you check to see if these students did

indeed have small vocabularies? Are there commercial tests you could use, or would you make up our own tests? If you did make up your own tests, how would you select the words to test and what sorts of test items would you construct?

3. Identify a word you might teach using Robust Vocabulary Instruction and a word you might teach with the Frayer method, and outline the instruction for each of them, much like is done in this chapter. Now, try creating Robust Vocabulary Instruction for the word for which you have previously used the Frayer method and visa versa. Consider your results, discuss them with a colleague, and make a tentative conclusion about the extent to which the two procedures can be used with the same words.

4. Choose two of the methods of introductory vocabulary instruction presented, create instruction for three or four words using each method, and try out the methods with your students. Afterward, jot down some notes on what you discovered about each of the methods or discuss what you discovered with a colleague.

NOTE

REFERENCES

American Educational Research Association. (2004). English language learners: Boosting academic achievement. *Research Points: Essential Information for Educational Policy, 2*(1), 1–4.

Anderson, R.C., & Nagy, W.E. (1992). The vocabulary conundrum. *American Educator, 16*(4), 14–18, 44–47.

Anglin, J.M. (1993). Vocabulary development: A morphological analysis. *Monographs of the Society for Research on Child Development, 58*(10, Serial No. 238).

Baumann, J.F., Edwards, E.C., Boland, E.M., Olejnik, S., & Kame'enui, E.J. (2003). Vocabulary tricks: Effects of instruction in morphology and context on fifth-grade students' ability to derive and infer word meanings. *American Educational Research Journal, 40*(2), 447–494.

Baumann, J.F., Edwards, E.C., Font, G., Tereshinski, C.A., Kame'enui, E.J., & Olejnik, S. (2002). Teaching morphemic and contextual analysis to fifth-grade students. *Reading Research Quarterly, 37*(2), 150–176.

Baumann, J.F., Font, G., Edwards, E.C., & Boland, E.M. (2005). Strategies for teaching middle-grade students to use word-part and context clues to expand reading vocabulary. In E.H. Hiebert & M.L. Kamil (Eds.), *Teaching and learning vocabulary: Bringing research to practice* (pp. 179–205). Mahwah, NJ: Erlbaum.

Baumann, J.F., & Kame'enui, E.J., (Eds.). (2004). *Vocabulary instruction: Research to practice*. New York: Guilford.

Baumann, J.F., Ware, D., & Edwards, E.C. (2007). "Bumping into spicy, tasty words that catch your tongue": A formative experiment in vocabulary instruction. *The Reading Teacher, 61*(2), 108–122.

Beck, I.L., & McKeown, M.G. (1991). Conditions of vocabulary acquisition. In R. Barr M.L. Kamil, P. Mosenthal, & P.D. Pearson (Eds.), *The handbook of reading research* (Vol. 2, pp. 789–814)

Beck, I.L., & McKeown, M.G. (2001). Text talk: Capturing the benefits of read-aloud experiences for young children. *The Reading Teacher, 55*(1), 10–20.

Beck, I.L., & McKeown, M.G. (2007). Increasing young low-income children's oral vocabulary repertoires through rich and focused instruction. *The Elementary School Journal, 107*(3), 251–273.

Beck, I.L., McKeown, M.G., & Kucan, L. (2002). *Bringing words to life: Robust vocabulary instruction*. New York: Guilford.

Beck, I.L., Perfetti, C.A., & McKeown, M.G. (1982). The effects of long-term vocabulary instruction on lexical access and reading comprehension. *Journal of Educational Psychology, 74*(4), 506–521.

Becker, W.C. (1977). Teaching reading and language to the disadvantaged—What we have learned from field research. *Harvard Educational Review, 47*(4), 518–543.

Biemiller, A. (1999). *Language and reading success*. Cambridge, MA: Brookline books.

Biemiller, A. (2001). Teaching vocabulary: Early, direct, and sequential. *American Educator, 25*(1), 24–28, 47.

Biemiller, A. (2004). Teaching vocabulary in the primary grades: Vocabulary instruction needed. In J.F. Baumann & E.J. Kame'enui (Eds.), *Vocabulary instruction: Research to practice* (pp. 28–40). New York: Guildford.

Biemiller, A. (in press). *Words worth teaching*. Columbus, OH: SRA/McGraw-Hill.

Biemiller, A., & Boote, C. (2006). An effective method for building meaning vocabulary in the primary grades. *Journal of Educational Psychology, 98*(1), 44–62.

Blachowicz, C.L.Z., & Fisher, P. (1996). *Teaching vocabulary in all classrooms*. Columbus, OH: Merrill.

Blachowicz, C.L.Z., & Zabroske, B. (1990). Context instruction: A metacognitive approach for at-risk readers. *Journal of Reading, 33*(7), 504–508.

Blachowicz, C.L.Z., Fisher, P.J., Ogle, D., & Watts-Taffe, S.M. (2006). Vocabulary: Questions from the classroom. *Reading Research Quarterly, 41*(4), 524–539.

Buikema, J.A., & Graves, M.F. (1993). Teaching students to use context cues to infer word meanings. *Journal of Reading, 36*(6), 450–457.

Carlo, M.S., August, D., McLaughlin, B., Snow, C.E., Dressler, C., Lippman, D.N., et al. (2004). Closing the gap: Addressing the vocabulary needs of English-language learners in bilingual and mainstream classrooms. *Reading Research Quarterly, 39*(2), 188–215.

Cassidy, J., & Cassidy, D. (2008, February). What's hot, what's not for 2007. *Reading Today, 25*(4), 1, 10–11.

Chall, J.S., & Dale, E. (1995). *Readability revisited: The new Dale-Chall readability formula.* Cambridge, MA: Brookline Books.

Chall, J.S., & Jacobs, V.A. (2003). Poor children's fourth-grade slump. *American Educator, 27*(1), 14–15, 44.

Coyne, M.D., Simmons, D.C., & Kame'enui, E.J. (2004). Vocabulary instruction for young children at risk of experiencing reading difficulties: Teaching word meanings during shared story book reading. In J.F. Baumann & E.J. Kame'enui (Eds.), *Vocabulary instruction: Research to practice* (pp. 41–59). New York: Guilford.

Cunningham, A.E., & Stanovich, K.E. (1997). Early reading acquisition and its relationship to reading experience and ability 10 years later. *Developmental Psychology, 33*(6), 934–945.

De Temple, J.M., & Snow, C.E. (2003). Learning words from books. In A. van Kleeck, S.A. Stahl, & E.B. Bauer (Eds.), *On reading books to children* (pp. 16–36). Mahwah, NJ: Erlbaum.

Edwards, E.C., Font, G., Baumann, J.F., & Boland, E.M. (2004). Unlocking word meanings: Strategies and guidelines for teaching morphemic and contextual analysis. In J.F. Baumann & E.J. Kame'enui (Eds.), *Vocabulary instruction: Research to practice* (pp. 159–176). New York: Guilford.

Folse, K.S. (2004). *Vocabulary myths: Applying second language research to classroom teaching.* Ann Arbor: University of Michigan Press.

Frayer, D.A., Frederick, W.D., & Klausmeier, H.J. (1969). *A schema for testing the level of concept mastery* (Working Paper No. 16). Madison: Wisconsin Research and Development Center for Cognitive Learning.

Goswami, U. (2001). Early phonological development and the acquisition of literacy. In S.B. Neuman & D.K. Dickinson (Eds.), *Handbook of early literacy research* (pp. 111–125). New York: Guilford.

Graves, M.F. (1984). Selecting vocabulary to teach in the intermediate and secondary grades. In J. Flood (Ed.), *Understanding reading comprehension* (pp. 245–260). Newark, DE: International Reading Association.

Graves, M.F. (1992). The elementary vocabulary curriculum: What should it be? In M.J. Dreher & W.H. Slater (Eds.), *Elementary school literacy: Critical issues* (pp. 101–131). Norwood, MA: Christopher-Gordon.

Graves, M.F. (2000). A vocabulary program to complement and bolster a middle-grade comprehension program. In B.M. Taylor, M.F. Graves, & P. van den Broek (Eds.), *Reading for meaning: Fostering comprehension in the middle grades* (pp. 116–135). New York: Teachers College Press.

Graves, M.F. (2004). Teaching prefixes: As good as it gets? In J.F. Baumann & E.J. Kame'enui (Eds.), *Vocabulary instruction: Research to practice* (pp. 81–99). New York: Guilford.

Graves, M.F. (2006). *The vocabulary book: Learning and instruction.* New York: Teachers College Press.

Graves, M.F. (in press). *Teaching individual words: One size does not fit all.* New York: Teachers College Press; Newark, DE: International ReadingAssociation.

Graves, M.F., Juel, C., & Graves, B.B. (2007). *Teaching reading in the 21st century* (4th ed.). Boston: Allyn & Bacon.

Graves, M.F., & Watts-Taffe, S.V. (in press). For the love of words: Fostering word consciousness in young readers. *The Reading Teacher, 62*(3).

Hart, B., & Risley, T.R. (1995). *Meaningful differences in the everyday experience of young American children*. Baltimore: Paul H. Brookes.

Hart, B., & Risley, T.R. (2003). The early catastrophe: The 30 million word gap. *American Educator, 27*(1), 4–9.

Heimlich, J.E., & Pittelman, S.D. (1986). *Semantic mapping: Classroom applications*. Newark, DE: International Reading Association.

Hiebert, E.H., & Kamil, M.L. (Eds.). (2006). *Teaching and learning vocabulary: Bringing research to practice*. Mahwah, NJ: Erlbaum.

Juel, C., & Deffes, R. (2004). Making words stick. *Educational Leadership, 61*(6), 30–34.

Klare, G.R. (1984). Readability. In P.D. Pearson, R. Barr, M.L. Kamil, & P. Mosenthal (Eds.), *Handbook of reading research* (pp. 681–794). New York: Longman.

Miller, G.A., & Wakefield, P.C. (2000). Commentary on Anglin's analysis of vocabulary growth. In J.M. Anglin, *Vocabulary development: A morphological analysis* (167–175). Boston: Blackwell. (Original work published in 1993).

Nagy, W.E. (2005). Why vocabulary instruction needs to be long-term and comprehensive. In E.H. Hiebert & M.L. Kamil (Eds.), *Teaching and learning vocabulary: Bringing scientific research to practice* (pp. 27–44). Mahwah, NJ: Erlbaum.

Nagy, W.E., & Anderson, R.C. (1984). How many words are there in printed school English? *Reading Research Quarterly, 19*(3), 304–330.

Nagy, W.E., & Herman, P.A. (1987). Breadth and depth of vocabulary knowledge: Implications for acquisition and instruction. In M.C. McKeown & M.E. Curtis (Eds.), *The nature of vocabulary acquisition* (pp. 19–35). Hillsdale, NJ: Erlbaum.

Nation, I.S.P. (2001). *Learning vocabulary in another language*. Cambridge, UK: Cambridge University Press.

National Institute of Child Health and Human Development. (2000). *Report of the National Reading Panel. Teaching children to read: An evidence-based assessment of the scientific research literature on reading and its implications for reading instruction* (NIH Publication No. 00-4769). Washington, DC: U.S. Government Printing Office.

Petty, W., Herold, C., & Stoll, E. (1967). *The state of knowledge about the teaching of vocabulary*. Urbana, IL: National Council of Teachers of English.

Pittelman, S.D., Heimlich, J.E., Berglund, R.L., & French, M.P. (1991). *Semantic feature analysis: Classroom applications*. Newark, DE: International Reading Association.

RAND Reading Study Group. (2002). *Reading for understanding: Toward an R&D program in reading comprehension*. Santa Monica, CA: Rand Education.

Scarborough, H.S. (1998). Early identification of children at risk for reading disabilities: Phonological awareness and some other promising predictors. In B.K. Shapiro, P.J. Accardo, & A.J. Capute (Eds.), *Specific reading disabilities: A review of the spectrum* (pp. 75–119). Timonium, MD: York Press.

Scott, J.A., & Nagy, W.E. (2004). Developing word consciousness. In J.F. Baumann & E.J. Kame'enui (Eds.), *Vocabulary instruction: Research to practice* (pp. 201–217). New York: Guilford.

Stahl, S.A., & Fairbanks, M.M. (1986). The effects of vocabulary instruction: A model-based meta-analysis. *Review of Educational Research, 56*(1), 72–110.

Stahl, S.A., & Nagy, W.E. (2006). *Teaching word meanings*. Mahwah, NJ: Erlbaum.

Sternberg, R.J. (1987). Most vocabulary is learned from context. In M.G. McKeown & M.E. Curtis (Eds.), *The nature of vocabulary acquisition* (pp. 89–105). Hillsdale, NJ: Erlbaum.

Templin, M.C. (1957). *Certain language skills in children, their development and inter-relationships.* Minneapolis: University of Minnesota Press.

Terman, L.M. (1916). *The measurement of intelligence: An explanation of and a complete guide for the use of the Stanford revision and extension of the Binet-Simon intelligence scale.* Boston: Houghton Mifflin.

Wagner, R.K., Muse, A.E., & Tannenbaum, K.R. (2007). *Vocabulary acquisition: Implications for reading comprehension.* New York: Guilford.

White, T.G., Graves, M.F., & Slater, W.H. (1990). Growth of reading vocabulary in diverse elementary schools: Decoding and word meaning. *Journal of Educational Psychology, 82*(2), 281–290.

White, T.G., Power, M.A., & White, S. (1989). Morphological analysis: Implication for teaching and understanding vocabulary growth. *Reading Research Quarterly, 24*(3), 283–304.

White, T.G., Sowell, J., & Yanagihara, A. (1989). Teaching elementary students to use word-part clues. *The Reading Teacher, 42*(4), 302–308.

Whitehurst, G.J., Arnold, D.S., Epstein, J.N., Angell, A.L., Smith, M., & Fischel, J.E. (1994). A picture book reading intervention in day care and home for children from low-income families. *Developmental Psychology, 30*(5), 697–689.

Whitehurst, G.J., Falcon, F., Lonigan, C.J., Fischel, J.E., DeBaryshe, D.B., Valdez-Menchaca, M.C., et al. (1988). Accelerating language development through picture book reading. *Developmental Psychology, 24*(4), 552–559.

Zevenbergen, A.A., & Whitehurst, G.J. (2004). Dialogic reading: A shared picture book reading intervention for preschoolers. In A. van Kleeck, S.A. Stahl, & E.B. Bauer (Eds.), *On reading books to children: Parents and teachers* (pp. 177–200). Mahwah, NJ: Erlbaum.

LITERATURE CITED

Bridwell, N. (1977). *Clifford at the circus.* New York: Scholastic.

Gillman, P. (1997). *Jillian Jiggs.* New York: Scholastic.

Khalsa, D. (1989). *Julian.* Montreal: Tundra Books.

Lionni, L. (1969). *Alexander and the wind-up mouse.* New York: Scholastic.

McLellan, S. (2000). *The chicken cat.* Ontario: Fitzhenry & Whitside.

Schertle, A. (1995). *Down the road.* San Diego: Brownder Press.

Chapter 4

Teaching Vocabulary-Learning Strategies: Word Consciousness, Word Connection, and Word Prediction

Ula C. Manzo and Anthony V. Manzo

Vocabulary-learning strategies are habits of mind that help one learn and remember words and word meanings. We acquire vocabulary-learning strategies as an aspect of general language acquisition and cognitive development. Typically, at least in early stages of language development, we aren't consciously aware of the vocabulary-learning strategies we acquire and use. Many children acquire these strategies naturally as an outcome of immersion in a language-rich environment. The same outcomes can be achieved much more efficiently by identifying and directly teaching the strategies that some advantaged children acquire naturally, but over a longer period of time.

This chapter proposes three categories of vocabulary-learning strategies, and details research-based methods for teaching each. In a review of the research on vocabulary instruction, Blachowicz, Fisher, Ogle, and Watts-Taffe (2006) found consensus among researchers on three necessary components of an effective and comprehensive program of vocabulary instruction. These three components, detailed more fully in the following pages, are (1) fostering word consciousness, (2) intentionally teaching selected words, and (3) teaching generative elements of words. These program components align well with the vocabulary-learning strategies or habits of mind of effective vocabulary learners: strategies for noticing new words and nuances of meaning, strategies for remembering newly encountered and considered words, and strategies for applying existing word knowledge to wrest possible meanings from unknown words. The importance of viewing vocabulary instruction as the teaching of strategies rather than the teaching of words is nested in fairly recent understandings about the conceptual constructs of schema,

What Research Has to Say About Vocabulary Instruction, edited by Alan E. Farstrup and S. Jay Samuels. © 2008 by the International Reading Association.

IQ, learning strategy acquisition in general, and social constructivists' insights into the nature of school literacy learning of students of diverse backgrounds.

Vocabulary and Schema

Vocabulary is more than words. Vocabulary is the "stuff" of which schema is made. Schema can be defined as an individual's personal organization of information and experiences about a topic (Manzo, Manzo, & Thomas, 2005). If you were asked what you know about the desert, for instance, your response would most likely begin with the vocabulary that represents your knowledge of and experiences related to that topic: hot, dry, cactus, sand, and so forth. If schema is pictured as a mental net in which we catch new information and ideas—as a large fisherman's net sprawled about a ship's deck—then vocabulary is the fibers of the rope that make the net: some fibers may be short and loosely connected, some long and intricately woven.

Continuing the schema–net analogy, a measure of a person's vocabulary, a snapshot of their entire schema net, would amount to a measure of all that they have learned, experienced, felt, and reflected upon. It would also be a good indicator of what one is capable of learning; in other words, the more finely woven a particular section of our schema net is—or, the more words we know that are associated with the topic— the easier it is to catch new bits of information we encounter that are related to that topic, and attach these to existing schema in personally meaningful ways. If one's schema for *desert* includes the importance of aridity, more so than heat, as a defining feature of deserts, it is easier to comprehend, connect, and remember the term *snow pack* encountered in a sentence such as, "There is very little precipitation in cold deserts, and even that small amount remains frozen as snow pack."

A person's vocabulary, then, reflects where they have been, who they are now, and what they are prepared to become. The analogy of vocabulary as a schema net makes short work of explaining why a test of vocabulary has the highest correlation with virtually every cognitive factor that can be measured. Every test is, in large measure, a test of vocabulary. Is vocabulary, then, essentially the same as IQ? The general public tends to think of someone with a large vocabulary as more intelligent than someone with a meager one. Several studies suggest that this clearly is not the case, and we focus on these studies in the next section.

Vocabulary and IQ

It does seem that some people have a stronger natural inclination than others to notice and acquire new words; however, as with most human characteristics, innate inclinations interact with experience. The effect of experience upon vocabulary acquisition is much greater than early constructs of IQ assumed. Graves, Brunetti, and Slater (1982) found that, on average, the vocabulary of lower SES (socioeconomic status) first graders is half the size of that of their higher SES peers. This speaks clearly to the point that vocabulary acquisition has at least as much to do with nurture as with nature. Hart and Risley (1995) found a similar disparity by age 3; White, Graves, and Slater (1990) found that the difference increased from grade to grade.

Hart and Risley followed up by going inside the homes of the two groups of children and making careful records on interactions between parents and children. They found that children's vocabulary size was most closely related to a single factor: how many times parents spoke to children. In the higher SES homes, children were spoken to approximately 487 times an hour (counting a single word, a phrase, or a longer language stream as a single utterance). In lower SES homes, 178 utterances were addressed to children per hour. The sheer number of words encountered, then, appears to be an enormous factor in vocabulary acquisition. Therefore, vocabulary acquisition is not a product of IQ, or innate intellectual capacity, but rather almost the opposite: What is generally thought of as intelligence can more correctly be thought of as the product of having acquired, and habitually used, effective vocabulary-learning strategies.

Vocabulary and Learning-Strategy Instruction

Some literacy experts have insisted that once children have learned to read, direct instruction in vocabulary is less effective than simply increasing the number of words they encounter by encouraging wide reading (Cunningham & Stanovich, 1998; Goodman, 1994; Nagy & Herman, 1984). Other experts disagree. Beck and McKeown's (1991) analysis of the research on the extent to which vocabulary is acquired through wide reading found little evidence that significant numbers of words are acquired in this incidental way. They found fairly consistent evidence, however, that good readers learn more words than poor readers from the same amount of reading. They concluded, "The point of these comments is certainly not to discourage the practice of wide reading but to question whether it can be relied upon to enhance vocabulary development for all students" (p. 809). In other words, wide reading was not found to result in vocabulary growth.

We suggest that these contradictory findings may be fundamentally due to the following dynamics:

- Learners who have not acquired effective vocabulary-learning strategies are not likely to acquire much vocabulary through wide reading. Therefore, because learners' use of vocabulary-learning strategies has not been a factor in the research to date, it has been difficult to show that wide reading results in vocabulary growth.

- Learners who have acquired comprehension strategies are likely to have also acquired vocabulary-learning strategies since these processes are analogous (and it is their vocabulary-learning strategies—not their reading abilities—that cause good readers to acquire more vocabulary from the same amount of reading than poor readers).

A learning strategy, in general, is an intentionally and flexibly applied phrase that reminds the learner to construct, respond to, and retain new information and ideas. When a learning task is easy, strategies are used subconsciously and effortlessly—and are more appropriately referred to as *skills*. When a learning task is difficult, strategies need to be sought and applied consciously and with greater mental effort. Vocabulary-learning strategy phrases remind the learner to notice, connect, and predict meanings of new words.

Study-reading comprehension strategies, and methods for teaching these, frequently are categorized as either *prereading* schema activation strategies, *during-reading* metacognitive monitoring and comprehension fixup strategies, and *postreading* schema-building strategies (Manzo & Manzo, 1990). Current understandings of comprehension instruction emphasize methods that permit the teacher to model meaning-making strategies at these three phases of the reading process and encourage students to try out and practice using these strategies themselves. For example, prereading strategies such as predicting, recalling prior knowledge and experience related to the topic, and setting purposes for reading can be demonstrated when using methods such as Reciprocal Questioning (Manzo, 1969), in which the teacher and students take turns asking and answering questions, based on one sentence at a time, for the first few sentences of an assignment.

Vocabulary-learning strategies and methods for teaching vocabulary can also be categorized as pre-, during-, and postreading (cf. Manzo, Manzo, & Estes, 2001). However, the context of vocabulary learning is broader than reading, incorporating language heard outside as well as inside school, in home and community settings, and via an increasing array of media.

In developing this chapter, we have drawn on the conclusions of Blachowicz and colleagues' (2006) review of research on vocabulary instruction referenced above, which found a general consensus among researchers on the three necessary components of an integrated and comprehensive program of vocabulary instruction:

1. The classroom is a language- and word-rich environment that fosters word consciousness.

2. Selected words are taught through direct instruction, providing multiple types of information about each new word as well as regular review and practice.

3. Generative elements of words and word-learning strategies are taught to students' ability to learn new words independently.

Based on these findings, we have organized methods for teaching vocabulary-learning strategies into three parallel categories:

1. Word consciousness strategies—for heightening students' awareness of new words heard or read

2. Word connection strategies—for connecting a new word with its meaning and an additional schema element (such as personal experience)

3. Word prediction strategies—for using knowledge of word parts and language structures to predict possible meanings of new words encountered in print or speech

The shift in perspective from program components to a specific focus on the vocabulary-learning strategies we want learners to acquire is slight but, we believe, important. If we want students to acquire word consciousness strategies, for example, we need to do more than provide a language-rich environment. We need to focus on the specific strategy that a learner in such an environment acquires, then model that strategy and encourage learners to try it out themselves. If a video is shown in which the word *lariat* is spoken in passing, we want the learner to grab that word mentally and think something like "lariat, lariat, what is a lariat?"—rather than letting that moment slip past.

Strategy-based instruction is both direct and precise. Its aim is to identify and systematically teach the specific learning mechanisms that a learner might acquire over a much longer period of time if no specific interventions were offered. As such, it aligns with the concerns of social constructivism, and particularly as these relate to students from diverse backgrounds, including English-language learners.

Vocabulary and Diverse Social Constructivism

The findings from the studies of lower and higher SES first graders' vocabulary levels can be interpreted from the perspective of vocabulary-learning strategy acquisition. Most likely, children in the higher SES, language-rich homes are acquiring not just words, but habits for learning words—vocabulary-learning strategies such as: *noticing* when an unfamiliar word is encountered; *connecting* new words and their meanings with personal experiences, attitudes, images, and feelings; and *predicting* possible meanings of unfamiliar words based on context. Shifting the emphasis from how many words have been encountered to the strategies that have been acquired is an important distinction because it offers a much more viable means of intervention. If vocabulary-learning were simply a matter of being exposed to words, or even being directly taught words, it would be unreasonable to expect children to double their vocabularies in first grade—actually they would need to more than double the size, since their more advantaged peers continue to learn words throughout that year. However, if we identify and teach the strategies that those more advantaged children had opportunity to acquire in their early years at home—if we provide, directly and systematically, the tools to learn words—it is not unreasonable to expect that they will catch up to their peers within a few years.

This interpretation illustrates the distinction between social constructivism, per se, and the concerns of diverse social constructivists. Social constructivist theory proposes that reality is created through social interaction; thus, literacy learning should be grounded in authentic experiences and learners immersed in language-rich environments. Diverse social constructivists' concern is that this approach is insufficient to meet the needs of students of diverse backgrounds. Au (1998) applied Cummins's (1986) "theoretical framework for the empowerment of minority students" (p. 54) to literacy learning, to propose a "framework for improving the school literacy learning of students of diverse backgrounds." With respect to instructional methods, Au's essential point was,

> The school literacy learning of students of diverse backgrounds will be improved as educators provide students with both authentic literacy activities and a considerable amount of instruction in the specific literacy skills needed for full participation in the culture of power. (pp. 305–306)

Enriched environments and authentic activities must be supplemented with direct instruction in what needs to be learned from these experiences.

Specific instruction in learning strategies, to the point that these become skills, benefits learners across ages, grades, and disciplines. At each higher grade level, and in content area reading especially, a key factor in the increasing difficulty of text is the increasing number of new vocabulary words. This means that even students who have become comfortable with using vocabulary-learning strategies in the early grades are likely to have difficulty with higher grade materials unless they are able to consciously call upon these strategies—intentionally and flexibly—as they continue to encounter more and more challenging text. Thus, a practical and integrated program for teaching vocabulary-learning strategies serves developmental and advanced learners equally, as well as delayed learners.

This chapter provides research-supported approaches and methods for incorporating each of these components into a program of direct and systematic instruction across grades and subject areas, and in ways that support all levels of learners. The first section provides two approaches for systematically teaching word consciousness strategies. In the next section, three methods are provided for teaching three-way word connection strategies—connections among a new word, its meaning, and other schema components. Three final methods address teaching learners to use known elements of words and language to acquire word prediction strategies to pry out possible meanings of new words.

Methods for Teaching Word Consciousness Strategies

Logically, a language rich environment would facilitate language learning. And logically, young children who are spoken to twice as often as other children are likely to acquire twice as many words, which has indeed been shown in the studies cited above. It would seem to follow that immersing the older learner in authentic activities involving the language of a discipline—science, mathematics, social sciences, for example—would facilitate learning in that subject. Practically, this is difficult to achieve above primary grade levels. There are literally too many words to be learned for the available amount of time. However, it may not be immersion, in and of itself, that builds language and vocabulary. The reason that immersion builds language and vocabulary may be, instead, that when one is immersed in language, one is more likely to begin to consciously notice features of words and language—and particularly to simply notice when one has encountered an unfamiliar word. This habit of noticing words, or word consciousness, can be taught systematically and efficiently, without leaving it to develop or not develop by chance, through immersion.

We might begin by asking, how could one not be word conscious? The answer is surprisingly easily. Most people can recall instances when they have encountered a new word, found out its meaning by asking or perhaps even looking it up, wondered why the speaker or writer used that word rather than a more familiar one, and then seemed to hear and read that very word everywhere. The word was there all along—we just didn't perceive it because it was unfamiliar. That's the way the human brain works. It helps keep us sane, one might say, by filtering out masses of unfamiliar stimuli to permit us to focus on the things that are most important to reasonable functioning in a given situation. Word consciousness is a habit that can be taught and practiced.

Teaching students, across grades and subject areas, to simply begin to notice unfamiliar words they encounter in speech and print is a quintessential component of vocabulary instruction. Poor word learners tend also to be poor comprehenders, and poor comprehenders are much more likely than good readers to read right past unfamiliar words without noticing they have skipped them. Two practical classroom approaches for teaching students strategies for noticing unfamiliar words are Community of Language and Secret Language.

Community of Language

Community of Language (Manzo & Manzo, 1990) is a fundamental approach to teaching word consciousness that can be applied in a variety of ways. The basic formula is simple: The teacher identifies a set of vocabulary words that will be important to upcoming instruction and then intentionally uses these words as often as possible when interacting with the students. The approach may be implemented by a single teacher or any combination of teachers who have students in common. For example, an elementary grade teacher might identify three to five key vocabulary words from each of five subject areas from the content of the next three weeks' lessons. Or a middle school interdisciplinary team of teachers might identify five vocabulary words each from their next few weeks of lesson plans and combine their words into one interdisciplinary list that each teacher then begins to use in interactions with the students they have in common. Teachers might tape the list to their desk or inside their lesson plan book for easy reference throughout the day.

Typically the first time the approach is used, students will notice the list at some point and ask whether they will have to look up the words or whether they will have a test on the words. When these questions come up, the teacher should take advantage of the opportunity to call the rest of the class's attention to the list and explain the purpose of Community of Language: to help students develop the habit of (and strategies for) noticing new words around them and to learn the meanings of new words by hearing them repeatedly in similar and differing contexts.

Students should not be required to look up and define the words and there should not be a test on the words, per se, other than as the words come up naturally in instructional materials and as part of the regular test on the material from which the words were drawn. An exception to this latter point might be to occasionally discuss the effectiveness of the Community of Language approach with students at the end of the time period in which they have been used and follow this discussion with a test on the word list to permit students to discover for themselves how well they have learned.

Secret Language

The Secret Language Approach was originally published as the Secret Language Police (Baines, 1998), but this name has tended to strike a sour note with many, possibly because of it evokes the term "secret police"—undoubtedly an unintended association. In any case, the term *police* is replaced here with the word *tutor*. The Secret Language approach is a good complement to Community of Language because it turns over responsibility for teaching new vocabulary words to students. Like Community of Language, it is a basic approach with many possible variations. Two or more students are selected as Secret Language Tutors, whose (secret) job is to communicate the meaning of a key vocabulary word to the rest of the class without explicitly stating "These are the vocabulary words and they mean...." Rather, each Tutor tries to find opportunities, as often as possible, to use his or her word in appropriate contexts in comments during class.

Some variations on the basic approach include extra credit for the tutors for asking the principal (or whoever makes the school announcements) to use the words on the public address system or for finding one or both of their words in a newspaper, magazine, book, or website and showing the example to the class before the day of the test.

Methods for Teaching Word Connection Strategies

The traditional approach to teaching vocabulary, and probably still the most widely used approach, could be called list/look up/practice/test. A *list* of words appears on the board on Monday; the students' task is to *look up* the words in the dictionary and copy a definition. There may be some additional *practice*, such as using the word in a sentence at that point or later in the week, and the definitions are to be studied for a *test* on Friday. This approach bears little resemblance to the way words are learned naturally, but it is relatively effective because, in any given class, some students will make the extra effort to translate the dictionary definition into a meaning that they understand and then connect the new word meaning to their existing knowledge and experiences. The relative effectiveness of this approach is dangerously deceptive, since it is the same few students who benefit from this approach in class after class, year after year, and the same greater number of students for whom it is much less or completely ineffective. For most students, this approach could more accurately be referred to as list/look up/practice/test/*forget*. If our job as teachers is to make *more* learning *more* accessible to *more* students, then we need to look to better-informed approaches to vocabulary instruction.

To do so, we can begin by looking closely at the traditional approach just described and the vocabulary-learning strategies that those few students are applying to make it effective. Then, we can shift the emphasis from requiring students to memorize definitions of words to teaching students to use vocabulary-learning strategies such as translating dictionary definitions into understandable meanings and connecting meanings of new words to existing information and experiences.

The analogy of schema as a net, the fibers of which are vocabulary, helps to explain why the list/look up/practice/test approach is ineffective for so many students. We might add that while vocabulary words are, figuratively, the fibers of schema, it is the weaving of language patterns that holds the net together and personal subjective experience that gives it interesting textures and hues. When a word is truly learned, remembered, and available for use, it is woven into one's schema in several ways:

- It is connected with the relevant section (topic/category) of one's schema and understood in terms of similarities and differences with other words one knows on that topic.
- It is connected to the language patterns with which one is familiar and able to use when thinking or speaking about that topic or using words in that category.
- It is connected to the attitudes and emotions associated with the actual experiences one has had related to the topic or category in which the new word fits.

The interconnectedness of words, language patterns, and emotion are evident even in a child's first attempts to combine words to express thoughts. A number of years ago, we (the authors) were sitting on our back deck after lunch with our son, who was then barely a year old. It was time for the baby to go in for his nap, which he was inclined to resist. In one of the first actual sentences he ever spoke, he said, "Mommy...take...outside...inside." Two words he had known for less than a year (inside, outside), juxtapositioned in a simple language pattern using a more recently acquired word (take), created a charmingly impossible idea, made all the more endearing by the personal subjective emotions with which it was textured: safety (Mommy can do anything), love and belonging (they will enjoy this thought), confidence (they won't get mad), humor (it's impossible!), and a tinge of regret (but it still won't get me out of naptime).

The three methods in this section are designed to teach vocabulary words in ways that model strategies for connecting a new word to its meaning with existing schema structures. In the Subjective Approach to Vocabulary (SAV; Manzo, 1983), described first, the word is connected with a personal experience related to the new word meaning; in Motor Imaging (Casale, 1985), the word is connected with a relevant gesture; and in Keyword Vocabulary, the word is connected with a relevant mnemonic device.

These direct instructional methods for teaching word connection strategies may be used either to preteach a few words that appear in a particular reading assignment to facilitate comprehension or to introduce a traditional weekly word list (instead of having students look up and write dictionary definitions). Though some controversy remains regarding the usefulness of the former—preteaching vocabulary from a given reading assignment (Nagy & Herman, 1984; Nagy, Herman, & Anderson, 1985)—Stahl and Fairbanks's (1986) meta-analysis of 30 research studies of the effects of vocabulary instruction found that "vocabulary instruction does appear to have a significant effect on the comprehension of passages containing taught words" (p. 100). Regarding direct instruction in general vocabulary, this same analysis concluded that "vocabulary instruction generally facilitates growth in reading comprehension, both on measures containing and not containing taught words, possibly by increasing the students' interest in learning new words" (Stahl & Fairbanks, 1986, p. 100, referring to studies by Beck et al., 1982; McKeown, Beck, Omanson, & Pople, 1985). In other words, there is empirical support for the intuitively obvious hypothesis that interest in learning new words effectively carries the day's lesson outside the classroom and facilitates independent learning of words encountered in many contexts.

In each of the methods in this section, the teacher begins by preparing a statement of each word's meaning that is brief, clear, and appropriate for the grade level. Typically, this is a rephrasing of a dictionary-type definition, but it is an essential preparatory step because the language style and words used in many dictionary definitions are more difficult than the word defined.

Subjective Approach to Vocabulary (SAV)

Dictionary definitions are objective, emotionless, and dry. SAV (Manzo, 1983) teaches students to connect a new word meaning with a relevant personal experience as a way to more effectively learn and remember the word. Each word is introduced and taught as follows:

- The teacher writes the word on the board and tells the meaning. Students write the word and its "objective" meaning in their notes or vocabulary journal.
- The teacher asks, "When you hear this word and its meaning, what is a personal experience it reminds you of?" and takes four or five student suggestions; the teacher can interject images when student images appear vague.
- Students then write at least one subjective meaning under the objective meaning in their notes or journal. Students may write their own or another student's association.

Figure 4.1 presents an example transcript of SAV in a classroom.

As a variation, instead of simply recording objective and subjective meanings, students may be shown how to make a four-section box for each word, including the word, its objective meaning, its subjective meaning, and a drawing to illustrate its meaning. This option can include having students form small groups to share and compare their drawings and select one to share with the rest of the class.

Silent reading follows next when SAV is used for prereading vocabulary introduction. When it is being used for general vocabulary

Figure 4.1. Classroom example of SAV

Teacher:	This word is magnetic, and it means being charming and attractive in ways that draw people to you, as in having a "magnetic personality."
	[pause to have students write the word and its meaning]
Teacher:	When you hear the word *magnetic* and its meaning, what personal experience comes to mind?
Student A:	My brother Billy. Our neighbor, Mr. Alba, is a grump. But he gave Billy some of his old golf clubs. Everyone likes Billy, and they just give him things.
Teacher:	I guess you'd say that he had a "*magnetic* personality?"
Student A:	He has a *lot* of "*magnetic* personality."
Teacher:	Another way to say that is, "He has a great deal of *personal magnetism*." Who else has a personal experience to connect with this meaning of the word *magnetic*?
Student B:	Well, my dad says being pleasant is important to selling stuff.
Teacher:	Being *magnetic*?
Student B:	Right.
Teacher:	Have you used that technique in trying to sell something?
Student B:	When my scout troop sold popcorn in front of the grocery story, we tried to be real *magnetic*!
Teacher:	I can picture that. Anyone else?
Student C:	Everyone who sees my dog just loves her. She makes you smile.
Teacher:	Ah, doggie *magnetism*! Great. Go ahead and write a personal association under your meaning of the word *magnetic*. It's best to use something you've experienced yourself, but you can add someone else's also, or use someone else's if you just can't think of anything for this one.

development, students are given 5 to 10 minutes to study and rehearse new and previously recorded word meanings.

This simple strategy of connecting a new word and its meaning to personal experience can offer diagnostic opportunities for the teacher to discover how students think and what they might be saying to themselves that may be enriching or unsettling. It also gives students a chance to hear the views of others, affording multicultural knowledge and insights to occur in a natural and authentic manner.

Motor Imaging

Motor Imaging (Casale, 1985) teaches the strategy of connecting a new word with its meaning and a relevant gesture, as in making the shape of a steeple when learning the word *cathedral* or connecting the word *amorphous* with the gesture of wiggling the fingers of one hand while moving the hand back and forth, right and left. When this connection is made, the gesture becomes an aide to recalling the meaning of the word when it is encountered again and an aide to recalling the word when it is needed in speech or writing. A 1998 *Newsweek* article reporting psychologist Robert Krauss's research into the connection between gestures and language, opened with a story:

> When Robert Krauss was a boy, 50 years ago, his grandfather told him a story about two men walking down a street one cold winter's day. One man babbled incessantly, while his companion, frigid hands stuffed in his pockets, merely nodded here and there. Finally, the talker asked, "Samuel, why aren't you saying anything?" To which the friend replied, "I forgot my gloves."

By monitoring electrodes attached to people's arms, Krauss found that people "gesture" even when they don't think they are. When subjects were given a definition and asked to think of the word defined, the electrodes detected small muscle movements related to the word meanings. Words that connoted movement, such as *castanets*, elicited more muscle movement than abstract words like *mercy*. These findings support a central tenet of Piaget's (1953) theory of cognitive development. Piaget observed that preverbal infants appear to use gestures to represent meanings, and, as speech is acquired, these gestures are not replaced by words, but simply diminish in size and eventually are "interiorized" and retained in connection with word meanings. In a similar vein, Paivio's (1986) dual coding theory proposed that human functioning is based on equal weightings for verbal and nonverbal learning. Using Paivio's principles and techniques, Frick-Horbury and Guttentag (1998) investigated vocabulary availability by telling the subject the definition of a word, then asking him or her to think of the word defined. Subjects asked to perform this task while grasping a bar with both hands were less accurate and took longer to think of the words than subjects who had free use of their hands.

To evaluate the effectiveness of Motor Imaging, a study was conducted that compared three approaches with vocabulary learning: a conventional dictionary/worksheet technique, SAV, and Motor Imaging. Fifth and sixth grade students were rotated through each of these three treatments in different orders. Motor Imaging and SAV resulted in statistically significantly greater word learning than the dictionary/worksheet technique, both in immediate testing and after two weeks, and this effect was maintained across ability levels (Casale & Manzo, 1983).

Motor Imaging, like SAV, can be used either to introduce a weekly word list or to preteach a few difficult vocabulary words from a reading assignment to facilitate comprehension. Each word is introduced and taught as follows:

- The teacher writes the word on the board and tells the meaning. Students write the word and its meaning in their notes or vocabulary journal.
- The teacher says, "If you were to make a gesture to use when speaking this word, think of what that gesture might be. When I point to the class, go ahead and make the gesture you are thinking of."
- After observing students' gestures for similarities, the teacher selects one that seems to best represent the word meaning and shows the selected gesture to the class.
- The teacher then tells students to say the word and make the gesture when the word is pointed to; this can be repeated several times if it seems necessary.
- When all the words have been introduced and connected with gestures, the teacher points to one word at a time, in random order, and has students say the meaning of the word while making the gesture for it.

Table 4.1 provides a few examples of Motor Imaging words and gestures.

Table 4.1. Motor Imaging examples

New word	Language meaning	Motor meaning
Appropriate	right or fit for a certain purpose	both palms together matching perfectly
Convey	take or carry from one place to another	both hands together, moving from one side to the other
Woe	great sadness or trouble	one or both hands over the eyes, head slanted forward
Dazzle	shine or reflect brightly	palms close together, facing outward, fingers spread
Utmost	the very highest or most	one or both hands reaching up as far as possible
Abode	place where you live	hands meeting above the head in a triangular roof shape

If Motor Imaging is used for prereading vocabulary introduction, silent reading of the assignment would follow next. If used for general vocabulary development, students are given 5 to 10 minutes to study and rehearse new and previously recorded word meanings.

Keyword Vocabulary

This approach teaches students to identify a known keyword that is suggested by the sound of the target word and to connect the target word, its meaning, and a visual image of a connection between the word meaning and the keyword. For example, the word *plateau* might evoke, from the sound of the word alone, the familiar word *plate*. Given the meaning of *plateau*, as a "raised flatland," the word (*plateau*) and its meaning (raised flatland) would be connected with a visual image of a plate being carried on a raised hand (the way a waiter might carry a tray at shoulder level). Steps in using the keyword approach are:

- The teacher writes the target word on the board and says, "Listen to this word. Just from its sound, what picture comes to mind?"

- Students make suggestions, and the teacher writes some or all of these on the board.

- The teacher gives the word meaning and asks how one of the images might be modified to represent the actual meaning of the word.

- On later encounters with the word, the teacher reminds students to remember their keyword image and its connection to the word meaning.

The keyword method is based on ancient wisdom. The basic principle dates back thousands of years to when a messenger had to travel over long distances to convey messages in preliterate times. It has been adapted and studied by several researchers in modern times. It was employed by Atkinson (1975) as a technique for teaching and learning foreign language vocabulary and has received much attention in the literature for English as a second language (ESL) instruction and developmental education (Mastropieri, 1988; McCarville, 1993). It has been reported as effective with learning disabled (LD) students (Condus, Marshall, & Miller, 1986; Gutherie, 1984) and in learning content material (Konopak & Williams, 1988; Levin, Morrison, McGivern, Mastropieri, & Scruggs, 1986). Students in grades 3, 4, 7, and 8 who used the keyword method performed higher on recall of definitions and sentence and story comprehension usage than students who used a sentence context method (Levin, Levin, Glasman, & Nordwall, 1992). Pressley and associates studied the keyword strategy the most extensively and maintained that it helps students learn how to form connections and to develop elaborations on concepts (Pressley, Johnson, & Symons, 1987; Pressley, Levin, & McDaniel, 1987; Pressley, Levin, & Miller, 1981). They did note, however, that it can be demanding for children under 11 years old because young children tend to require several explicit examples (Pressley et al., 1981).

Some critics have maintained that the keyword method is cumbersome and artificial (Moore, 1987). However, when vocabulary learning is thought of as a several-stage continuum, this method does a good job of moving word knowledge from zero or minimal into the midrange of having to pause a moment to recall the word meaning so that it can progress to the final stage of full and automatic word knowledge.

Keyword can create an interesting instructional conversation in which the teacher and students come to the workbench thinking through a word together, and it inculcates a potentially useful memory training device with much wider applications.

Methods for Teaching Word Prediction Strategies

Vocabulary Self-Collection Strategy

The Vocabulary Self-Collection Strategy (Haggard, 1982, 1985) is a co-operative structure that provides practice in identifying unfamiliar vocabulary words in a reading assignment and using context to predict meaning. It is best used with concept-rich reading selections that contain several important vocabulary terms. After students have completed the reading assignment and some type of comprehension check, student teams of two to five members are formed and directed through the following steps:

1. The teacher instructs each group to nominate one vocabulary word from the reading assignment that is both likely to be unfamiliar to most of the class and important to the meaning of the reading selection. Each group's word should be different from the other groups' selections.

2. The teacher next instructs each group to prepare a presentation about their word for the class and pick a spokesperson from the group to present it. (When this activity is new to a group, the teacher gives a prepared example.) The spokesperson should (a) read the word in context (from the reading assignment), (b) tell what the group thinks the word means (they may use context or any other resources available in the classroom for this purpose), and (c) explain why the group thinks the word should be emphasized.

As each group presents, the teacher facilitates by writing the words and meanings on the chalkboard, along with any additional information and clarifications provided by the class, and students record the information from the chalkboard in their vocabulary notebooks or journals.

Incidental Morpheme Analysis

Approximately 80% of the words in the English dictionary contain Greek or Latin prefixes, suffixes, or roots. These word parts, called morphemes, are units of language that cannot be further divided without losing meaning. Some morphemes have meanings only when attached to other word parts. Examples of such bound morphemes include *ed, ing, tele,* and *cide.* Other morphemes, such as *cover, graph,* and *stand,* called free morphemes, can stand alone, that is, they are words in themselves.

Noticing and using morphemes without necessarily labeling these as such is an important strategy for predicting possible meanings of unfamiliar words. Incidental Morpheme Analysis (Manzo & Manzo, 1990) raises students' sensitivity to word parts and provides direct instruction in the strategy of using known word parts to predict meanings of unknown words. The method is incidental in the sense that it can only be used to teach words that have prefixes, suffixes, or root parts that students might recognize in words they already know. Words beginning with the prefix *bi-*, for example, would be good candidates, because students will know or easily learn that *bi-* in *bicycle* means two, and they can use this tool to predict meanings of other words beginning with that prefix. The morpheme *vid* can be predicted to mean *see* from the word *video*. However, not all words we wish to teach have familiar word parts. The recommended use of Incidental Morpheme Analysis is for the teacher to watch for words in content reading assignments that are likely to be unfamiliar and have meaningful word parts that lend themselves to this method, with a goal of teaching a word with this method about every other week.

When a word has been identified, the teacher prepares two levels of clues. The Level 1 clue—minimal help clue—is to provide an easy word that uses the same word part for each meaningful word part in the target word. For *seismograph*, Level 1 clues could include the word *seizure* (for *seis*) and the word *graph* (for *graph*). The Level 2 clue—greater help clue—is the meaning of the Level 1 clue words, such as "to shake" (for *seis*) and "written form" (for *graph*). The method is a game-like challenge to predict a word meaning in the following way:

1. The teacher writes the target word on the chalkboard or overhead and underlines meaningful word parts, or morphemic elements, that might help students predict the word meaning.

   <u>seis</u> mo <u>graph</u>

2. The teacher asks students if they can use the underlined parts to predict the word meaning and why. Write predicted meanings to the side. If the word meaning is predicted correctly, do not tell students that the prediction is correct; write the correct prediction along with other predictions and continue to work through the steps as practice in using this strategy.

3. The teacher can give students clues for predicting (or confirming) the word meaning. For instance, beneath the underlined word

parts, write "Level 1 clues" and then list other, easier words using those morphemes. If students have not yet correctly predicted the word meaning, the teacher continues to ask for predictions.

<u>seis</u> mo <u>graph</u>

Level 1 clues—seizure graph, photograph

4. Beneath Level 1 clues, the teacher can write "Level 2 clues," which are word part meanings, and continue to ask for predictions until the correct definition is reached and written below the clues.

<u>seis</u> mo <u>graph</u>

Level 1 clues—seizure graph, photograph

Level 2 clues—to shake written

Meaning—An instrument that makes a written record of the direction, time, and intensity of earthquakes

Words that have been prepared and used for Incidental Morpheme Analysis may be posted, with Level 1 and 2 clues, on the board, overhead, or PowerPoint during the lesson. A grade-appropriate list of prefixes, suffixes, and roots may also be posted. As students become familiar with the routine, pairs or small groups of students can be given a morpheme-rich word to develop Level 1 and Level 2 clues and guide the class in predicting their word meaning.

Blachowicz and Fisher (2004) recommend Incidental Morpheme Analysis for building vocabulary in remedial settings. We agree that this method, as well as all of the methods in this chapter, is especially appropriate for students who have not yet acquired vocabulary-learning strategies of word consciousness, word connection, and word prediction. (See also Chapter 7, this volume, for discussion of Incidental Morpheme Analysis for teaching content area vocabulary.)

Possible Sentences

Possible Sentences (Moore & Moore, 1986, 1992) builds on students' knowledge of language structures by asking them to use several teacher-selected words from an upcoming reading assignment in sentences. Stahl and Kapinus (1991) found Possible Sentences to be an easy-to-use approach to vocabulary development in a content class or remedial setting that is effective in teaching vocabulary and promoting recall of passage information. Stahl and associates have emphasized that it appears to be the discussion generated by this method that makes it particularly effective (Stahl & Kapinus, 1991; Stahl & Vancil, 1986):

1. The teacher lists several key concept words from a selection, including words likely to be familiar to students, and words likely to be unfamiliar.

2. Students are asked to suggest sentences containing at least two of the words listed that could possibly appear in the textual material. Students' sentences are recorded on the board, overhead, or projector.

3. Students read the textual material to check the appropriateness of their predicted sentences; their sentences should use the target words in ways that are similar to, though not identical to, how the words are used in the text.

4. The students' sentences are then revisited, evaluated, and corrected as needed.

5. New sentences are invited that reflect the sum of learnings from the prediction, reading, and sentence analysis steps.

Possible Sentences teaches students to more expertly use whatever context may be available to predict unfamiliar word meanings by challenging them to produce context themselves. Comparing the sentences they produce with those in the actual text helps to develop and fine tune awareness of language structures and the ways in which context reveals meanings either directly or in subtle shadings.

Conclusions

In this chapter, previously published methods for teaching vocabulary-learning strategies have been aligned with the three components that Blachowicz and her colleagues (2006) found to be necessary in an integrated and comprehensive program of vocabulary instruction. The real focus here, however, has been on the vocabulary-learning strategies that learners need to acquire, more so than on the methods for teaching these or aspects of program design. Our working definition of *vocabulary-learning strategy* is an intentionally and flexibly applied phrase that reminds the learner to notice, connect, and predict meanings of new words. It should be reitterated also that when a learning task is easy, strategies are used subconsciously and effortlessly—and are more appropriately referred to as skills. When a learning task is difficult, however, strategies need to be sought and applied consciously and with greater mental effort.

Looking ahead, we predict that research on teaching vocabulary-learning strategies will support a streamlined approach that is analogous to the approach we are developing for comprehension instruction. We would call this streamlined approach Vocabulary Prompts, to parallel our work on Comprehension Prompts. Comprehension Prompts provide a way to model comprehension strategies so that these are more easily and quickly internalized by students for independent use. Comprehension Prompts are strategy phrases that an individual teacher word-crafts to be personally comfortable to use frequently at appropriate times during text-based instruction (Manzo, 2007). Rather than only modeling prereading questions tied to a particular text in any prereading lesson segment, the teacher would also say or ask one or two Comprehension Prompts. One teacher might use the phrase "I wonder why the author chose this title." Another teacher might like to say "Think about the title, before you read on." However they craft their own Comprehension Prompts, each teacher would use just a handful of Prompts as often as appropriate and seek to create opportunities to do so. The goal is for students to begin to speak and think exactly these phrases—worded and often even inflected exactly as the teacher speaks them—as they begin to read, while they read, and in reflecting upon what they have read.

Similarly, to develop Vocabulary Prompts, teachers would consider types of vocabulary-learning strategies, word-craft their own individual phrase or two for each, and seek opportunities to use the prompts frequently in interactions with students. Examples include the following:

- Word Consciousness Prompt: "Wait—*what* was that word?"
- Word Connection Prompt: "How can I *show* this word meaning with a gesture?"
- Word Prediction Prompt: "If *tri-* in *tricycle* means *three*, then *tri-* in *tripartite* might mean *three*."

The idea of Vocabulary Prompts is for the teacher to carefully select and hone a few such phrases and to intentionally watch for opportunities to use these repeatedly in many contexts. The teacher will model phrases such as these naturally, within the structures of methods like the SAV and the keyword approach. The phrases might be posted on the wall or occasionally written on the board. The teacher should point them out to students and discuss the purpose of using these Prompts. The goal is to begin to overhear students using Prompts appropriately; this means soon they will be using them easily and effectively, as natural habits of mind.

Questions for Discussion

1. Think of an unfamiliar word you recently encountered, or a word that someone asked you to define. In considering the word meaning, did you associate it with prior experiences? Did it evoke any mental images or call up any emotional response? Have you used or encountered the word since? How does your own word-learning example illustrate the importance of word connection strategies?

2. A number of years ago, we conducted a pilot study of Motor Imaging with college students in which we also administered a standardized vocabulary test. One finding in the study was that students who scored in the lowest 10% on the vocabulary test reported that they strongly disliked Motor Imaging, whereas students who scored in the highest 10% reported that they strongly liked the method. How would you explain this finding?

3. The experts disagree about the effects of wide reading on vocabulary acquisition, although wide reading tends to benefit good readers more than poor readers. If we could identify one group of students who had acquired good vocabulary-learning strategies (call these group A) and another group who had not acquired these strategies (group B), which group would likely acquire more vocabulary through wide reading? Why? What are the implications for instruction of group A and of group B? How might we evaluate students' vocabulary-learning strategies?

4. When our son was a preschooler, a question we often found ourselves asking was, "Where did you learn that word?" We were always amazed at the specificity of his reply. Not only would he know, for example, the cartoon series that it was in but also the specific episode and the image associated with the word. What are some effects of being asked this question, and how does this relate to the discussion in the chapter of the disparity in size of upper and lower SES first graders? What are some other vocabulary-learning phrases that caregivers and teachers might use with young children?

REFERENCES

Atkinson, R.C. (1975). Mnemotechnics in second-language learning. *American Psychologist, 30*(8), 821–828.

Au, K.H. (1998). Social constructivism and the school literacy learning of students of diverse backgrounds. *Journal of Literacy Research, 30*(2), 297–319.

Baines, L. (1998). The future of the written word. In J.S. Simmons & L. Baines (Eds.), *Language study in middle school, high school, and beyond: Views on enhancing the study of language* (pp. 190–214). Newark, DE: International Reading Association.

Beck, I.L., & McKeown, M.G. (1991). Conditions of vocabulary acquisition. In R. Barr, M.L. Kamil, P.B. Mosenthal, & P.D. Pearson (Eds.), *Handbook of reading research* (Vol. 2, pp. 789–814). White Plains, NY: Longman.

Beck, I.L., Perfetti, C.A., & McKeown, M.G. (1982). The effects of long-term vocabulary instruction on lexical access and reading comprehension. *Journal of Educational Psychology, 74*(4), 506–521.

Blachowicz, C.L.Z., & Fisher, P. (2004). Building vocabulary in remedial settings: Focus on word relatedness. *Perspectives, 30*(1).

Blachowicz, C.L.Z., Fisher, P., Ogle, D., & Watts-Taffe, S.M. (2006). Vocabulary: Questions from the classroom. *Reading Research Quarterly, 41*(4), 524–539.

Casale, U. (1985). Motor imaging: A reading-vocabulary strategy. *Journal of Reading, 28*(7), 619–621.

Casale, U., & Manzo, A.V. (1983). Differential effects of cognitive, affective, and proprioceptive approaches on vocabulary acquisition. In G.H. McNinch (Ed.), *Reading research to reading practice: The third yearbook of the American Reading Forum* (pp. 71–73). Athens, GA: American Reading Forum.

Condus, M.M., Marshall, K.J., & Miller, S.R. (1986). Effect of the keyword mnemonic strategy on vocabulary acquisition and maintenance by learning disabled children. *Journal of Learning Disabilities, 19*(10), 609–613.

Cummins, J. (1986). Empowering minority students: A framework for intervention. *Harvard Educational Review, 56*(1), 18–36.

Cunningham, A.E., & Stanovich, K.E. (1998). What reading does for the mind. *American Educator, 22*(1–2), 8–17.

Frick-Horbury, D., & Guttentag, R.E. (1998). The effects of restricting hand gesture production on lexical retrieval and recall. *The American Journal of Psychology, 111*(1), 43–62.

Goodman, K.S. (1994). Reading, writing, and written texts: A transactional sociopsycholinguistic view. In R.B. Ruddell, M.R. Ruddell, & H. Singer (Eds.), *Theoretical models and processes of reading* (4th ed., pp. 1903–1130). Newark, DE: International Reading Association.

Graves, M.F., Brunetti, G.J., & Slater, W.H. (1982). The reading vocabularies of primary-grade children of varying geographic and social backgrounds. In J.A. Niles & L.A. Harris (Eds.), *New inquiries in reading research and instruction* (pp. 99–104). Rochester, NY: National Reading Conference.

Gutherie, J.T. (1984). Lexical learning. *The Reading Teacher, 37*(7), 660–662.

Haggard, M.R. (1982). The vocabulary self-collection strategy: An active approach to word learning. *Journal of Reading, 27*(3), 203–207.

Haggard, M.R. (1985). An interactive strategies approach to content reading. *Journal of Reading, 29*(3), 204–210.

Hart, B., & Risley, T. (1995). *Meaningful differences in the everyday experience of young American children.* Baltimore: Paul H. Brookes.

Konopak, B.C., & Williams, N.L. (1988). Using the keyword method to help young readers learn content material. *The Reading Teacher, 41*(7), 682–687.

Levin, J.R., Levin, M.E., Glasman, L.D., & Nordwall, M.B. (1992). Mnemonic vocabulary instruction: Additional effectiveness evidence of the keyword method. *Contemporary Educational Psychology, 17*(2), 156–174.

Levin, J.R., Morrison, C.R., McGivern, J.E., Mastropieri, M.A., & Scruggs, T.E. (1986). Mnemonic facilitation of text-embedded science facts. *American Educational Research Journal, 23*(3), 489–506.

Manzo, A.V. (1969). The ReQuest procedure. *Journal of Reading, 13*(2), 123–126.

Manzo, A.V. (1983). Subjective approach to vocabulary acquisition (or, "...I think my brother is arboreal!"). *Reading Psychology, 3*(2), 155–160.

Manzo, A.V., & Manzo, U.C. (1990). *Content area reading: A heuristic approach.* Upper Saddle River, NJ: Merrill/Prentice Hall.

Manzo, A.V., Manzo, U.C., & Estes, T.H. (2001). *Content area literacy: Interactive teaching for active learning.* New York: John Wiley & Sons.

Manzo, A.V., Manzo, U.C., & Thomas, M.T. (2005). *Content area literacy: Strategic teaching for strategic learning.* Hoboken, NJ: Wiley/Jossey-Bass.

Manzo, U.C. (2007, March). *Comprehension prompts: For teaching instructional level comprehension across grade levels and subject areas, K–12.* Paper presented at the meeting of the Orange County Reading Association, California State University, Fullerton.

Mastropieri, M.A. (1988). Using the keyword method. *Teaching Exceptional Children, 20*(2), 4–8.

McCarville, K.B. (1993). Keyword mnemonic and vocabulary acquisition for developmental college students. *Journal of Developmental Education, 16*(3), 2–4.

McKeown, M.G., Beck, I.L., Omanson, R.C., & Pople, M.T. (1985). Some effects of the nature and frequency of vocabulary instruction on the knowledge and use of words. *Reading Research Quarterly, 20*(5), 552–535.

Moore, D.W. (1987). Vocabulary. In D.E. Alvermann, D.W. Moore, & M.W. Conley (Eds.), *Research within reach: Secondary school reading* (pp. 64–79). Newark, DE: International Reading Association.

Moore, D.W., & Moore, S.A. (1986). Possible sentences. In E.K. Dishner, T.W. Bean, J.E. Readence, & D.W. Moore (Eds.), *Reading in the content areas: Improving classroom instruction* (2nd ed., pp. 174–179). Dubuque, IA: Kendall/Hunt.

Moore, D.W., & Moore, S.A. (1992). Possible sentences: An update. In E.K. Dishner, T.W. Bean, J.E. Readence, & D.W. Moore (Eds.), *Reading in the content areas: Improving classroom instruction* (3rd ed., pp. 196–202). Dubuque, IA: Kendall/Hunt.

Nagy, W.E., & Herman, P.A. (1984). *Limitations of vocabulary instruction* (Technical report No. 326). Paper presented at the 68th annual meeting of the American Educational Research Association, New Orleans, LA.

Nagy, W.E., Herman, P.A., & Anderson, R.C. (1985). Learning words from context. *Reading Research Quarterly, 20*(2), 233–253.

Paivio, A. (1986). *Mental representations.* New York: Oxford University Press.

Piaget, J. (1953). *The origins of intelligence in children.* London: Routledge & Kegan Paul.

Pressley, M., Johnson, C.J., & Symons, S. (1987). Elaborating to learn and learning to elaborate. *Journal of Learning Disabilities, 20*(2), 76–91.

Pressley, M., Levin, J.R., & McDaniel, M.A. (1987). Remembering versus inferring what a word means: Mnemonic and contextual approaches. In M.G. McKeown & M.E. Curtis (Eds.), *The nature of vocabulary acquisition* (pp. 107–129). Hillsdale, NJ: Erlbaum.

Pressley, M., Levin, J.R., & Miller, G.E. (1981). How does the keyword method affect vocabulary comprehension and usage? *Reading Research Quarterly, 16*(2), 213–225.

Stahl, S.A., & Fairbanks, M. (1986). The effects of vocabulary instruction: A model based meta-analysis. *Review of Educational Research, 56*(1), 72–110.

Stahl, S.A., & Kapinus, B.A. (1991). Possible sentences: Predicting word meanings to teach content area vocabulary. *The Reading Teacher, 45*(1), 36–43.

Stahl, S.A., & Vancil, S.J. (1986). Discussion is what makes semantic maps work in vocabulary instruction. *The Reading Teacher, 40*(1), 62–67.

White, T.G., Graves, M.F., & Slater, W.H. (1990). Growth of reading vocabulary in diverse elementary schools: Decoding and word meaning. *Journal of Educational Psychology, 82*(2), 281–290.

Chapter 5

The Nature, Learning, and Instruction of General Academic Vocabulary

Elfrieda H. Hiebert and Shira Lubliner

Scholars have characterized school texts, especially those in content areas, as using a special register called academic language. Cummins (1979, 1984), in particular, distinguished between basic interpersonal communicative skills and cognitive academic language. For instance, the comment "Hey, that's a good point," while appropriate in a conversation between coauthors about an academic paper, would not be anticipated in a review by an editor. An editor would likely say, "The explanation in the second paragraph is noteworthy." The former illustrates the nature of language that Cummins describes as interpersonal communication, while the latter is a form of cognitive academic language.

Cognitive academic language is not simply a function of whether language is oral or written. Biber (1988) demonstrated that, even within oral language, a lecture that consists of a scientific exposition will be considerably more complex than an intimate interpersonal interaction. Typically, however, written language genres have more sophisticated vocabulary than oral language (Hayes & Ahrens, 1988). Even within the written language that appears in school texts, however, the nature of vocabulary can differ substantially across genres. The two excerpts that appear below illustrate two text types. Excerpt 1 (from a fourth-grade language arts text) falls into the category of general narrative exposition, and Excerpt 2 (from a fourth-grade social studies text from the same publisher) illustrates scientific exposition.

> Excerpt 1: "Get that dog in," the pilot hollered. "I want to get out of here before the storm hits!" Akiak jumped and pulled and snapped. All she wanted was to get back on the trail. To run. To win. Then all at once, the wind gusted, the plane shifted, and Akiak twisted out of the handler's grip. (Blake, 1997, in Cooper et al., 2003)

> Excerpt 2: Geography is the study of the people and places of Earth. It explains the forces that shape the land. It explores how living things are

What Research Has to Say About Vocabulary Instruction, edited by Alan E. Farstrup and S. Jay Samuels. © 2008 by the International Reading Association.

connected to the places where they live. Geography helps us understand our environment. An environment includes all the surroundings and conditions that affect living things. (Viola et al., 2005)

While both texts that these excerpts represent have approximately the same percentage of rare words (around 23% for the narrative; 20% for the expository) (Hayes & Ahrens, 1988), the rare words in the two genres are different in kind. The narrative excerpt has synonyms for words that most fourth graders know (Dale & O'Rourke, 1981) such as *hollered* (yelled, shouted) and *gusted* (blew). By contrast, the synonyms for the rare words in the social studies texts are themselves likely not known by fourth graders: *affect* (have an effect on or influence) and *geography* (topography or natural features).

There is also a difference between the words *geography* and *affect* within the social studies text. Nation (1990) has distinguished between words specific to a content area (e.g., *geography*) and words that appear in numerous content areas (e.g., *affect*). This distinction, Nation has observed, is an important one to consider in the design of instruction. Words within the former group are likely to be addressed by content area specialists teaching a course or writers of textbooks and teachers' guides. Words of the second type—which Nation has called general academic words—are used to communicate the content of the topic and are not often addressed by either teachers or textbook writers of content areas.

General academic vocabulary has often been identified as an obstacle for many students, especially the students of poverty who depend on schools to become literate (Corson, 1997; Cummins, 1984). This argument has been made particularly for students who are English-language learners (ELLs) (Bailey, 2006). Reasons for this challenge may lie in the abstract content of much of this vocabulary and the shifts in meaning these words show in different conceptual contexts. Our inability to find instructional studies of general academic vocabulary suggests that this abstract and polysemous content may become an even greater challenge because these words are infrequently the focus of instruction. While the meaning of *geography* is likely to be addressed in social studies instruction, it is unlikely that instructional attention would be paid to *contain*, *certain*, and *cause*. In reading and language arts (in which most vocabulary instruction occurs), words such as *contain*, *certain*, and *cause* will be passed over to attend to unfamiliar words such as *hollered* or *gusted*.

Attention to general academic vocabulary has the potential for being a particularly productive area of instruction and learning because many of these words belong to rich morphological families. When the word *connect* is taught, the members of its morphological family such as *connection, connective, disconnect, reconnect, connectible,* and *connectibility* can also be addressed. Another feature of general academic vocabulary that we report in this chapter is the presence of many words within this group that have cognates in Spanish. Since a substantial percentage of these cognates are more common in Spanish conversation than in English, attention to this group of words in instruction could build on a potential fund of knowledge held by Spanish-speaking students.

For these reasons, we have chosen to make the focus of this chapter on general academic vocabulary and not the content-specific vocabulary of content areas or the literary vocabulary of narratives. We develop four topics related to general academic language: (1) defining general academic language relative to other types of academic language, (2) describing general academic language through the lenses of two corpora, (3) reviewing available research on the learning and instruction of morphology and cognates, and (4) suggesting applications and extensions of this review on general academic vocabulary for educators and researchers.

Defining Academic Vocabulary

General academic vocabulary needs to be understood in relation to three other types of vocabulary that occur in school texts and tasks: content-specific vocabulary, school-task vocabulary, and literary vocabulary Illustrations of words in each of these groups appear in Table 5.1. The type of vocabulary most commonly associated with academic learning consists of the technical words around which content area instruction typically focuses, words such as *geography* and *democracy* in social studies and *photosynthesis* and *erosion* in science. Marzano (2004) has produced a vocabulary curriculum of content-specific words by drawing on (a) standards documents from 13 national organizations, including the major content areas (i.e., mathematics, language arts) and secondary areas (e.g., health), (b) a synthesis of more than 100 national and state documents (Kendall & Marzano, 2000), and (c) the Council for Basic Education's (1998) synthesis of 22 national and state documents. From these documents, Marzano identified 7,923 terms that can be classified into 14 subject areas and, within each subject area, at one of four grade-level spans: K–2, 3–5, 6–8, and 9–12. A sample of terms from Marzano's analysis for seven primary subject areas for grades 3–5 is included in Table 5.2.

Table 5.1. Examples of words within different vocabulary groups

Vocabulary group	Examples	Frequency	Dispersion
Content-specific (social studies)	landforms	2	.21
	geography	9	.44
	continents	20	.57
	globe	24	.63
	Meridian	3	.41
	hemispheres	2	.54
	equator	24	.51
	X	9.7	.47
School-task	preview	1	.56
	draft	11	.60
	statement	52	.63
	concluding	2	.72
	summarize	4	.74
	outline	24	.83
	opinion	52	.89
	X	20.8	.71
Literary	blizzard	4	.67
	hollered	1	.32
	burrowed	3	.43
	handler's	.02	0
	pilot	19	.72
	cautiously	6	.61
	refuge	5	.65
	X	5.4	.45
General academic	affect	63	.85
	features	48	.88
	conditions	107	.91
	created	65	.91
	reasons	91	.93
	specific	97	.93
	experienced	31	.97
	X	71.7	.91

The content-specific vocabulary in Table 5.2 for social studies, mathematics, and science illustrates the focus of instruction at the target grade level. For example, a topic such as ecosystems is evident in the term

Table 5.2. Illustrative vocabulary of seven subject areas for grades 3–5

Content area	Sample words
Civics	abuse of power, campaign, elected representative, geographical representation, individual liberty, Labor Day, national origin, patriotism, school board, Uncle Sam, welfare
Economics	barter, division of labor, firm, household, limited budget, natural resource, rent, tax, wage
English language arts	abbreviation, capitalization, e-mail, genre, illustration, learning log, paragraph, reading strategy, table, verb
Geography	billboards, discovery, fall line, harbor, Japan, land clearing, national capital, Pacific rim, rainforest, technology, vegetation region
History	ballad, Daniel Boone, factory, Hanging Gardens of Babylon, Jackie Robinson, labor, Nathan Beman, the Pacific, race relations, tactic, vaccine, Zheng He
Mathematics	addend, capacity, equation, gram, improbability, mass, obtuse angle, quotient, sample, unit conversion
Science	bedrock, Earth's axis, gases, inherited characteristic, magnetic attraction, ocean currents, recycle, technology, water capacity

rainforest for geography. A unit on geometry is evident with the term *obtuse angle* among the mathematics terms. The vocabulary for English language arts in Table 5.2 is of a different type than the vocabulary for social studies, science, and mathematics. Prominent terms for English language arts are *learning log, reading strategy*, and *capitalization*. Unlike a concept that may underlie a selection of literature (e.g., *survival, bravery*), a term such as *learning logs* is used in instructional tasks including the directions in workbooks and tests. None of the words for the English language arts in Table 5.2 pertain to the content of texts that students might read—words that describe themes of literature or words that describe how characters might move or what or how they might speak or act. As is evident in Excerpt 1, children's literature has an abundance of unique vocabulary (e.g., *hollered, gusted*).

Within English language arts standards, the emphasis has been on instructional and reader processes, not on the content of literature (Hirsch, 2006). Hirsch's (1992) Core Knowledge program for grade 4 English language arts illustrates one form that a content-specific English language arts curriculum could take. Among the topics are characters in literature (Merlin, Robinson Crusoe), titles and authors/poets/playwrights (e.g., "Dreams" by Langston Hughes, *Treasure Island* by Robert Louis Stevenson), genres (e.g., myths, epics, speeches), forms of language (e.g., phrases, proverbs, idioms), and grammatical terms (e.g., prepositions, interjections, adverbs).

Scholars have labeled vocabulary such as many of the terms that are now presented within English language arts standards in Table 5.1 (e.g., *learning logs, reading strategy*) as the school-task vocabulary. Downing (1970) was the first to identify the many terms that teachers use as part of reading instruction or that writers of textbook programs use to describe instructional processes and tasks. Downing observed that often times teachers may be oblivious to the fact that their students do not know the terms and that some students' reading acquisition can be negatively affected as a result. Some of these terms, such as *capitalization*, have to do with features of written language (e.g., *letter, alphabet, phrase, sentence, vowel*). Others have to do with reading processes such as *reread* and *summarize*. Such terms influence students' performances on comprehension questions (Cunningham & Moore, 1993) as well as on standardized tests (Butler, Stevens, & Castellon, 2006).

The vocabulary of the excerpt from children's literature illustrates a third kind of academic language—literary vocabulary. In addition to the content of literature that Hirsch (1992) identified in his Core Knowledge curriculum, literature uses particular verbs, nouns, and adjectives to describe the states of characters, their actions, and the settings in which these actions occur. Many of these words occur infrequently in conversations and in texts (e.g., *hollered, gusted*, in Excerpt 1). While the same concept may be repeated in a poem or story, writers of literary texts will typically use synonyms or words that connote slightly different meanings for the concept. In a story on a character finding himself unprepared for the wilderness in which he is lost such as *Hatchet* (Paulson, 1987), various words will be used to describe the character's disposition—*terrified, frightened*, and *discouraged*. Each of these words appears only a single time in the text. While students may understand the concept *afraid*, they may not have encountered the synonyms for the concept before.

The final group of words found in school texts consists of general academic vocabulary. Similar to the literary words that characterize narrative texts, these words are not apparent in the content-specific vocabulary sampled in Table 5.2. Within Excerpt 2 from the social studies text (see p. 106), such words are prominent (e.g., *contain, certain, cause*). These are words whose meanings often change in different content areas (e.g., *form, process*). Further, writers of texts as well as teachers often assume that students know their meanings.

An analysis of the four groups of words in Table 5.1 illustrates the manner in which the general academic words differ from the other three groups. The frequency and the dispersion index was obtained from the *Word Frequency Book* (Zeno, Ivens, Millard, & Duvvuri, 1995) for the words illustrating each of the four groups of words. Frequency in Table 5.1 is a prediction of the number of appearances of a word per one million words of text (Zeno et al., 1995). The dispersion index reflects how widely a word is used in different subject areas (Carroll, Davies, & Richman, 1971). Words that appear in only one content area have a D value of 0; words that appear in many content areas (e.g., social sciences, science, mathematics, fine arts, literature) could have a D value as large as 1.0 (Carroll et al., 1971).

Two groups—the literary words and the content-specific words—have similar frequency (5.4 and 9.7, respectively) and dispersion indices (0.45 and 0.47, respectively). Overall, these words appear rarely in texts and do not appear in many subject areas. The school-task words have a moderate number of appearances (approximately 21 per million words of text) and the dispersion index is also moderately high (0.71), indicating that they appear across several content areas.

The general academic words have high frequency ratings and dispersion indices. On average, these words appear 71.7 times per million words of text and have an average dispersion index of 0.91, indicating that they appear across numerous subject areas. In the following section, we expand on this description by examining the words on two lists of general academic words.

Characteristics of General Academic Words

An exhaustive review of literature produced no studies of the effects of instruction of general academic vocabulary, even among scholars who have highlighted the role of these words in the success of university students who are non-native English speakers (Coxhead, 2000; Nation, 1990). As we will demonstrate with analyses of two corpora of general academic vocabulary, however, these words have certain features that have been considered in instructional interventions: morphological richness and English–Spanish cognates. While research on effects of instruction on general academic vocabulary is not yet available, studies have been conducted on these two features of vocabulary.

The first corpus consists of the Academic Word List (AWL) developed by Coxhead (2000) as part of a long-standing program of work to support English reading proficiency of university students who are non-native English speakers. Recently this list has begun to be used for middle and high school interventions as well (Snow, 2007). Recognizing that the general academic vocabulary in the elementary and middle school may differ from that found in college texts (Hyland & Tse, 2007), Hiebert (2007) developed the Core Academic Word List (CAWL). The CAWL consists of 400 morphological families in which at least one word is among the 5,586 most-frequent words in samples of written English from grades kindergarten through college (Zeno et al., 1995). Further, morphological families were selected in which at least one member had a dispersion index of 0.8 or higher. These choices were made to ensure that experiences with the 400 morphological families would extend to students' reading in the content areas during the upper grades of the elementary school and middle school.

To demonstrate the feasibility of suggesting that research on instruction of morphology and cognates can be a resource for advocating and designing instruction of general academic vocabulary, we have analyzed these two corpora for their morphological richness and the presence of cognates.

Morphological Richness

Morphemes—the smallest meaning units in English—are of two types: free and bound. Examples of free morphemes are *type* and *morpheme*. In the words *types* and *morphemes*, the -*s* illustrates a bound morpheme. The addition of inflected endings (e.g., plurals [-*s*, -*es*], verb tenses [-*s*, -*ed*, -*ing*], comparatives [-*er*, -*est*]) changes the meaning of a base word only slightly. Some words take derivational suffixes that change the part of speech of a word (e.g., *construct* to *constructive* to *constructively*). When a derivational prefix is added to a word, the meaning of the base word is changed (e.g., *deconstruct*, *reconstruct*). Whether a word has both inflected and derivational affixes is a function of the historical origins of a word. Unlike French/Latin words, which use derivational affixes to change the meaning of the base word, words with origins in Anglo-Saxon combine base words to form new words (i.e., compound words). An example of a compound word is *coldblooded* (*cold* akin to the German word *kalt* and *blood* to the German word *Blut*). The addition of derivational affixes (e.g., -*ion*, *non*-) is characteristic of words that came into English through French and Latin (Barber, 2000).

As texts become more complex with students' movement through school, derived words become more frequent (Nagy & Anderson, 1984; White, Power, & White, 1989). Nagy and Anderson (1984) analyzed a sampling of English vocabulary according to the criterion that, if the base or root word is known, readers have the potential to understand an unfamiliar word based on knowledge of the base or root word in the context of a text. Based on this criterion (the fourth of six categories that describe the transparency of the meaning of derived words), Nagy and Anderson predicted that 60% of the unfamiliar words students encounter in texts are derived words that students may be able to understand based on their knowledge of a member of the word's morphological family. (See Chapter 1, this volume, for more information on teaching vocabulary to young learners using word roots.)

Since morphological relationships contribute substantially to students' word learning, identifying words with rich morphological families was a key factor in the development of the CAWL (Hiebert, 2007). Hiebert used the fifth of Nagy and Anderson's (1984) categories (i.e., derived words that require an explicit extension such as *apart/apartment* and *artifice/artificial)* to establish inclusion within morphological families. Hiebert made this extension a priority because the focus of the CAWL is on instruction in morphology at the upper elementary grades. With this inclusive definition of morphological families and with the requirement that a head word represent a morphological family, it should come as no surprise that the 400 words on the CAWL represent morphological families with an average of 5.4 members.

Coxhead (2000) defined a word family according to all inflections and frequent, productive, and regular prefixes and suffixes of a base or stem word. On average, head words on the AWL represent morphological families of 5.5 words. Of the 570 words on the list, 76% had a morphological family of three or more words and 24% represented one or two words. These analyses show that, overall, a characteristic of general academic words is that they come from rich morphological families.

Cognates

The number of derivational affixes represented within the morphological families of general academic words suggests that the majority of these are French-Latin in origin (Barber, 2000). The Romance origins of general academic words are relevant for the many native-Spanish speaking students in American schools because Spanish has closer ties to French and Latin—Romance languages—than to German. French was a source for many of the words that comprise the academic layer of English (Barber, 2000). Analyses have shown that more than one third of the words in academic texts are Spanish-English cognates (Nash, 1997) and that knowledge of cognates mediates reading comprehension achievement (Nagy, García, Durgunoglu, & Hancin-Bhatt, 1993).

Lubliner and Hiebert (2008) developed a category scheme to analyze English-Spanish cognates based on specific spelling patterns. The scheme consists of five clusters that attend to regular orthographic shifts from English to Spanish. In the first cluster (*same*), the English and Spanish words are spelled the same in English and Spanish (e.g., *total/total; popular/popular*). The second, and largest, cluster (*add/change*) includes 11 cognate patterns characterized by minor spelling differences such as an additional letter(s) at the end of the Spanish word (e.g., *art/arte, family/familia*). The third cluster (*verbs*) is characterized by a common base of a verb followed by inflectional endings that signify tense, number, and formality in Spanish (e.g., *accepted/aceptado*). The fourth cluster (*es*) consists of words that begin with *s* in English and change to *es* in Spanish (e.g., *student/estudiante*). The fifth cluster (*other*) is a catchall of words that have a variety of spelling differences (e.g., *benefit/beneficio*).

Using this category scheme, Lubliner and Hiebert (2008) established that nearly 70% of the 570 head words on the AWL were morphologically transparent English-Spanish cognates. Hiebert (2007) used the same category scheme to identify head words on the CAWL that had morphologically transparent English-Spanish cognates. Of the 400 words on the CAWL, 61% of the English words were of this type.

An additional analysis was conducted to determine how many of the cognates on the AWL had higher frequencies in Spanish than in English. Lubliner and Hiebert (2008) conducted this analysis because of the distinction of Bravo, Hiebert, and Pearson (2007) between high-frequency and low-frequency cognates. An illustration of a high-frequency Spanish-English cognate is *facil*, which is the common word in Spanish for the English word *easy*. *Facilitation* (a word on the AWL) and members of its morphological family—*facilitator, facilitate*—are used in academic texts and speeches but not common speech in English. Of the 268 AWL cognate pairs for which frequency rankings in both Spanish and English could be obtained, 85% were more frequent in Spanish than English. Provided that Spanish-speaking students can recognize an English word in a text as a word in their spoken language, the higher frequency of Spanish words that correspond to English academic vocabulary words could provide them with a linguistic advantage.

The analyses of these two lists of general academic words indicate that many are French-Latin in origin. This origin means that these words typically represent rich morphological families and have cognates to Spanish words.

Learning and Instruction of General Academic Vocabulary

We could not find any studies on how well students perform with general academic vocabulary nor could we find any studies of interventions on general academic vocabulary. There are studies, however, of learning and instruction of words based on both morphology and cognates. Because descriptive analyses have shown that many general academic words have rich morphological families and cognates, we consider the literature on these two topics.

Learning and Instruction: Morphology

As the analyses of the general academic vocabulary corpora showed, derivational affixes (prefixes and suffixes) are more important to academic vocabulary than inflected suffixes. Native English speaking children have generally acquired most inflected forms in their oral language (both receptive and productive) before they start school (Anglin, 1993; Carlisle & Fleming, 2003; Tyler & Nagy, 1989). Typically, children who are beginning school also know some derivational suffixes, such as -er (e.g., *runner, teacher*) and the -y adjective (e.g., *smelly*) (Berko, 1958). However, most derivational suffixes are acquired between first and fifth grades. Based on an extensive study of derivational knowledge, Anglin (1993) reported that students learned about 4,000 base words and about 14,000 derived words during the period from grades one through five. Explicit knowledge of the morphemic structure of words (also described as morphological awareness) continues to develop through the high school years (Anglin, 1993; Carlisle, 2000; Mahony, 1994; Tyler & Nagy, 1989; Wysocki & Jenkins, 1987). Even with orthographic and phonological abilities accounted for, morphological awareness and vocabulary knowledge correlate highly. Nagy, Berninger, Abbott, Vaughnn, and Vermeulen (2003) reported that this correlation was highest at grades 4 and 5 ($r = 0.83$). Beyond this level into high school, the correlation decreased slightly (Nagy, Berninger, & Abbott, 2006). Morphological awareness also contributes to reading comprehension, independent of its relation to vocabulary (Katz, 2004; Nagy et al., 2006).

Findings of a recent study suggest that instruction that fosters morphological awareness may be appropriate for many students, not simply learning disabled students. Nagy et al. (2006) reported a substantial amount of variation among students in the speed with which students decoded morphologically related words even within a sample where 98% of the students were of European-American descent and only 8% qualified for free or reduced lunch. Morphological awareness proved to be a powerful predictor of reading comprehension, reading vocabulary, and spelling through the last grade that they tested (grade 9). Nagy et al. speculated that higher levels of morphological awareness are associated with greater accuracy and fluency in decoding morphologically complex words, which in turn contribute to greater comprehension.

The research team that produced these descriptions of students' morphological knowledge has studied an intervention to support the development of morphological awareness in learning-disabled students. Berninger et al. (2003) contrasted a morphological condition with a phonological one. The activities of the morphological condition were designed to build sensitivity to morphological composition of words, such as word building (producing written words by combining base words and affixes) and unit finding (identifying base words and affixes in written words). Students also received instruction in the meaning of prefixes and suffixes, had opportunities to highlight and discuss unfamiliar words, and practiced oral reading fluency and text comprehension. The program in phonological knowledge had the same goals, but activities focused on the level of phonemes and graphemes rather than morphemes. Berninger et al. reported that, while both the phonological and morphological interventions produced an increase in accuracy of phonological decoding for students with reading disabilities, those in the morphological intervention had higher performances on nonsense word reading. Effects on vocabulary and comprehension measures were unclear since these measures were not administered.

Baumann et al. (2002) implemented a project to establish which aspects of morphological training produce the greatest benefits. The National Reading Panel (NICHD, 2000) had identified a shortcoming of much vocabulary research to be the confounding of numerous instructional components, making it uncertain as to which components produce the greatest effects. To isolate variables, Baumann et al. compared fifth graders' performance as a function of morphological instruction of prefixes, instruction in contextual clues, a combined treatment of morphological and contextual knowledge, or an instructed control group. The morphology instruction focused on eight sets of prefixes, clustered according to similar meaning such as the not family (*dis, un, in, im*) and the number family (*mono, bi, semi*). The context group was taught eight ways of using context such as appositives or synonyms. Following 12 fifty-minute lessons, students were tested on their ability to recall the meanings of words used in the instructional lessons (lesson words) and their ability to correctly identify the meaning of either uninstructed words using taught morphological elements or words in texts using taught context clues (transfer words). Both immediate and delayed effects of morphological and contextual analysis instruction were found for lesson words and an immediate effect for both treatments for transfer words. However, instruction in morphological or contextual analysis, whether in isolation or combination, did not significantly affect text comprehension. Further, the morphological and contextual instruction in combination was as effective as either form of instruction conducted separately.

Henry's (1989) structural-historical approach took another direction in research on morphological training. Because letter–sound correspondences and syllabic and morphemic patterns differ according to word origin (Anglo-Saxon, French/Latin, and Greek), students in Henry's study were taught to distinguish between letter–sound correspondences and morpheme patterns on the basis of words' origins. In Henry's study, upper elementary grade students who received decoding instruction made significant gains in word structure knowledge and in decoding and spelling achievement. Those students receiving decoding instruction based on word structure and word origin learned more about the structure of English orthography and also made similar gains in reading and spelling performance. In that the instruction provides information at both the phoneme and morpheme levels, it is difficult to determine the degree to which morphological instruction is useful.

A final example of directions of research on morphology is that of Nunes and Bryant (2006). While Nunes and Bryant have only recently begun to include measures of vocabulary with those of spelling that have been their primary interest, the underlying stance of the project is that morphology, like phonology, needs to be taught explicitly if many students are to develop appropriate knowledge and strategies. Further, the systematic progression of the project from laboratory to large-scale implementation provides a model for research on morphology instruction. Nunes and Bryant began with quasi-experimental studies in a laboratory setting (instructor student ratio of 1:2) and in classroom settings taught by members of the research team. These studies were of limited duration and addressed limited content (i.e., two suffixes). Based on positive effects on spelling in this initial phase (with a significant, although weaker, effect in the classroom), a second phase was initiated in which classroom teachers conducted the instruction on a wider range of affixes and spellings with members of the research team at hand (Nunes, Bryant, & Olsson, 2003). A significant positive effect of this instruction on students' spelling led to a larger classroom intervention where teachers received a CD-ROM that contained tasks or games and a small amount of professional development. This larger classroom intervention also produced strong effects on students' spelling (Nunes & Bryant, 2006).

Finally, the research program attended to the effects of teachers' participation in a course about morphemes and spelling. The course did increase teachers' awareness of morphology and its links with spelling. Further, students' spelling improved when teachers used at least some of the project tasks. More recently, intervention tasks were presented in a training program designed to improve students' vocabulary. The program, administered with minimal constraints, improved students' knowledge and understanding of polymorphemic words.

While the review of the National Reading Panel (NICHD, 2000) indicated that evidence for large-scale efforts of vocabulary instruction were limited, an increasing number of projects are showing that instruction in morphology can have a positive effect on students' learning of vocabulary and spelling. Further, these studies provide models for instructional content, strategies, and tasks. In that rich morphological families characterize general academic vocabulary, these studies demonstrate the benefits and also the means that can be used to facilitate general academic vocabulary.

Learning and Instruction: Cognates

Students who are ELLs face particular challenges learning English vocabulary. The historical antecedents of academic vocabulary, however, may mean that native Spanish speakers have resources to draw upon that are not as readily available as speakers of other native languages, including English. Many native Spanish speakers learning to read in English, however, need to be made aware of these connections through instruction. Nagy et al. (1993) found that the relationship between first-language vocabulary and second-language comprehension of texts containing cognates was positive for those students who recognized the most cognate relationships and negative for those who recognized the fewest cognate relationships.

Factors such as ability, biliteracy, and age appear to affect bilingual students' ability to recognize and use cognates. Successful Spanish-speaking bilingual students make effective use of cognates while less proficient students do not know how to apply their knowledge of Spanish to reading tasks in English (Jiménez, García, & Pearson, 1996). Biliteracy confers an advantage to students in terms of their ability to transfer strategies across languages, including enhanced ability to use cognates (Proctor, August, Carlo, & Snow, 2006). Student age also appears to influence the successful use of cognates. Middle school grade students are more successful in cognate recognition tasks than elementary students, suggesting that cognate awareness increases with age and cognitive maturity (Hancin-Bhatt & Nagy, 1994).

Several studies have identified factors such as orthographic and phonological overlap and word frequency in Spanish and English that may be salient in students' ability to recognize and use cognate information. According to Bowers, Mimouni, and Arguin (2000), cognate relatedness is based on the overlap of orthographic features. Findings reported by Nagy et al. (1993) confirm this argument in that students were more successful in identifying cognates with clear orthographic overlap; even small spelling differences reduced students' ability to recognize English-Spanish cognate pairs.

For native Spanish speakers who are being taught to read in English and not in Spanish, however, the degree of phonological transparency between cognates may be particularly critical. For example, when confronted with the word *possible* [**pos**-uh-buhl] in a text, students may not recognize that the word is the same as the word *possible* [po-**see**-blay] due to differences in pronunciation and accent. This prediction is confirmed by findings from a study by Carlo, August, and Snow (2005) who reported that fourth graders' ability to correctly identify low-frequency English words that are cognates to Spanish was predicted by performances on measures of Spanish reading. Students who were not fluent readers in Spanish were not able to recognize cognates in English text to the same degree as fluent Spanish readers, regardless of the language of instruction.

Research on the amount of instruction required to bring native Spanish speaking students to relatively high levels of cognate recognition in reading English is based primarily on information from research on the Vocabulary Improvement Project (VIP) first reported on by McLaughlin, August, and Snow (2000) and subsequently by Carlo et al. (2004) and Carlo et al. (2005). Because this research program includes an array of vocabulary strategies, the specific effects of cognate instruction in the development of morphological awareness and proficiency with academic vocabulary is not clear. However, results of the project are indicative of the kinds of instruction that can support the learning of academic vocabulary.

In its initial implementation (Carlo et al., 2005; Lively, August, Carlo, & Snow, 2003), VIP was conducted with a set of fables (Lobel, 1980). A group of 10–12 target words from a different fable provided the focus of each of the eight lessons. After 10 weeks of instruction, large differences were found on all measures for language status (ELLs versus English-only students) and geographic site. Impact of the intervention was found only for the mastery test that measured whether students had retained the vocabulary words taught in the curriculum.

Carlo et al. (2004) tested VIP next with fifth graders, making the instruction more rigorous by extending the length of the intervention to 15 weeks and by using social studies content (immigration). This more rigorous version produced significantly higher performances for the intervention than comparison students on generalization measures of word association, polysemy, and cloze as well as on the mastery test of taught vocabulary.

The topic of immigration and the use of informational text also meant that the vocabulary was challenging. Unlike the fourth-grade intervention with narrative text where approximately 20% of the target words had clear Spanish cognates, approximately two thirds of the words in the fifth-grade social studies instruction were cognates. We conducted an analysis of the number of general academic words in the Carlo et al. (2004) study. A substantial number of the words were content-specific words (e.g., *transcontinental, treaty, tenement*). Since some of the texts that Carlo and colleagues used were trade books, literary words were also prominent among the vocabulary (e.g., *fledging, straddle, ominous, scorn*). However, general academic words were also present. Of the 169 words that Carlo and colleagues taught as part of the immigration unit, 23% were on the AWL and 16% were on the CAWL.

Studies of the ability of native Spanish-speaking students to use their knowledge of Spanish cognates in reading English indicate that many do not make these connections without at least a modicum of explicit instruction. When they are guided in using this knowledge as part of instruction, however, their knowledge of English vocabulary expands. While research to date has not attended to the learning of general academic vocabulary as part of interventions, efforts such as the VIP illustrate ways in which native Spanish-speaking students can be taught to use their knowledge of cognates in understanding academic words in English.

Implications and Extensions

While specialists who instruct university students who are non-native English speakers have emphasized the importance of general academic vocabulary, a similar emphasis has not been apparent in curricula for students learning to read in their first language or of students learning to read in English. Many educators with a specialty in reading may never have received or taught a lesson in general academic vocabulary. This lack of attention to general academic vocabulary is indicative of the atheoretical nature of the vocabulary curriculum that Pearson, Hiebert, and Kamil (2007) have described. However, analyses such as those of Hiebert (2007) indicate that general academic vocabulary consumes a sufficiently critical portion of content area texts, even in the upper elementary grades, to make it a factor in proficient reading.

An unanswered question is whether general academic words, with their often variable meanings in different content areas and contexts, can be taught effectively and efficiently. Even among those who have emphasized the need to attend to general academic vocabulary with university students who are non-native English speakers, the nature and effects of instructional programs that focus on general academic vocabulary have not been documented. A research project that focuses specifically on general academic vocabulary in middle schools is currently underway (Snow, 2007), components of which will be described subsequently to illustrate the form that instruction of general academic vocabulary can take. However, effects of this project have not been reported to date. What we know at present about the learning of general academic vocabulary is based on studies of morphology and cognates. While the findings are not specific to general academic vocabulary, these studies have shown that students' knowledge of words in reading and spelling can be improved by instruction that focuses on morphology, including cognates. This instruction makes a difference to general groups of students, in addition to those who typically have lower levels of morphological awareness such as learning-disabled students. When instruction has emphasized cognates with native Spanish-speaking students, the learning of non-native English speakers who often have lower vocabulary performances is also enhanced.

We anticipate that instruction of general academic vocabulary will increase morphological awareness as well as facility with general academic vocabulary. Carlisle (2006) and Nunes and Bryant (2006) have raised the need for increased attention to morphological knowledge within the school curriculum, especially in the middle grades and beyond. As Carlisle (2006) stated,

> Leaving morphological analysis to be discovered by students on their own means that those who are in some way challenged by language learning are likely to be left behind by their peers in the development of vocabulary, word reading, and reading comprehension. (p. 90)

The presence of the cognates among general academic vocabulary also means that these words are a potentially rich fund of knowledge for Spanish-speaking students. The finding that 70% of the head words on the AWL are transparent cognates and 50% of these words are either highly or moderately frequent in Spanish means that these words are used commonly in oral Spanish discourse. However, it is unlikely that Spanish-speaking students will automatically make the connections between languages if they are learning to read in English (and not in Spanish first). Although orthographic similarities may appear obvious, the differences in phonological representation need to be considered. That is, students may not recognize that a Spanish word that they use commonly in conversations is very similar to an English word in their texts. Spanish-speaking students likely require explicit cognate instruction if they are to realize the potential value of their linguistic fund of knowledge.

What form might instruction of general academic vocabulary take? The first response to this question is the form that such instruction should *not* take. Instruction should not take the form of distributing word lists that teachers are asked to systematically instruct from top to bottom— and that students are asked to learn or memorize. There is no evidence that such learning or instructional experiences will develop the facility with this vocabulary that is necessary for success in the content areas. Further, there is no evidence of which words among the general academic vocabulary require support and in what content areas. At present, the data on which words are within students' vocabularies are from an outdated and methodologically flawed source (Dale & O'Rourke, 1981). Studies that establish levels of students' knowledge of general academic words in particular content areas are needed. Studies of the extent to which students can generalize their knowledge of base words and derivational affixes within morphological families are also needed. In all likelihood, however, there are substantial numbers of general academic words that would benefit from instructional attention. The review of studies of morphological awareness and of cognates indicate that explicit instruction is needed for students to develop their capacity to expand their vocabularies on the basis of morphological characteristics.

In addition to the previously reviewed studies where morphological knowledge and cognates were the focus, there is a project that is currently examining effects of instruction of specific words on the AWL (Coxhead, 2000) to middle school students (Snow, 2007). In this project titled Word Generation, a group of five words from the AWL is the focus for a week. These words appear in a text that students read (or that is read to students) on Mondays as part of their homeroom period. The texts pertain to topics such as cloning or drug testing in the workplace that are viewed as interesting and controversial to adolescents and young adults. During the homeroom periods of a week (approximately four days a week), students are involved in an experience with the texts, content, and words. The science, social studies, and mathematics teachers as well as the English language arts teachers are given information on how the words apply to their content. Students end the week by writing their response or opinions about the topic.

Middle schools have homeroom periods in which instruction such as Word Generation (Snow, 2007) can occur. But where should instruction of general academic vocabulary occur in the upper grades of the elementary school? We suggest that, starting in grades 3 or 4, this instruction should occur in the reading or language arts period. The reading and language arts are consuming more and more of the school day in elementary schools. Regardless of claims, narrative text continues to consume the curriculum (Walsh, 2003). As the examples in Table 5.1 (see page 109) illustrate, there are critical differences in the vocabularies of narrative and informational texts. One of these differences is in the presence of general academic vocabulary within informational text. General academic vocabulary needs to be situated firmly within the reading and language arts block and then extended to other subject areas across the curriculum. The fact that general academic vocabulary has a high frequency rating and a high dispersion index underscores the value of this instruction. General academic vocabulary words are likely to appear often in a broad array of texts that students read in school, making instruction of this vocabulary essential across content areas. Instruction in these words can provide students with the opportunities to develop understandings of the morphological features of vocabulary within the French/Latin layer of English and the polysemous nature of vocabulary.

Conclusions

In this chapter, we distinguished general academic vocabulary from the content-specific vocabulary of subject areas such as social studies (e.g., *geography, environment*), school-task vocabulary that teachers and students need to communicate about tasks (e.g., *learning logs, adverb*), and the literary vocabulary of narrative texts (e.g., *gusted, hollered*). There is evidence that general academic vocabulary is prominent in content area texts. There is also evidence that students benefit from instruction that promotes morphological awareness. In the decade to come, we are hopeful that reports of instructional projects and interventions on general academic vocabulary will increase. We predict that such attention to the linguistic patterns and meanings of general academic words will contribute to higher levels of comprehension with content area texts and content for many students, particularly students who are English-language learners as well as those who struggle in becoming proficient readers.

Questions for Discussion

1. Identify a lesson from the beginning, middle, and end of the teachers' manuals for the primary reading/language arts program that your educational agency uses. Follow the same procedure for the science program used by your educational agency. Make a list of the words that are the focus of vocabulary instruction in both of the programs.

    (a) Sort the words in each list according to the four categories that are described in this chapter.

    (b) How consistent is the representation of different categories in the two lists to the information presented in this chapter?

    (c) How well-represented is general academic vocabulary in the words that are identified for instruction?

2. Next, locate the text that accompanies the lessons that you have just analyzed. Study these texts for the presence of general academic words (e.g., *conditions, process, reasons, specific*). If

possible, enter sample portions of the texts into one of the available analyzers on the Internet.

(a) What portion of the words in the texts consists of general academic text?

(b) How attentive is instruction in the teachers' manuals to the presence of this general academic text?

3. Using the same lessons from the teachers' manuals and the accompanying student texts, examine treatment of morphological connections across words.

(a) How many words within the student texts belong to morphological families, which have similar meanings but differ in affixes and inflected meanings (e.g., *reason, reasonable*)?

(b) How many words within the student texts are compound words (where two free morphemes form a new word such as *rainforest*)?

(c) How many instances can you find where several words occur together consistently to convey a special meaning as in *scientific method* or *learning log*?

(d) What is the nature of instruction that addresses these different forms of morphological complexity?

REFERENCES

Anglin, J.M. (1993). Vocabulary development: A morphological analysis. *Monographs of the Society for Research in Child Development, 58*(10), 1–166.

Bailey, A.L. (2006). Teaching and assessing students learning English in school. In A.L. Bailey (Ed.), *The language demands of school: Putting academic English to the test* (pp. 1–26). New Haven, CT: Yale University Press.

Barber, C. (2000). *The English language: A historical introduction.* Cambridge, UK: Cambridge University Press.

Baumann, J.F., Edwards, E.C., Font, G., Tereshinski, C.A., Kame'enui, E.J., & Olejnik, S. (2002). Teaching morphemic and contextual analysis to fifth-grade students. *Reading Research Quarterly, 37*(2), 150–176.

Berko, J. (1958). The child's learning of English morphology. *Word, 14*(3), 150–177.

Berninger, V.W., Nagy, W.E., Carlisle, J.F., Thomson, J., Hoffer, D., Abbott, S., et al. (2003). Effective treatment for children with dyslexia in grades 4–6: Behavioral and brain evidence. In B. Foorman (Ed.), *Preventing and remediating reading difficulties: Bringing science to scale* (pp. 281–347). Baltimore: York Press.

Biber, D. (1988). *Variation across speech and writing.* New York: Cambridge University Press.

Bowers, J.S., Mimouni, Z., & Arguin, M. (2000). Orthography plays a critical role in cognate priming: Evidence from French/English and Arabic/French cognates. *Memory & Cognition, 28*(8), 1289–1296.

Bravo, M.A., Hiebert, E.H., & Pearson, P.D. (2007). Tapping the linguistic resources of Spanish/English bilinguals: The role of cognates in science. In R.K. Wagner, A. Muse, & K. Tannenbaum (Eds.), *Vocabulary development and its implications for reading comprehension* (pp. 140–156). New York: Guilford.

Butler, F.A., Stevens, R., & Castellon, M. (2006). ELLs and standardized assessments: The interaction between language proficiency and performance on standardized tests. In A.L. Bailey (Ed.), *The language demands of school: Putting academic English to the test* (pp. 27–49). New Haven, CT: Yale University Press.

Carlisle, J.F. (2000). Awareness of the structure and meaning of morphologically complex words: Impact on reading. *Reading and Writing, 12*(3–4), 169–190.

Carlisle, J.F. (2006). Fostering morphological processing, vocabulary development, and reading comprehension. In R. Wagner, A. Muse, & K. Tannenbaum (Eds.), *Vocabulary acquisition: Implications for reading comprehension* (pp. 78–103). New York: Guilford.

Carlisle, J.F., & Fleming, J.E. (2003). Lexical processing of morphologically complex words in the elementary years. *Scientific Studies of Reading, 7*(3), 239–253.

Carlo, M.S., August, D., McLaughlin, B., Snow, C.E., Dressler, C., Lippman, D.N., et al. (2004). Closing the gap: Addressing the vocabulary needs of English-language learners in bilingual and mainstream classrooms. *Reading Research Quarterly, 39*(2), 188–215.

Carlo, M.S., August, D., & Snow, C.E. (2005). Sustained vocabulary-learning strategy instruction for English language learners. In E.H. Hiebert & M.L. Kamil (Eds.), *Teaching and learning vocabulary: Bringing research to practice* (pp. 137–153). Mahwah, NJ: Erlbaum.

Carroll, J.B., Davies, P., & Richman, B. (1971). *The American heritage word frequency book.* Boston: Houghton Mifflin.

Cooper, J.D., Pikulski, J.J., Ackerman, P.A., Au, K.H., Chard, D.J., Garcia, G.G., et al. (2003). *Houghton Mifflin reading (Grade 4).* Boston: Houghton Mifflin.

Corson, D. (1997). The learning and use of academic English words. *Language Learning, 47*(4), 671–718.

Council for Basic Education. (1998). *Standards for excellence in education: A guide for parents, teachers, and principals for evaluating and implementing standard for education.* Washington, DC: Author.

Coxhead, A. (2000). A new academic word list. *TESOL Quarterly, 34*(2), 213–238.

Cummins, J. (1979). Cognitive/academic language proficiency, linguistic interdependence, the optimum age question, and some other matters. *Working Papers on Bilingualism, 19*(2), 121–129.

Cummins, J. (1984). *Bilingualism and special education: Issues in assessment and pedagogy.* Clevedon, UK: Multilingual Matters.

Cunningham, J.W., & Moore, D.W. (1993). The contribution of understanding academic vocabulary to answering comprehension questions. *Journal of Reading Behavior, 25*(2), 171–180.

Dale, E., & O'Rourke, J. (1981). *Living word vocabulary: A national vocabulary inventory.* Chicago: World Book/Childcraft International.

Downing, J. (1970). Children's concepts of language in learning to read. *Educational Research, 12*(2), 106–112.

Hancin-Bhatt, B., & Nagy, W.E. (1994). Lexical transfer and second language morphological development. *Applied Psycholinguistics, 15*(3), 289–310.

Hayes, D.P., & Ahrens, M. (1988). Vocabulary simplification for children: A special case of "motherese"? *Journal of Child Language, 15*(2), 395–410.

Henry, M.K. (1989). Children's word structure knowledge: Implications for decoding and spelling instruction. *Reading and Writing: An Interdisciplinary Journal, 2*(3), 135–152.

Hiebert, E.H. (2007, November). *A core academic word list for the middle grades.* Paper presented at the 52nd annual meeting of the International Reading Association, Toronto, ON.

Hirsch, E.D., Jr. (1992). *What your 4th grader needs to know: Fundamentals of a good fourth-grade education.* New York: Dell.

Hirsch, E.D., Jr. (2006). *The knowledge deficit: Closing the shocking education gap for American children.* Boston: Houghton Mifflin.

Hyland, K., & Tse, P. (2007). Is there an "academic vocabulary"? *TESOL Quarterly, 41*(2), 235–253.

Jiménez, R.T., García, G.E., & Pearson, P.D. (1996). The reading strategies of bilingual Latina/o students who are successful English readers: Opportunities and obstacles. *Reading Research Quarterly, 32*(1), 90–112.

Katz, L.A. (2004). *An investigation of the relationship of morphological awareness to reading comprehension in fourth and sixth grades.* Unpublished doctoral dissertation, University of Michigan.

Kendall, J.S., & Marzano, R.J. (2000). *Content knowledge: A compendium of standards and benchmarks for K–12 education* (3rd ed.). Alexandria, VA: Association for Supervision and Curriculum Development.

Lively, T., August, D., Carlo, M.S., & Snow, C.E. (2003). *Vocabulary improvement program for English language learners and their classmates.* Baltimore: Paul H. Brooks.

Lubliner, S., & Hiebert, E.H. (2008, March). *An analysis of English-Spanish cognates.* Paper presented at the annual meeting of the American Educational Research Association, New York, NY.

Mahony, D.L. (1994). Using sensitivity to word structure to explain variance in high school and college level reading ability. *Reading and Writing: An Interdisciplinary Journal, 6*(1), 19–44.

Marzano, R.J. (2004). *Building background knowledge for academic achievement.* Alexandria, VA: Association for Supervision and Curriculum Development.

McLaughlin, B., August, D., & Snow, C.E. (2000). *Vocabulary knowledge and reading comprehension in English language learners. Final performance report.* Washington DC: Office of Educational Research and Improvement.

Nagy, W.E., Berninger, V.W., & Abbott, R.B. (2006). Contributions of morphology beyond phonology to literacy outcomes of upper elementary and middle school students. *Journal of Educational Psychology, 98*(1), 134–147.

Nagy, W.E., & Anderson, R.C. (1984). How many words are there in printed school English? *Reading Research Quarterly, 19*(3), 304–330.

Nagy, W.E., Berninger, V.W., Abbott, R.B., Vaughan, K., & Vermeulen, K. (2003). Relationship of morphology and other language skills to literacy skills in at-risk second-grade readers and at-risk fourth-grade writers. *Journal of Educational Psychology, 95*(4), 730–742.

Nagy, W.E., García, G.E., Durgunoglu, A.Y., & Hancin-Bhatt, B. (1993). Spanish-English bilingual students' use of cognates in English reading. *Journal of Reading Behavior, 25*(3), 241–259.

Nash, R. (1997). *NTC's dictionary of Spanish cognates.* Lincolnwood, IL: NTC Publishing.

Nation, I.S.P. (1990). *Teaching and learning vocabulary.* Boston: Heinle & Heinle.

National Institute of Child Health and Human Development. (2000). *Report of the National Reading Panel. Teaching children to read: An evidence-based assessment of the scientific research literature on reading and its implications for reading instruction* (NIH Publication No. 00-4769). Washington, DC: U.S. Government Printing Office.

Nunes, T., & Bryant, P. (2006). *Improving literacy by teaching morphemes.* New York: Taylor Francis Group.

Nunes, T., Bryant, P., & Olsson, J. (2003). Learning morphological and phonological spelling rules: An intervention study. *Scientific Studies of Reading, 7*(3), 289–307.

Pearson, P.D., Hiebert, E.H., & Kamil, M.L. (2007). Vocabulary assessment: What we know and what we need to learn. *Reading Research Quarterly, 42*(2), 282–296.

Proctor, C.P., August, D., Carlo, M.S., & Snow, C.E. (2006). The intriguing role of Spanish language vocabulary knowledge in predicting English reading comprehension. *Journal of Educational Psychology, 98*(1), 159–169.

Snow, C.E. (2007, October). *Word generation: An approach to promoting academic language.* Paper presented at the conference of the Center for Research on the Educational Achievement and Teaching of English Language Learners, Oak Brook, IL.

Tyler, A., & Nagy, W.E.(1989). The acquisition of English derivational morphology. *Journal of Memory and Language, 28*(6), 649–667.

Viola, H.J., Bednarz, S.W., Cortés, C.E., Jennings, C., Chug, M.C., White, C.S., et al. (2005). *Houghton Mifflin social studies (Grade 4).* Boston: Houghton Mifflin.

Walsh, K. (2003). The lost opportunity to build the knowledge that propels comprehension. *American Educator, 27*(3), 24–27.

White, T.G., Power, M.A., & White, S. (1989). Morphological analysis: Implications for teaching and understanding vocabulary growth. *Reading Research Quarterly, 24*(3), 283–304.

Wysocki, K., & Jenkins, J.R. (1987). Deriving word meanings through morphological generalization. *Reading Research Quarterly, 22*(1), 66–81.

Zeno, S.M., Ivens, S.H., Millard, R.T., & Duvvuri, R. (1995). *The educator's word frequency guide.* New York: Touchstone Applied Science Associates.

LITERATURE CITED

Blake, R.J. (1997). *Akiak: A tale from the Iditarod.* New York: Philomel Books.

Lobel, A. (1980). *Fables.* New York: HarperTrophy.

Paulson, G. (1987). *Hatchet.* New York: Simon & Schuster.

Chapter 6

Teaching Vocabulary Through Text and Experience in Content Areas

Marco A. Bravo and Gina N. Cervetti

Content area vocabulary presents both a set of challenges and pos-sibilities for word learning. On the one hand, content areas expose students to a large corpus of challenging and often abstract words, many of which require the use of other equally challenging words to define and exemplify them. Yet content areas also present students with multiple, multimodal, thematically related, and contextualized experiences with target words, all of which can increase student opportunities to build active control of generative academic language.

This chapter illustrates the importance of vocabulary teaching and learning in content areas, outlines the challenges of vocabulary learning in these contexts, and suggests possibilities for rich vocabulary teaching in the content areas.

Importance of Vocabulary in Content Areas

With increased attention to integration of literacy with content area instruc-tion (Hapgood, Magnusson, & Palincsar, 2004; Hopkins, 2007; Hilve, 2006), vocabulary teaching and learning in these contexts has gained considerable visibility. In part, interest in the role of vocabulary learning in content area instruction stems from the understanding that word knowledge is essential to reading for comprehension of content area texts (Anderson & Freebody, 1981; Nagy, 1988) just as appropriate vocabulary use is essential to high-quality content area writing (Jones & Thomas, 2006; Rothstein, Rothstein, & Lauber, 2006). The link between word knowledge and comprehension of content area text and quality writing makes common sense and is well established by research (Beck, Perfetti, & McKeown, 1982; Blachowicz & Fisher, 2000). For example, Carney, Anderson, Blackburn, and Blessing (1984) found that preteaching social studies vocabulary to fifth-grade students resulted in significantly improved reading comprehension of

What Research Has to Say About Vocabulary Instruction, edited by Alan E. Farstrup and S. Jay Samuels.
© 2008 by the International Reading Association.

passages that contained the target words. Similarly Amaral, Garrison, and Klentschy (2002) found an increase in the quantity and quality of writing produced by elementary grade students in science when the vocabulary of science was a focus of instruction.

Moreover learning the language of the content area is as important as learning the content itself; one can argue that words are, in fact, the surface level instantiations of the deeper underlying concepts and that, as such, they provide the connections to the everyday discourse that makes the concepts transparent. Gaining control over disciplinary vocabulary is critical for conceptual understanding; knowing disciplinary terms is fundamental to the comprehension of content area concepts. To deal effectively with the content of content area textbooks, it is critical to understand the terminology of the discipline. Readence, Bean, and Baldwin (1985) suggest that students are often "outsiders" to subjects like math, science, and social studies and that by demystifying the vocabulary of these disciplines, we can help students become "insiders" (p. 149) with the concepts of the domain. Armbruster (1992) notes that, in content area instruction, new words are typically closely tied to the major purpose of the lesson, which is typically the acquisition of new knowledge; in fact it would be surprising if the words were not related to the primary goal of knowledge acquisition. While challenging terms in literature are often peripherally related to important themes, challenging content area words are more often labels that describe, or stand for, the key content area concepts (Armbruster, 1992; Cervetti, Pearson, Bravo, & Barber, 2006). Collectively concepts compose areas of study within content matter (Harmon, Hedrick, & Wood, 2005). Concepts such as *polygon, convex, equilateral,* and *vertex,* for example, make up a section of the study of geometry in math. These concepts build upon each other to construct the conceptual knowledge of the content area. Not knowing concepts or having passive understanding of concepts can leave gaps in areas of study and can negatively affect future learning in that discipline (Blachowicz & Obrochta, 2005). For example, not understanding the term *square* will make understanding terms like *perimeter* and *area* much more difficult. While this relationship between vocabulary and comprehension is well established by research, precious little vocabulary instruction uses conceptual relatedness as a basis for content area vocabulary instruction particularly across content areas (Ryder & Graves, 1998).

Acquiring technical terminology of content areas is also tied to successful functioning in the domain (Schleppegrell, 2007; Spencer & Guillaume, 2006; Vacca & Vacca, 2002); in other words, it is hard to engage in key cognitive activities unless one knows enough of the key vocabulary to transform what could be empty processes into meaningful participatory structures. Lemke (1990) suggested that to do science it is essential to know the language of science. In science, precision with specialized language is essential for understanding and supports students' ability to participate in disciplinary inquiry and to communicate the results of the inquiry. For example, the use of the term *observe* instead of *see* is critical to the practice of science. While the distinction between this pair of words may be unimportant in everyday conversation, in science a term like *observe* invokes other elements not present in the everyday term *see*, including looking at something with attention to detail, extending the examination for a prolonged period of time, and using all of one's senses to imbue the activity with meaning. Not knowing the terminology of the content compromises students' ability to inquire in the discipline and makes students "outsiders" to the discipline (Readence, et al., 1985).

Challenges of Content Area Vocabulary

Some of the challenges associated with content area vocabulary learning include the fact that disciplinary words are typically numerous (Schell, 1982), often abstract (Nagy, Anderson, & Herman, 1987), frequently carry more than one meaning (Kopriva & Saez, 1997), and are likely to be new labels for unknown ideas even when their form is recognizable (Armbruster, 1992). These features combine to create a lexical overload for students in content areas that can only be overcome by demystifying the meanings and interrelationships of key vocabulary (Beck & McKeown, 1985).

Copious Vocabulary

One common vocabulary feature across disciplines is the sheer number of complex terms students are exposed to. According to Armstrong and Collier (1990), an introductory biology textbook averages 738 pages and presents over 3,500 new terms, which is around 45%–50% more new words than are presented in a semester of foreign language instruction. Similarly, math texts have been found to include "more concepts per word, per sentence, and per paragraph than any other [subject] area" (Schell, 1982, p. 544). Harmon, Hedrick, and Fox (2000) examined the nature and representation of vocabulary instruction in the teachers' editions of social studies textbooks for grades 4–8 and also found a heavy vocabulary demand. Encountering this number of words independently within one content area would be difficult, but because students will experience all content areas, this multiplies the dilemma (Harmon et al., 2005).

Abstractness of Content Area Vocabulary

An additional challenge of teaching and learning content area vocabulary stems from the fact that many important words in subject matter domains are abstract (Vacca & Vacca, 2002), making them more difficult to acquire (Schwanenflugel & Noyes, 1996). Levels of concreteness or abstractness have been found to influence how well students learn target words (Gentner, 1982; Nagy et al., 1987; Schwanenflugel, Stahl, & McFalls, 1997). For example, Schwanenflugel et al. (1997) in their study of fourth-grade students examined whether vocabulary knowledge changed as a function of story reading and found that for partially known words, word concreteness (defined by degree of imageability) was positively related to students' learning of targeted words. The researchers attributed easier access to concrete words to three related factors: (1) the "imageability" (p. 541) of the words, (2) the capacity of "imageable" (p. 541) words to allow students to use all, or at least some, of the five senses to make sense of the concept, and (3) the stronger likelihood that more concrete words will, in general, permit greater student reliance on prior knowledge to access target concepts. Nagy et al. (1987) also found that degree of abstractness influenced word learning; for complex, abstract words, there was little evidence of incidental word learning, indicating that for such words students could make only very generic distinctions among their meanings.

Multiple-Meaning Words

Many unfamiliar and challenging disciplinary words carry more than one meaning, which opens the possibility, perhaps the likelihood, that comprehension will be complicated (Kopriva & Saez, 1997). A word like *operation*, for example, can reference what takes place in a hospital or a mathematical process in which particular rules are applied. Words that have one meaning in everyday language and a more specialized meaning in content area learning are especially vulnerable to misunderstanding and semantic "interference." Multiple meaning words abound in the English language. Johnson, Moe, and Baumann (1983) found that among the identified 9,000 critical vocabulary words for elementary-grade students, 70% had more than one meaning. These words are not limited to written language: teachers' talk also includes words with multiple meanings. Lazar, Warr-Leeper, Nicholson, and Johnson (1989) found that 36% of teacher utterances from kindergarten to grade 8 contained at least one word that had a multiple meaning.

The interference potential of multiple-meaning words (Marzano, 2004) can be particularly challenging to the growing population of English learners (Carlo, August, & Snow, 2005; Graves, 2006). Consider the shades of meaning in the terms *expression* in math, *current* in science, and *capital* in social studies. All of these terms have an everyday meaning familiar to students, along with a specialized meaning in their respective fields that is less likely to be known by students. Complicating the issue a bit more, the same multiple-meaning words can be found across content areas where within each domain a different specialized meaning is intended. The term *solution* in science, for example, can mean when one thing is dissolved in another. In mathematics, the term refers to the answer and steps taken to solve a problem; in social studies, the intended meaning can be the act of ending a dispute or the payment of a debt. As students move through instruction across content areas, an extra level of analysis is necessary to choose the intended meaning in the respective subject matter. Other terms that fall into this category include *property*, *add*, and *climate*.

New Labels for Unknown Words

Armbruster (1992) suggested that a primary difference between vocabulary encountered in content areas and those encountered in literature-focused instruction is the degree of conceptual familiarity. They note that, while learning vocabulary in narrative-dominant reading lessons often involves learning new labels for known concepts (i.e., *stunning* for *beautiful*), content area vocabulary learning is more challenging because the vocabulary in these contexts is less often associated with a familiar concept. The technical vocabulary that students encounter in content areas is likely to be new labels for new ideas (Armbruster, 1992); consequently, as students are learning new words, they are also learning new and challenging concepts (Graves & Prenn, 1986).

Graves (2000), in his typology of vocabulary learning tasks, found that this process was mediated by whether students are learning to read known words, learning new words that represent known concepts, or learning new words representing new concepts. Learning to read known words includes words students possess in their listening or speaking vocabulary but not in their reading or writing vocabularies. Words for which a concept already exists in the students' lexicon are exemplified by the situation when students already have a concept but are confronted with an unfamiliar synonym. These synonyms often invoke a nuanced meaning that is different from the original word, but students will likely have some background knowledge that they can leverage to make sense of the target concept (Bravo, Hiebert, & Pearson, 2006). Some examples of this type include the word pairs *equivalent/same* and *solution/answer*. The final category, which best describes the bulk of content area vocabulary, includes words where both the label and the concept are foreign to students. For example, students' first encounters with terms such as *polygon* and *isosceles* are likely to take place in a math class and both the label and concept are likely to be unfamiliar.

These differing vocabulary-learning tasks bear different instructional implications (Hiebert, 2005). Teaching new labels for known concepts can require different levels of instructional involvement than teaching unknown labels for challenging concepts. Instruction for these tasks can range from pronouncing a word for students—a word that they already possess in their listening vocabularies—as they read so that they make an association between the word they know and the target word, to having in-depth and extended discussions coupled with contextual definitions to illustrate new words and concepts.

Vocabulary Learning Possibilities in Content Areas

The challenges notwithstanding, several key factors make content areas a potentially rich and interesting context for vocabulary development. A saving grace of content area writing is that novel words, because they are conceptually central to the topic under study, are likely to be repeated in text designed to explain the topic. Hence students are likely to encounter multiple instances of the word in varied contexts, and both multiple and varied exposures are important to acquiring new vocabulary. Conceptually core words in content areas are also likely to be thematically related, making for a rich contextualized word-learning experience. Moreover content areas lend themselves to the use of multiple modalities (written, oral, and experiential language contexts) to acquire vocabulary knowledge. All of these conditions conspire to present students with an optimal word-learning experience.

Multiple and Varied Exposures

Existing research not only suggests that vocabulary learning is dependent on multiple exposures to target words (Beck et al., 1982; Nagy, 1988;

Stahl & Fairbanks, 1986), but also that it is related to the nature of the exposures (Graves & Prenn, 1986). Approaches that provide meaningful information about words—both definitional and contextual information—appear to be more powerful than approaches that focus on only one kind of information (Nagy & Scott, 2000).

Research suggests that definitional information is important, but insufficient for word learning. Several studies compare some version of definitional instruction in which students memorized, looked up in dictionaries, or discussed the definitions of a set of words with approaches that provide more contextual and semantic information about the words (e.g., Anders, Bos, & Filip, 1984; Stahl, 1983; Stahl & Kapinus, 1991). Taken together, this research suggests that approaches that provide more information about the words, particularly about the relationships among words, result in increased word learning and often in stronger comprehension of texts that use the target words. For example, Stahl (1983) compared two approaches to teaching text-based words to fifth-grade students: a definitional approach, in which students looked words up in a dictionary and discussed the words, and a mixed approach, in which students were given words and definitions, discussed the definitions, and generated sentences with the words. Both of these groups performed better on posttest measures of vocabulary learning than a group that received no special instruction on measures of vocabulary and comprehension. The mixed approach group scored higher on the vocabulary measures (but not the comprehension measure) than the definitional group.

Bos and Anders (1990) studied the science vocabulary learning of learning-disabled junior high school students using three semantic mapping and semantic feature analysis approaches and a definitional approach. Students in the semantic mapping and semantic feature analysis groups outperformed the students in the definitional group on measures of vocabulary learning and comprehension. Bos, Anders, Filip, and Jaffe (1989) compared two approaches to prereading vocabulary instruction in social studies among learning-disabled high school students: a dictionary method of vocabulary instruction, in which students used a dictionary to write definitions of words then wrote sentenceswith the words, and an approach using semantic feature analysis. Students who received instruction using semantic feature analysis performed significantly better on a comprehension measure after reading. (See Chapter 3, this volume, for more detail on semantic mapping and semantic feature analysis.)

There are several possible limitations to approaches that rely on definitions alone: Definitions do not provide enough information to support students in acquiring more than partial understanding; definitions do not provide very much information about context of use, limiting students' ability to recognize and use the words in various contexts; and definitional approaches teach words as isolated units, even though deep, flexible word knowledge involves a process of integrating new words into semantic networks with a range of known words. In content areas in particular, simple definitions often will not suffice (Armbruster, 1992). Even so, context in and of itself does not fare much better as a solo word-learning strategy. For example, Brett, Rothlein, and Hurley (1996) found that fourth graders who listened to stories and were provided with an explanation of the meaning of unfamiliar words were more likely to learn the words than students who listened to the words read in the context of the stories without explanation of their meaning. Biemiller and Boote (2006) found that grade K–2 students who encountered words through repeated readings of fictional stories learned about 12% of words' meanings. When repeated readings were accompanied by explanations of the word meanings, students learned about 22% of the words. Notably children with smaller vocabularies benefited more from explanations of words (during encounters in text) than children with larger vocabularies. We, the authors, would like to point out that part of the advantage of direct explanation may be that it draws attention to words that might otherwise be overlooked by young readers: It can be difficult for these readers to attend to individual words while reading or listening to connected text.

In addition to providing multiple encounters with conceptually core vocabulary, content areas also typically supply students with exposures in varied contexts, the kinds of exposures that are meaningful and in context, critical for in-depth understanding of target words. Due to the central role content area vocabulary plays in content area learning, important terms tend to appear often in the texts and talk surrounding instruction (Spencer & Guillaume, 2006). Hiebert (2005) has found, for example, that conceptually important words are repeated often in nonfiction science books for young readers. Since word meanings are accumulated gradually (Nagy & Scott, 2000), getting more than one shot at deciphering the meaning of terms can lead to more sophisticated understandings of target words. McKeown, Beck, Omanson, and Pople (1985), for example, found that more than 10 encounters with target words, reliably predicted fourth-grade students' increased reading comprehension.

Each subsequent encounter with target words, especially when that encounter is different from a previous encounter, serves as an opportunity to accumulate information about that word. This can include understanding the appropriate contextual usage of a term, the word's grammatical form, and nuanced conceptual meanings (Nation, 1990). For example, in an initial encounter with the science term *adaptation* in the sentence "These plants and animals have many adaptations," students may understand that the term is in noun form and understand that it is something that a plant or animal possesses. In later encounters, as in the sentence "Those plants and animals adapted to their environment by way of certain behaviors and structures that develop over time," students gain access to additional information about the term, including the fact that the term can also be used in verb form and that the term refers to certain actions and body parts that plants and animals need in their environment and that it takes time to develop those behaviors and structures.

Content areas, by their very nature, lend themselves to these two key conditions—varied contexts and rich explanations—necessary to develop in-depth and enduring understanding of vocabulary. Given that word learning is multifaceted, that content area vocabulary is often abstract, and that both the labels and the ideas are likely to be new, multiple exposures are vital to content vocabulary learning. In addition, the treatment of important and challenging words in content areas often has a more conceptual focus that provides both definitional and contextual information. Definitional and contextual information provide the type of meaningful information needed to access key content area concepts and subsequently assist in building the conceptual knowledge in the domain.

Teaching Words as Thematically Related Concepts

Teaching words as related concepts appears to add value to vocabulary instruction. Semantic mapping, broadly defined as any approach that makes explicit the relationships among sets of words, has been shown to have positive effects beyond definitional and contextual vocabulary instruction alone. Margosein, Pascarella, and Pflaum (1982) compared two approaches to vocabulary learning among seventh- and eighth-grade students: (1) a semantic mapping approach that tied new words to known words through discussion of the similarities and differences between the new and related, familiar words and (2) a context approach that presented each target word in three-sentence passages where the target word was used in each sentence and defined. The semantic mapping intervention produced significantly higher scores than the context group on weekly vocabulary tests, treatment tests, and the Gates-MacGinitie vocabulary subtest. The results of two other subtests of the Gates-MacGinitie (comprehension and definition tests) likewise showed slightly higher scores for the semantic mapping intervention.

While the Margosein et al. (1982) study did not focus on content area vocabulary, the implications for vocabulary instruction in content areas were apparent. Smith (1990) and Armbruster (1992) noted that viewing vocabulary instruction as a study of relationships is particularly relevant in content area reading. In science, social studies, and mathematics, words index important concepts and those concepts are organized in thematically related networks. Terms like *community*, *culture*, *custom*, and *tradition* are introduced in social studies texts not separate from, but in relation to, each other. These terms are linked to other areas of study within the discipline, which together construct the overall conceptual flow of the content area. The nature of this organization of concepts highlights the association between terms. Recognizing how terms are related to one another suggests high degrees of word knowledge (Stahl, 1999) since students have to situate the term's particular meaning in the context of the meanings of other terms.

This web of concepts affords students a rich context from which they can learn the new technical terminology offered by content areas. Yet, students must be challenged to consider the semantic relationship among the core set of words. Under this approach, a term like *organism* would be semantically introduced as referencing such living things as plants and animals. An example of such is an *isopod*, an animal characterized by its seven pairs of legs, flattened body, and existence in forest floor *habitats*, which is the place where it gets what it needs to *survive*, including *shelter*, *food*, *protection*, *moisture*, and so forth. These italicized words tied semantically together assemble a structure of knowledge within the life science domain.

Exploiting the inherent organization of content area concepts can facilitate vocabulary learning and subsequently content area learning. Assisting students in recognizing and understanding the thematic relationship between core vocabulary within the discipline helps build established levels of word knowledge (Johnson & Pearson, 1984) while helping students construct a knowledge base of the domain as an organized network of related information, assuring more in-depth understanding of important concepts (Glynn & Muth, 1994).

Multimodal Experiences With Content Area Vocabulary

Experiences with vocabulary in modalities other than reading and writing also advance word learning (Carlisle, Fleming, & Gudbrandsen, 2000;

Stahl & Clark, 1987; Stahl & Kapinus, 1991). In particular, discussion and experience seem to support word learning because they demand a high level of involvement, or deep processing, of information about the words and because they call on both contextual and definitional understanding. Stahl and Kapinus (1991) found that students who participated in a possible sentences intervention made greater growth in vocabulary than students in semantic mapping and no-treatment interventions. In possible sentences, the teacher chooses words (usually key concepts) that are used to generate sentences. Students discuss whether the sentences are true or not based on their reading and, if not, how they could be modified to be made true. Stahl and Kapinus suggest that the power of the possible sentences strategy lies in its ability to draw upon students' prior knowledge of the topic and requires that students think about and discuss relations between word concepts rather than treating each word as a separate entity. They also suggest that, because possible sentences involves interactions among students, it encourages active processing of information. In addition, Stahl and Vancil (1986) compared word learning among sixth graders in three conditions: (1) discussion of words, (2) mapping of words, and (3) full semantic mapping involving the physical map and discussion. The discussion group and full semantic mapping group outperformed the word mapping group on a posttest of vocabulary learning. In a related study, Stahl and Clark (1987) studied the learning of science vocabulary with fourth- and fifth-grade students in an instructional intervention involving semantic mapping and discussion. Students who were told they would participate in discussion and those who were called on to participate performed significantly better on a test of vocabulary learning than students in the same classes who did not participate in the discussions.

Similarly Carlisle, Fleming, and Gudbrandsen (2000) found that involvement in discussions and firsthand experiences in fourth- and eighth-grade science led to word learning particularly for students who had partial knowledge of the words. These gains were attributed to students' ability to connect with words through varied sensory representations that allowed students to use multiple codes for understanding target words. Students not only made growth on their recognition of the meaning of the topical words but also on the quality of the explanation of word meanings during open-ended interviews (e.g., what does the word _____ mean?).

Beck, McKeown, and Kucan (2002) concluded that students who engage with words by hearing them, using them, manipulating them semantically, and playing with them are more likely to learn and retain new vocabulary. Opportunities for students to learn and encounter difficult words through reading, writing, talk, and experience are widely available in content area learning.

Research Implications: Some Principles for Content Area Vocabulary Instruction

Informed by the research reviewed, we offer several suggestions for helping students gain word knowledge in content areas. We have organized our suggestions into four "lessons" for solid vocabulary instruction.

Word Selection Is Key to Shaping Vocabulary Instruction

The initial challenge when confronting a large corpus of content area vocabulary is to identify words to target for instruction. We recommend selecting words that are high-utility, necessary for understanding the domain, and connected with one other conceptually.

Select words that are high-utility in the discipline. Beck et al.'s (2002) classification of terms provides some guidance for the selection of high-utility terms. Beck et al. classified terms into three tiers: Tier 1 words are those that are highly frequent in everyday talk (e.g., *pencil, paper*); tier 2 words, which occur with regularity across domains and are used by adults in literate discourse, are essentially uncommon labels for common ideas (predict rather than guess; habitat rather than home); tier 3 words (e.g., *trapezoid, stoma)* are the highly specialized, rare words that often occur solely within content areas. Beck and her colleagues suggested targeting tier 2 words for instruction because they are high-utility words and appear frequently in a variety of academic contexts. Tier 2 words in content areas might be thought of as those that are high-utility and ubiquitous within the discipline and across subfields of the discipline even if they are not necessarily part of the lexicon of everyday adult speech. In science, for example, terms associated with science inquiry, such as *hypothesis, evidence,* and *model,* occur often across life, earth, and physical science. Similarly *mean, expression*, and *product* occur regularly in arithmetic, algebra, and geometry. In social studies, words such as *demand, region, culture*, and *modify* have utility in geography, history, and civics studies. These "intradisciplinary" words may not be used by adults outside of the domain, yet they appear in textbooks and in tests and will be encountered by students throughout their school careers and, therefore, deserve explicit attention. They support students' ability to participate in the discourse of science (Cervetti & Bravo, 2005), discussions in social studies (Hess, 2004), or problem solving in math (Schleppegrell, 2007).

Select words that are necessary for understanding the concepts and processes of the domain. While tier 2 terms are critical, more specialized tier 3 words are equally, if not more, important to content area understanding. These terms are often unique to a content area and necessary for understanding of the subject matter concepts. Select words for study that represent the most important concepts or processes. Words like *decomposition, habitat,* and *adaptation* in a second-grade earth science unit are specialized terms that index some of the most important concepts in the domain. Renewed interest in generating word lists for subject areas may be one way to identify terms that are conceptually core (Marzano, Kendall, & Paynter, 2005). Also, Ryder and Graves (1998) found it helpful to allow students (with teacher guidance) to be involved in determining which terms are essential to describe and talk about the learning goals. While conceptually core vocabulary may appear frequently within a domain of study (Spencer & Guillaume, 2006), they are not likely to travel across subject matter domains. Hence instruction around these terms must be focused, direct, and true to each term's role in subject matter learning (Ryder & Graves, 1998).

Select words that together represent important related concepts in the domain. Learning the vocabulary of a discipline should be thought of as learning about the interconnectedness of ideas and concepts indexed by words. Select words that help students develop rich networks of related word and concepts and those words that assist them in discussing and participating in disciplinary inquiry. One way to do this is to create a map of important concepts for instruction and then to associate one or more words with each concept. For example, in the domain of science the words *transmit, reflect,* and *absorb* can be mapped in relation to one another as different ways that light interacts with materials.

Provide Many Opportunities to Learn Target Words

Knowing a word is not an all or nothing phenomenon (Anderson & Freebody, 1981; Nagy & Scott, 2000). Vocabulary knowledge is multifaceted and students come to content areas with varying degrees of vocabulary knowledge (Ryder & Graves, 1998). Vocabulary knowledge can include at least three levels of word knowledge: unknown, acquainted, and established (Beck, McKeown, & McCaslin, 1983). When a term is unknown, the student has never heard nor seen the word. For example, a term like *habitat* may be at the unknown level for kindergarten students.

For some purposes, such as reading a story, an acquaintance level of vocabulary understanding in which a student can decode the word and provide a basic definition may suffice. Content area texts, which usually involve informational texts, are much more dependent on specific terms that are crucial for content area understanding (Blachowicz, Fisher, Ogle, & Watts-Taffe, 2006). Harmon et al. (2005) pointed out that, while partial knowledge of unfamiliar words may be sufficient to support comprehension in the reading of a narrative text, content area reading often demands a higher level of word knowledge because the words are labels for important concepts. Harmon and colleagues further noted that not knowing the precise definition of terms in content areas has the potential to create much more frustration for students than when encountering unclear meanings in narrative texts.

To support students, develop word knowledge at a depth of understanding that is appropriate to content area instruction and provide opportunities for students to encounter important words often and in contexts that provide varied and meaningful information about the words, including definitional, contextual, and relational information. Create a classroom environment where the selected words are present in print and in talk and where the opportunities to use domain-appropriate language in place of everyday language are common. Use texts, charts, concept walls, discussions, and writing experiences to create an environment that is rich in the language of the domain.

Introduce Target Words in Relation to Other Related Words and Connect Known to Unknown Words

Approaches that connect new words to known words treat word learning in content areas as the building of conceptual understanding. Using semantic maps and related word mapping approaches can help students recognize the relationships among words/concepts. Semantic feature analysis (Johnson & Pearson, 1984) uses a table to represent the similarities and differences between examples of the same category, such as the similarities and differences between different forms of government.

It is also important to distinguish between new content area words and other words with which they might be confused including synonyms in everyday language and words with the same orthography but different meanings.

Involve Students in Domain-Appropriate Experiences

Students learn new words when they are engaged with words in ways that involve them personally in constructing meanings (Vogel, 2003). In many ways, content areas are ideal contexts for this kind of engagement with words. Using experiences in the domain as opportunities for vocabulary learning can support flexible and expressive control over important content words. Science, for example, provides natural opportunities for authentic, repeated, and varied encounters with new words and concepts—and ways of using them to talk, explain, and argue—during firsthand experiences, through texts, and in discussions and written activities. All of these contexts provide students opportunities to encounter words, to make personal meaning with the words, to tie word knowledge to experience, and to practice using the words in appropriate ways. In any content area domain, it is appropriate to encourage students to describe and discuss their inquiry and problem-solving experiences using the words of the discipline. The discourse of disciplines includes a particular and specialized vocabulary, but it is more than specialized words—it also includes ways of using these words in arranging arguments and leveraging evidence for explanations and conclusions. Binding the use of words to experiences provides opportunities for students to practice using these words in the interest of important practices in the domain.

Conclusions

In this chapter, we have championed vocabulary in content area learning, including the need for students to control content area vocabulary to promote literacy in content area learning. We have also illustrated some of the challenges of content area vocabulary learning. The fact that content area vocabulary terms are numerous, abstract, polysemous, and conceptually unfamiliar can potentially derail content area learning. Yet, the research also demonstrates that content area instruction also offers opportunities for rich and powerful word-learning experiences. In the content areas, students are likely to have multiple, meaningful, and multimodal experiences with vocabulary, all of which are needed to build enduring understanding of challenging subject matter vocabulary.

Explicit instructional measures are surely needed to reap the benefits of such favorable word-learning conditions. This includes being judicious with the number of words targeted for instruction and choosing words with clear criteria in mind—utility, domain centrality, and semantic relatedness. Vocabulary instruction must also actively involve students in uncovering nuanced and deep meanings of target words through domain-appropriate experiences. Recognizing the importance and navigating the challenges of content area vocabulary can help to demystify word learning for students who can otherwise be overwhelmed by the demands of reading in subject matter domains.

Questions for Discussion

1. What does research tell us about selecting content area vocabulary for instruction?

2. What challenges do students confront in learning content area vocabulary?

3. What possibilities are presented in content areas for rich vocabulary learning?

REFERENCES

Amaral, O.M., Garrison, L., & Klentschy, M. (2002). Helping English learners increase achievement through inquiry-based science instruction. *Bilingual Research Journal, 26*(2), 213–239.

Anders, P.L., Bos, C.S., & Filip, D. (1984). The effect of semantic feature analysis on the reading comprehension of learning-disabled students. *Changing perspectives in research on reading/language processing and instruction* (33rd yearbook of the National Reading Conference, pp. 162–166). Rochester, NY: National Reading Conference.

Anderson, R.C., & Freebody, P. (1981). Vocabulary knowledge. In J. Guthrie (Ed.), *Comprehension and teaching: Research reviews.* Newark, DE: International Reading Association.

Armbruster, B.B. (1992). Vocabulary in content area lessons. *The Reading Teacher, 45*(7), 550–551.

Armstrong, J.E., & Collier, G.E. (1990). *Science in biology: An introduction.* Prospect Heights, IL: Waveland Press.

Beck, I.L., & McKeown, M.G. (1985). Teaching vocabulary: Making the instruction fit the goal. *Educational Perspectives, 23*(1), 11–15.

Beck, I.L., McKeown, M.G., & Kucan, L. (2002). *Bringing words to life: Robust vocabulary instruction.* New York: Guilford.

Beck, I.L., McKeown, M.G., & McCaslin, E.S. (1983). Vocabulary development: All contexts are not created equal. *The Elementary School Journal, 83*(3), 177–181.

Beck, I.L., Perfetti, C.A., & McKeown, M.G. (1982). The effects of long-term vocabulary instruction on lexical access and reading comprehension. *Journal of Educational Psychology, 74*(4), 506–521.

Biemiller, A., & Boote, C. (2006). An effective method for building vocabulary in primary grades. *Journal of Educational Psychology, 98*(1), 44–62.

Blachowicz, C.L.Z., & Fisher, P. (2000). Vocabulary instruction. In M.L. Kamil, P.B. Mosenthal, P.D. Pearson, & R. Barr (Eds.), *Handbook of reading research* (Vol. 3, pp. 503–523). Mahwah, NJ: Erlbaum.

Blachowicz, C.L.Z., Fisher, P., Ogle, D., & Watts-Taffe, S.M. (2006). Vocabulary: Questions from the classroom. *Reading Research Quarterly, 41*(4), 524–539.

Blachowicz, C.L.Z., & Obrochta, C. (2005). Vocabulary visits: Virtual field trips for content vocabulary development. *The Reading Teacher, 59*(3), 262–268.

Bos, C.S., & Anders, P.L. (1990). Toward an interactive model: Teaching text-based concepts to learning disabled students. In H.L. Swanson & B. Keogh (Eds.), *Learning disabilities: Theoretical and research issues* (pp. 247–262). Hillsdale, NJ: Erlbaum.

Bos, C.S., Anders, P.L., Filip, D., & Jaffe, L.E. (1989). The effects of an interactive instructional strategy for enhancing learning disabled students' reading comprehension and content area learning. *Journal of Learning Disabilities, 22*(6), 384–390.

Bravo, M.A., Hiebert, E.H., & Pearson, P.D. (2006). Tapping the linguistic resources of Spanish–English bilinguals: The role of cognates in science. In R.K. Wagner, A. Muse, & K. Tannenbaum (Eds.), *Vocabulary development and its implications for reading comprehension* (pp. 140–156). New York: Guilford.

Brett, A., Rothlein, L., & Hurley, M. (1996). Vocabulary acquisition from listening to stories and explanations of target words. *The Elementary School Journal, 96*(4), 415–422.

Carlisle, J.F., Fleming, J.E., & Gudbrandsen, B. (2000). Incidental word learning in science classes. *Contemporary Educational Psychology, 25*(2), 184–211.

Carlo, M.S., August, D., & Snow, C.E. (2005). Sustained vocabulary-learning strategies for English-language learners. In E.H. Hiebert & M.L. Kamil (Eds.), *Teaching and learning vocabulary: Bringing research to practice* (pp. 137–153). Mahwah, NJ: Erlbaum.

Carney, J.J., Anderson, D., Blackburn, C., & Blessing, D. (1984). Preteaching vocabulary and the comprehension of social studies materials by elementary school children. *Special Education, 48*(3), 195–197.

Cervetti, G.N., & Bravo, M.A. (2005, May). *Designing and implementing literacy and science activities through discourse.* Paper presented at the 50th annual meeting of the International Reading Association, San Antonio, TX.

Cervetti, G.N., Pearson, P.D., Bravo, M.A., & Barber, J. (2006). Reading and writing in the service of inquiry-based science. In R. Douglas, M.P. Klentschy, & K. Worth (Eds.), *Linking science and literacy in the K–8 classroom* (pp. 221–244). Arlington, VA: National Science Teachers Association.

Gentner, D. (1982). Why nouns are learned before verbs: Linguistic relativity versus natural partitioning. In S.A. Kuczaj (Ed.), *Language development: Language, thought, and culture* (Vol. 2, pp. 301–334). Hillsdale, NJ: Erlbaum.

Glynn, S., & Muth, K.D. (1994). Reading and writing to learn science: Achieving scientific literacy. *Journal of Research in Science Teaching, 31*(9), 1057–1073.

Graves, M.F. (2000). A vocabulary program to complement and bolster a middle-grade comprehension program. In B.M. Taylor, M.F. Graves, & P.W. van den Broek (Eds.), *Reading for meaning: Fostering comprehension in the middle grades* (pp. 116–135). New York: Teachers College Press; Newark, DE: International Reading Association.

Graves, M.F. (2006). *The vocabulary book: Learning and instruction.* New York: Teachers College Press.

Graves, M.F., & Prenn, M.C. (1986). Costs and benefits of various methods of teaching vocabulary. *Journal of Reading, 29*(7), 596–602.

Hapgood, S., Magnusson, S.J., & Palincsar, A.S. (2004). Teacher, text and experience: A case of young children's scientific inquiry. *Journal of the Learning Sciences, 13*(4), 455–505.

Harmon, J.M., Hedrick, W.B., & Fox, E.A. (2000). A content analysis of vocabulary instruction in social studies textbooks for grades 4–8. *The Elementary School Journal, 100*(3), 253–271.

Harmon, J.M., Hedrick, W.B., & Wood, K.D. (2005). Research on vocabulary instruction in the content areas: Implications for struggling readers. *Reading & Writing Quarterly, 21*(3), 261–280.

Hess, D.E. (2004). Discussion in social studies: Is it worth the trouble? *Special Education, 68*(2), 151–168.

Hiebert, E.H. (2005). In pursuit of an effective, efficient vocabulary curriculum for the elementary grades. In E.H. Hiebert & M.L. Kamil (Eds.), *The teaching and learning of vocabulary: Bringing scientific research to practice* (pp. 243–263). Mahwah, NJ: Erlbaum.

Hilve, F. (2006). Creative writing in the social studies classroom: Promoting literacy and content learning. *Special Education, 70*(4), 183–186.

Hopkins, M.H. (2007). Adapting a model for literacy learning to the learning of mathematics. *Reading & Writing Quarterly, 23*(2), 121–138.

Johnson, D.D., Moe, A.J., & Baumann, J.F. (1983). *The Ginn word book for teachers: A basic lexicon.* Boston: Ginn.

Johnson, D.D., & Pearson, P.D. (1984). *Teaching reading vocabulary.* New York: Holt/Rinehart and Winston.

Jones, R.C., & Thomas, T.G. (2006). Leave no discipline behind. *The Reading Teacher, 60*(1), 58–64.

Kopriva, R., & Saez, S. (1997). *Guide to scoring LEP student responses to open-ended mathematics items.* Washington, DC: Council of Chief State School Officers.

Lazar, R.T., Warr-Leeper, G.A., Nicholson, C.B., & Johnson, S. (1989). Elementary school teachers' use of multiple meaning expressions. *Language, Speech, and Hearing Services in Schools, 20*(4), 420–429.

Lemke, J.L. (1990). *Talking science: Language, learning, and values.* Norwood, NJ: Ablex.

Margosein, C.M., Pascarella, E.T., & Pflaum, S.W. (1982). The effects of instruction using semantic mapping on vocabulary and comprehension. *The Journal of Early Adolescence, 2*(2), 185–194.

Marzano, R.J. (2004). The developing vision of vocabulary instruction. In J.F. Bauman & E.J. Kame'enui (Eds.), *Research and theory in vocabulary development* (pp. 100–117). New York: Guilford.

Marzano, R.J., Kendall, J.S., & Paynter, D.E. (2005). A list of essential words by grade level. In D.E. Paynter, E. Bodrova, & J.K. Doty (Eds.), *For the love of words: Vocabulary instruction that works, grades K–6* (pp. 127–202). San Francisco: Jossey-Bass.

McKeown, M.G., Beck, I.L., Omanson, R.C., & Pople, M.T. (1985). Some effects of the nature and frequency of vocabulary instruction on the knowledge and use of words. *Reading Research Quarterly, 20*(5), 522–535.

Nagy, W.E., & Scott, J.A. (2000). Vocabulary processing. In M.L. Kamil, P.B. Mosenthal, P.D. Pearson, & R. Barr (Eds.), *Handbook of reading research* (Vol. 3, pp. 269–284). Mahwah, NJ: Erlbaum.

Nagy, W.E. (1988). *Teaching vocabulary to improve reading comprehension.* Newark, DE: International Reading Association.

Nagy, W.E., Anderson, R.C., & Herman, P.A. (1987). Learning word meanings from context during normal reading. *American Educational Research Journal, 24*(2), 237–270.

Nation, I.S.P. (1990). *Teaching and learning vocabulary.* Boston: Heinle & Heinle.

Readence, J.E., Bean, T.W., & Baldwin, R.S. (1985). *Content area reading: An integrated approach* (2nd ed.). Dubuque, IA: Kendall/Hunt.

Rothstein, A.S., Rothstein, E., & Lauber, G. (2006). *Writing as learning: A content based approach.* Thousand Oaks, CA: Corwin.

Ryder, R.J., & Graves, M.F. (1998). *Reading and learning in content areas* (2nd ed.). New York: Merrill.

Schell, V.J. (1982). Learning partners: Reading and mathematics. *The Reading Teacher, 35*(5), 544–548.

Schleppegrell, M.J. (2007). The linguistic challenges of mathematics teaching and learning: A research review. *Reading & Writing Quarterly, 23*(2), 139–159.

Schwanenflugel, P.J., & Noyes, C.R. (1996). Context availability and the development of word reading skill. *Journal of Literacy Research, 28*(1), 35–54.

Schwanenflugel, P.J., Stahl, S.A., & McFalls, L. (1997). Partial word knowledge and vocabulary growth during reading comprehension. *Journal of Literacy Research, 29*(4), 531–553.

Smith, C.B. (1990). Vocabulary development in content area reading. *The Reading Teacher, 43*(7), 508–509.

Spencer, B.H., & Guillaume, A.M. (2006). Integrating curriculum through the learning cycle: Content based reading and vocabulary instruction. *The Reading Teacher, 60*(3), 206–219.

Stahl, S.A. (1983). Differential word knowledge and reading comprehension. *Journal of Reading Behavior, 15*(4), 33–50.

Stahl, S.A. (1999). *Vocabulary development.* Cambridge, MA: Brookline Books.

Stahl, S.A., & Clark, C.H. (1987). The effects of participatory expectations in classroom discussion on the learning of science vocabulary. *American Educational Research Journal, 24*(4), 541–555.

Stahl, S.A., & Fairbanks, M.M. (1986). The effects of vocabulary instruction: A model-based meta-analysis. *Review of Educational Research, 56*(1), 72–110.

Stahl, S.A., & Kapinus, B.A. (1991). Possible sentences: Predicting word meanings to teach content area vocabulary. *The Reading Teacher, 45*(1), 36–43.

Stahl, S.A., & Vancil, S.J. (1986). Discussion is what makes semantic maps work in vocabulary instruction. *The Reading Teacher, 40*(1), 62–69.

Vacca, R.T., & Vacca, J.L. (2002). *Content area reading: Literacy and learning across the curriculum.* Boston: Allyn & Bacon.

Vogel, E. (2003). Using informational text to build children's knowledge of the world around them. In N.K. Duke & V.S. Bennett-Armistead (Eds.), *Reading and writing informational text in the primary grades: Research-based practices* (pp. 157–198). New York: Scholastic.

Chapter 7

Vocabulary Instruction in Middle and Secondary Content Classrooms: Understandings and Direction From Research

Janis M. Harmon, Karen D. Wood, and Wanda B. Hedrick

We begin this chapter on vocabulary instruction in middle and secondary content classrooms by situating vocabulary within the larger arena of content area learning and teaching. By "zooming out," we gain a broader perspective of the importance of vocabulary across subject matter disciplines and the interplay between vocabulary knowledge and conceptual understandings in effective content area instruction.

Jetton and Alexander (2004) defined content areas as subject matter domains with "specific knowledge organized in a unique way" (p. 15). Students' academic achievement is measured by their competence in subject matter domains, especially at the middle and secondary school levels. Students demonstrate these competences in various domains, such as science, mathematics, and social studies, through their receptive and expressive communicative skills in listening, reading, speaking, writing, viewing, and visually representing (International Reading Association [IRA] & National Council of Teachers of English [NCTE], 1996). Thus, students need to be well versed in the language of each domain to gain conceptual knowledge. In regard to reading, the types of texts used in these academic domains place particular linguistic demands on student readers—demands that differ across different subject matter disciplines. As a result, students need both linguistic knowledge as well as content knowledge to successfully comprehend the texts of various subject matter areas (Fang, 2006; Jetton & Alexander, 2004).

While content knowledge encompasses a vast array of prior knowledge and experiences within a specific domain, the specialized grammar includes knowledge of language structures, such as subordinate clauses,

What Research Has to Say About Vocabulary Instruction, edited by Alan E. Farstrup and S. Jay Samuels.
© 2008 by the International Reading Association.

complex sentences, paragraph formations, and larger organizational structures of informational texts not found in less formalized language. Even at the semantic level, grammatical words, such as prepositions, conjunctions, and pronouns, may be used in ways unfamiliar to the novice informational text reader (Fang, 2006). All of this, in combination with specialized content vocabulary knowledge, can create challenges to readers. A rich receptive vocabulary, however, can enable learners to process texts more efficiently and fluently by providing them with the ability to make connections with what they read and hear and to articulate their understandings of any domain when they speak or write.

We want students in middle and secondary classrooms not only to develop conceptual knowledge but also to be able to handle the demands of text-based learning in various subject matter disciplines. We want them to be able to read like a scientist or a mathematician or a historian as they develop independent learning strategies that will serve them well as lifelong learners. However, for many students, both native speakers and English-language learners (ELLs), the specialized vocabularies of specific domains can be a daunting barrier, especially in light of the challenges of deriving word meanings independently in naturally occurring contexts, such as those found in content textbooks and informational books (Jenkins & Dixon, 1983).

This chapter will focus on challenges posed by the specialized vocabularies of content area texts. Students often express their frustration in attempts to read these kinds of texts by saying, "The words are too hard. I don't understand what I am reading." It is understandable how students can become overwhelmed by the literacy demands occurring during a typical school day in a middle school or high school. For example, on any given day, a student may be asked to read about different academic topics containing the following vocabulary. In mathematics class, the student may encounter words such as *probability, frequency, histogram, range, median, mode,* and *quartile.* As she moves to her science class, she is expected to read and understand the following words: *charge, current, voltage, electron, mass, matter.* Then after lunch break, she proceeds to her social studies class and is exposed to a new battery of specialized vocabulary such as *archaeology, archaeologist, culture, excavations,* and *digs.*

In this chapter, we examine current understandings of vocabulary learning and teaching through the lens of domain-specific areas to inform content area educators. We outline several key points about content area vocabulary and discuss the nature of content area vocabulary, including both general features across domains and features that are distinctive to particular subject matter areas. We then describe research-based instructional practices for supporting vocabulary and conclude with practical teaching suggestions that are applicable in content area classrooms.

The Nature of Vocabulary in the Content Areas

Our understandings of vocabulary teaching and learning in the content areas are grounded in the rich vocabulary research that has occurred in the past 25 years. We have learned much about vocabulary learning, including the nature of vocabulary and what it means to know a word, the role of incidental word learning and wide reading in vocabulary acquisition, and the features of effective classroom instruction (see Baumann, Kame'enui, & Ash, 2003, for a review of this research). Drawing from these investigations, we note four key points about vocabulary in the content areas:

1. **Vocabulary knowledge is critical for comprehending informational texts.** The impact of vocabulary on reading narratives, such as short stories and novels, differs from the impact of vocabulary on reading informational texts (Blachowicz, Fisher, Ogle, & Watts-Taffe, 2006). In many instances, students can still understand a story even though some words are unfamiliar. However, for comprehending informational texts, students must have a working knowledge of many context-specific terms. Without this background knowledge, students are hard-pressed to understand what they are reading. Expanding students' vocabulary is embedded in building background knowledge necessary for comprehending informational texts.

2. **Vocabulary instructional strategies used in language arts classrooms are applicable in the content areas.** In the most recent edition of *What Research Has to Say About Reading Instruction*, Vacca (2002) discussed what he termed the visible and invisible aspects of content area reading. The visible aspects include the place of direct, explicit instruction of reading in content classrooms. He urged teachers to include reading strategy instruction in their lessons, instruction requiring explanation, modeling, practice, and application of strategies. These strategies, such as predicting, questioning, summarizing, inferring, and clarifying word meanings, enable students to become independent learners as they grapple

with comprehending content area texts. The invisible aspects of content reading, on the other hand, are embedded within the context of content area instruction and are less direct. They include literacy support within an instructional framework that can consider before, during, and after reading tasks. Vacca also notes that the invisible aspects are evident in particular instructional techniques, including classroom discussions based upon the questioning the author techniques (Beck, McKeown, Hamilton, & Kucan, 1997). He goes on to say that invisible aspects are also evident in critical literacy stances that urge students to consider who wrote the text and why, who benefits, what impact word choices have on the author's intended meaning, and whose interests are being served, as well as in Socratic seminars that encourage socially constructed knowledge.

Vocabulary learning and teaching intersect both the visible and invisible aspect of content area reading. In regard to the visible aspects, we know that direct instruction of vocabulary terms in all content area domains plays a critical role in conceptual learning. Every day students need teachers to define terms, contextualize meanings, and demonstrate application of terms. Students also need explicit instruction in how to use independent word-learning strategies when they encounter unfamiliar terms or new meanings of known words in different subject matter domains. In addition, students build and strengthen their vocabulary knowledge base through the invisible aspects of content area reading. Before, during, and after reading tasks are arenas for vocabulary learning and reinforcement. Students also internalize word meanings as they engage in classroom discussions (e.g., questioning the author, Socratic seminars, instructional conversations) that require them to use the language of a domain.

3. **Informational text features affect vocabulary learning.** One important consideration in content area vocabulary learning is passage support offered by textbook authors. A few studies have examined ways in which texts can offer more contextual support to aid students in constructing word meanings (Cardinale, 1991; Gordon, Schumm, Coffland, & Doucette, 1992; Konopak, 1988). In her study of text passages, Konopak (1988) found that the use of explicit features for defining new terms in context positively affected eighth-grade students' understanding of what they read.

She argued that contextual clues for unlocking word meanings needed to be explicit and in close proximity to the word to make the text more considerate to the readers. In Gordon, Schumm, Coffland, and Doucette's (1992) replication of Konopak's work, they achieved similar, although not as solid, results with elementary-age students.

Cardinale's (1991) study on text-based features to support vocabulary acquisition, which upholds Konopak's findings, indicated that attention to cognitive processing is needed for determining effective ways of helping students construct passage meaning. She found benefits for several different types of term explanations including causal explications, where cause and effect relationships are clarified; analogical explications, in which concepts are compared with familiar ideas; and etymological explications, which provided the readers with information about Greek or Latin roots and affixes in the word. Cardinale noted that the use of these embedded explications is especially important in texts containing dense and challenging concepts.

These studies indicate the importance of examining text features in the books we ask students to read. We need to be cognizant of how textbook publishers and authors of other informational texts provide explanations for the domain-specific vocabulary needed for comprehension.

4. **Classroom instructional time is needed for learning vocabulary.** Learning and teaching vocabulary require classroom instructional time—sufficient time not readily given in many content area classrooms. In their observational study of 23 upper level classrooms in Canada, Scott, Jamieson-Noel, and Asselin (2003) found that only a minimal amount of time was spent on vocabulary instruction in both language arts classrooms and content area classrooms. In particular, only 1.4% of school time was spent on supporting vocabulary learning in science, social studies, and mathematics classrooms. Furthermore, the vocabulary instruction in these classrooms typically involved what Vacca and Vacca (2005) labeled "assigning and telling" with limited emphasis on conceptual understandings, word morphologies, and metacognition.

Other studies about time spent on vocabulary instruction in reading classrooms report similar results (Durkin, 1978/1979; Watts, 1995). The amount of time spent on vocabulary instruction in content area classrooms in particular is in need of investigation. Given that Durkin's observations (1978/1979) were in both reading and social studies and Scott et al.'s more recent study (2003) included content area classes, we question that the amount of time spent on vocabulary in content area classrooms, especially in secondary classrooms, is any higher than in reading classrooms in elementary and middle school classrooms.

From a broad perspective, language development needed for communicating in the various domains is inextricably connected to and intertwined with successful conceptual learning. Language and meaning, regardless of content area, develop simultaneously when new vocabulary representing new concepts is introduced and used in meaningful contexts (Vygotsky, 1934/1986). What do the vocabularies in each content area look like? What types of words are students expected to learn? What distinctions can we make among mathematics, science, and social studies vocabulary? How do these features inform effective instruction? What does research have to say about vocabulary instruction in particular content areas? To address these questions, we synthesize our findings for each content area by first discussing general features of vocabulary that are shared across domains and then presenting unique characteristics of vocabulary in mathematics, science, and social studies.

General Academic Vocabulary Features
Across Domains

Each domain-specific area (i.e., mathematics, science, social studies) has an esoteric vocabulary that is critical for communicating and for conceptual learning within that particular domain. These vocabularies contain not only the labels for specific concepts but also important phrases and language features that connect and hold ideas together. Drawing from descriptive sources in the body of literature about content area language and literacy (e.g., Itza-Ortiz, Robello, & Zollman, 2003; Monroe & Panchyshyn, 1995), we present four means of classifying domain-specific vocabulary: (1) academically technical terms, (2) nontechnical words, (3) word clusters or phrases, and (4) symbolic representations. Academically technical terms are unique to a particular subject matter area and are the labels for both simple and complex concepts. They are the low frequency words that appear in narrow, situational contexts, such as classrooms. While we may not have precise understandings of some of these terms, we can probably recognize the content area. For example, we can probably identify *absolute value, sine,* and *polynomial* as mathematical terms; *amino acid, DNA,* and *isotope* as science terms; and *gentrification, hinterland,* and *totalitarianism* as social studies terms, all representing specific concepts within each particular domain. Acquiring a solid knowledge base of these academically technical terms is synonymous to acquiring a solid knowledge base of the concepts themselves.

The second category, nontechnical terms, includes general words as well as polysemous words that appear across differing contexts but hold special meaning within a subject matter area. In many instances, students may be familiar with these terms in one context but may not necessarily know the meaning in another area. General words, such as *key, race, market, cabinet, bay,* and *legend,* have distinct meanings in social studies. In science, some polysemous words include *crust, degree, charge, wave, fault,* and *force.* A few words with multiple meanings in mathematics are *yard, root, mean, peck, product,* and *drill.* Common, nontechnical words can also carry different meanings in different content areas, such as the term *degree.* In science, *degree* is a unit for measuring temperature or pressure; in geometry, a *degree* is the 360th part of an angle; in algebra, *degree* refers to the sum of the exponents of the variables in an algebraic expression; in social studies, *degree* can refer to the classification of a crime in terms of its severity, such as *murder in the first degree*; and in the field of music, a *degree* refers to a tone or step of a musical scale. Nontechnical words deserve attention in content classrooms so that students do not become confused about how these terms are used.

The third category represents word clusters or phrases that appear frequently within a particular subject matter area. These function words and phrases are so commonplace that we sometimes mistakenly assume that students understand what they mean. Nevertheless, they are very important for constructing meaning because they signal relationships among ideas and link conceptually loaded words in context (Marco & Luzon, 1999). Examples in science include *is produced by, are composed primarily of,* and *that extends beyond.* In social studies, some examples are *another characteristic of, the result of,* and *helps to explain why.* In mathematics, phrases can indicate specific operations, such as *estimate the amount of, less than twice a number is,* and *the product of.* Students must understand the meanings of these phrases to construct appropriate understandings of what they read and hear in content area classrooms.

The last category, symbolic representations, involves precise meanings in a given content area. Special symbols and abbreviations, which simplify how concepts and ideas are depicted, are found in different content areas and can be a source of confusion for many students. The domain of mathematics not only uses regular words to convey ideas, but also numerical, "nonalphabetical" symbols that are highly abstract (Monroe & Panchyshyn, 1995). Furthermore, number representations can be read in different ways. For example, 5^3 can be read as five to the third power or five cubed. Science also makes use of symbols, especially in regard to chemical elements. Students must learn that NaCl stands for sodium chloride. Even the domain of social studies contains symbolic representations, such as states' abbreviations and map symbols. Obviously symbolic representations also need to be explicitly taught across all content areas.

Distinctive Vocabulary Features in Mathematics, Science, and Social Studies

In this section, we present research studies and noteworthy commentaries about the distinctive vocabulary in each content area.

Mathematics vocabulary. The four categories described above provide a thorough description of mathematics vocabulary. Mathematics contains many confusing terms, especially the polysemous words that have different meanings from everyday usage and that appear across grade levels, even beginning with young children (Durkin & Shire, 1991; Rubenstein & Thompson, 2002). Unfortunately students rarely encounter mathematics language outside of school in their everyday lives where vocabulary can be meaningfully used and reinforced (Thompson & Rubenstein, 2000). Furthermore, even generalized terms typically found in elementary reading materials differ from the generalized vocabulary words students encounter in mathematics textbooks (Monroe & Panchyshyn, 1995).

Yet the language used to convey mathematical concepts is inextricably woven into mathematical learning (Krussel, 1998; Steele, 1999; Tracy, 1994). In fact, in their study of the connection between language proficiency and algebra learning, MacGregor and Price (1999) found that students with low metalinguistic awareness, a cognitive component of language proficiency, were unable to attain high levels of achievement in learning algebraic notations. Along similar lines, Tracy (1994) contended that teachers need to use appropriate mathematical language to support students' conceptual understandings so that students become accustomed to new terminology in their listening and speaking vocabulary. Eventually, once concepts are internalized, students then are able to use new labels for new concepts in their reading and writing. Krussel

(1998) also viewed mathematics learning from a language perspective and posits that effective mathematics instruction is closely tied to language learning as well.

Mathematics vocabulary is consistently described as dense, highly abstract, very precise, and cumulative. The density of mathematics texts is a challenge to many students given that this discipline has, as Schell (cited in Monroe & Panchyshyn, 1995) so aptly pointed out, "more concepts per word, per sentence, and per paragraph than any other area" (p. 80). Furthermore, many mathematics terms, crossing all four categories described previously, are highly abstract with precise meanings. For example, the Pythagorean theorem is an abstract concept that explicitly describes the relationship among the three sides of a right triangle. An understanding of the Pythagorean theorem also requires cumulative, experiential knowledge, including knowledge of polygons, angles, triangles, not to mention the area of squares and the interrelatedness of these concepts. Clearly, as this example illustrates, effective vocabulary instruction builds upon previous knowledge and becomes even more imperative as students learn more sophisticated and complex mathematical concepts found in the middle and high school curriculum. Therefore, developing a solid vocabulary base is necessary for acquiring mathematical understandings and communicating within this discipline.

Science vocabulary. The language of science includes a tremendous body of vocabulary when you consider the different disciplines within science, such as physics, biology, earth science, psychology, medicine, and astronomy. Miller (2005) pointed out that student exposure to science terminology is no longer contained largely within school classrooms. Students today encounter science terms in commercials and ads for pharmaceutical drugs and products, in popular television programs, and other media events. As a result, many scientific terms are becoming part of students' everyday language even though they may have only a cursory understanding of some terms.

While such exposures enable students to acquire at least a low level of word knowledge, they can use this knowledge to move forward in their understandings of science concepts. In one study involving students in a conceptual physics course, Itza-Ortizet al. (2003) probed the effects of students' perceptions of word meanings used in everyday life (e.g., *force* and *momentum*) on their understanding of physics concepts. They found that students who had a more solid knowledge base about physics concepts were able to determine the finer distinctions between the physics words and their everyday meanings.

In addition to commonplace meanings of many science words, the vocabulary in this domain contains words with many common roots, a feature which makes science an almost universal language. Science texts contain a plethora of words based upon Greek and Latin roots, such as *arthr-* (relating to joints), *herbi-* (relating to plants), *hydro-* (relating to water), *osteo-* (relating to bone), and so forth. This feature of science vocabulary clearly implies the need to teach common roots to students. If they know that *hydro-* means water, then they can use this knowledge to understand many words, including *hydrology, hydrolysis, hydrometer, hydromagnetic, hydrokinetic, hydrographic, hydroelectric,* and *hydrodynamic,* to name a few.

The vocabulary words in some specific disciplines within the domain of science have distinctive features worth mentioning because of instructional implications. For example, some biology concepts are named using binominal nomenclature, a system for designating names for all species of plants and animals using two terms. The first term identifies the genus of the plant or animal and the second term is the species designation, such as *Speyeria cybele* for butterfly and *Asplenium ascensionis* for a fern. Furthermore, chemistry has its own special nomenclature for chemicals with letter symbols, numbers in front of symbols, numbers as subscripts, and arrows pointing in various directions. For example, labels for chemical compounds indicate the chemical and sometimes show the relationship between chemical families, such as iron chloride. Scientific measurement units are represented with letter abbreviations as well as symbols and may be common (e.g., *watt* or *measuring*) or not common (e.g., *candela* for measuring luminous intensity) (Fry, 2004).

Social studies vocabulary. Similar to other domains, social studies is language dependent. Many social studies teachers tend to depend extensively on teacher-centered classroom instruction, such as lecturing and student textbook reading (Short, 1995). Such instructional practices require students to understand the nature of social studies language, especially the vocabulary. Furthermore the domain of social studies includes specific fields, such as history, geography, economics, civics, all of which carry unique terms that can be new terms for familiar concepts or new terms for unfamiliar concepts (Graves, 2000).

In addition to the descriptors discussed previously, social studies vocabulary also has other features that warrant attention. This domain requires that students acquire a working knowledge of many specific names for places, people, and titles of events more so than for any other discipline. In addition, students must associate these specific names to particular time periods in history and/or geographic regions of the world. Place name geography, in particular, is a critical issue given the limited geographic knowledge of many Americans along with the scant attention given to place geography instruction in many textbooks (Smith & Larkins, 1990). Geography terms also include features, such as rivers and oceans, as well as geographic concerns (e.g., *climate, cultures, tectonics, biodiversity*) and even map terminology (e.g., *atlas, gazetteer, physical maps, political maps, satellite maps*) (Fry, 2004).

Social studies terms also represent abstract concepts, such as *negotiation, fundamentalism, democracy, taxation,* or *patriotism,* which require rich explanations and examples to be understood. Another feature of social studies vocabulary includes language function words—words and phrases that direct students to do something, such as *explain, sequence, define, compare, evaluate,* and *justify* (Short, 1995). Such words extend across all fields of social studies.

One final feature of note is the number of social studies words that contain common roots and affixes, a similar feature of science vocabulary. In their content analysis of five glossaries in elementary and secondary social studies textbooks, Milligan and Ruff (1990) found that approximately 71% of the terms contained meaningful affixes and roots. Examples include *inter-* (as in *international* and *interdependent*), *trans-* (as in *transportation* and *transnational*), and *mon-* (as in *monarchy* and *monotheism*).

Effective Content Vocabulary Instruction

Reading experts are not the only ones who understand and appreciate the importance of vocabulary acquisition and the need for appropriate vocabulary instruction. Our search for what experts in various contents areas, such as mathematics, science, and social studies, have to say about vocabulary acquisition and instruction uncovered similar beliefs (Harmon, Hedrick, & Wood, 2005). In fact, some sources readily acknowledged the role of literacy in content learning. For example, Gullatt (1987) argued that success in reading like a mathematician requires specific reading strategies and knowledge of technical vocabulary, an argument backed by Cloer (1981) who found that reading comprehension problems interfered with students' understanding of mathematical word problems. Along similar lines, Borasi, Siegal, Fonzi, and Smith (1998), in their study of the use of transactional reading strategies in mathematics classrooms, found that mathematical understandings were enhanced when secondary students used various sign systems, such as drama, drawing, writing, and discussion, to construct their own interpretations of concepts. Such activities provide students opportunities to use and internalize appropriate mathematics vocabulary.

Experts in other areas also note the need for a rich vocabulary program (Gomez & Madda, 2005; Groves, 1995). In their observations of instruction in a middle school science classroom, Gomez and Madda (2005) documented the difficulty and challenge one mainstream teacher faced in providing for the academic needs of English-language learner Latino students. The teacher viewed vocabulary as the greatest obstacle to the learning and teaching of science. An example from the area of social studies focused on the types of instruction (i.e., teacher-led direct instruction and computer-assisted instruction) for promoting student learning of place geography (Salsbury, 2006). While Salsbury found that the computer-assisted instruction appeared to be more effective than the teacher-led direct instruction, she advocates the use of both instructional types for teaching place geography.

While there is support for a rich vocabulary program in content area classrooms, what should this program look like? A list of guidelines for effective content vocabulary instruction can be extensive and can be configured in various ways depending upon who is developing the list. We chose to base our list of guidelines on the extensive work of Graves (2006) who provided four basic components of a comprehensive vocabulary program. Graves's four components represent research-based elements that should be universal practices for supporting vocabulary learning across all subject matter domains: (1) providing rich and varied language experiences, (2) teaching individual words (3) teaching word-learning strategies, and (4) promoting word consciousness. We examine each instructional component from the perspective of content area word learning, specifically targeting mathematics, science, and social studies. (See also Chapter 3, this volume, for general discussion of Graves's components.)

Providing Rich and Varied Language Experiences

There are several important instructional ideas for providing rich and varied language experiences in middle and high school content area classrooms. In his explanation of this component, Graves (2006) drew our attention to the role of incidental word learning as well as to the role of listening and discussion in helping primary children acquire vocabulary. Both apply to middle and high school students as they acquire content vocabulary as well. First, research shows us that students can learn many new words incidentally during normal reading (Nagy, Anderson, & Herman, 1987; Nagy, Herman, & Anderson, 1985; Swanborn & de Glopper, 1999). These studies serve as evidence for promoting wide reading, not just with narrative texts but also with informational texts. We are convinced that exposing students to a variety of texts about particular concepts and encouraging them to read the texts will have a positive impact on their vocabulary and learning.

One caveat, however, involves student familiarity with content topics. Some studies have shown that the more knowledge students have about a topic, the more apt they are to learn word meanings incidentally (Carlisle, Fleming, & Gudbrandsen, 2000; Swanborn & de Glopper, 1999). For example, in their studies of fourth-grade students and eighth-grade students in science classes, Carlisle, Fleming, and Gudbrandsen (2000) found evidence of incidental word learning when students were actively engaged in hands-on activities and class discussions. However, in both classes, students with some topical knowledge made more progress with word learning and concept learning than did the students with limited topical knowledge. Hence it is important to offer students a variety of texts that provide background for varying levels of concept knowledge and reading ability.

Graves's rich and varied language experiences also provide multiple opportunities for students to apply word meanings beyond a definitional level. Such opportunities include reading, writing, listening, speaking, viewing, and visually representing—all aspects of the English language arts supported by literacy teachers and researchers (IRA & NCTE, 1996). These aspects of the English language arts imply that students need to be active participants in classroom instruction and not passive receivers of information doled out by the teacher. They also support what we know about vocabulary learning in general, that is, the need for multiple opportunities to use words in varied and meaningful ways (Nagy, 1988). According to McKeown, Beck, Omanson, and Poole (1985), this means students need twelve or more encounters with the words to impact comprehension.

We found a few content area studies that support active engagement with vocabulary. In their study of fourth grade students, Lloyd and Contreras (1985) found that vocabulary knowledge and reading comprehension of science texts increased when students participated in hands-on experiences and class discussion as compared with traditional dictionary work. The students in the hands-on/discussion instruction significantly out-performed the dictionary group and a control group that received no special instruction. In another science study, Stahl and Clark (1987) also reported the benefits of discussion for promoting vocabulary learning with fifth-grade students as compared with having no discussion about vocabulary terms. Furthermore, Stahl and Kapinus (1991) found that using the possible sentences strategy, a teaching technique that directs students to use two or more vocabulary terms in a sentence, proved to be effective in learning science vocabulary and in recalling science facts. Grubaugh and Metzer (1986) also supported active engagement with their spoken word activity in which students participate in class discussions by defining words and then providing representative examples based upon their own personal or vicarious experiences. Even in mathematics, active participation in vocabulary learning is encouraged through student explanations, writing activities, and cooperative learning techniques to encourage classroom talk (Miller, 1993).

Therefore, a comprehensive vocabulary program in a content area should include opportunities for wide reading, access to a variety of texts at differing levels of conceptual understanding and reading ability, and multiple opportunities to use words in active ways that include reading, writing, speaking, listening, viewing, and visually representing.

Teaching Individual Words

Although teachers have particular beliefs about vocabulary learning and orientations toward vocabulary teaching (Hedrick, Harmon, & Linerode, 2004; Konopak & Williams, 1994), all would probably agree that vocabulary is an important part of their instructional program. In the content areas, direct teaching of individual words is very closely tied to actual content instruction when words are considered labels for concepts. Hence, vocabulary instruction is difficult to separate from effective content instruction.

For this component of a comprehensive vocabulary program, Graves (2006) urged educators to consider several important facets of vocabulary learning and teaching that are applicable in the content areas. First, he recommended initiating vocabulary teaching with a student-friendly definition and a meaningful context based upon the students' experiential knowledge. These contexts can be written texts, concrete objects, pictures, and even video clips. Graves also made the point that words are known in varying degrees and that not all words need to be learned to the highest level of word knowledge for rich, decontextualized understanding (Beck, McKeown, & Kucan, 2002). Sometimes having a general understanding of a term is enough to keep comprehension intact. Given time constraints, Graves also pointed out the need to be diligent and selective in the words that warrant instruction. These words should be the ones that are important for understanding the concepts being taught and perhaps transferable and useful in other areas. Another facet of vocabulary learning and teaching is the type of word-learning task associated with word meanings. Although Graves described several types of word learning tasks, two in particular hold critical implications in the content areas: new words that represent familiar concepts and new words that represent new and difficult concepts. Both types of word learning tasks require different instructional approaches. For example, geography instruction in place names would be different than the instruction needed to explain concepts, such as *urbanization* and *gentrification.*

There are many empirically grounded techniques for teaching individual content words, including preteaching strategies, keyword mnemonics, graphic representations, and other specific vocabulary activities. Some have been tested in particular content areas. For example, preteaching vocabulary, while sometimes difficult to measure for effectiveness (Seaver, 1991), has received support in different subject matter areas. Carney, Anderson, Blackburn, and Blessing (1984) reported improvement in the reading comprehension of fifth-grade students after preteaching social studies vocabulary terms found in the passages they were asked to read. In addition, studies in science also support preteaching vocabulary (Moran, 1990; Snouffer & Thistlethwaite, 1979) as well as the use of keyword mnemonics techniques for helping struggling readers learn and remember science vocabulary to increase the likelihood of success for understanding and acquiring science content (King-Sears, Mercer, & Sindelar, 1992).

Visual representations, such as structured overviews, concept mapping, and semantic grids, have also gained support as viable instructional techniques for teaching content area vocabulary. Some examples from the literature on content area vocabulary include the following: (a) Structured overviews as a preteaching device work well in science and social studies (Snouffer & Thistlethwaite, 1979); (b) Graphic organizers, such as the concept of definition map, used in conjunction with rich discussions, are effective in helping students learn mathematics vocabulary (Monroe & Pendergrass, 1997); and (c) Graphic organizers make use of both meaningful contexts and direct instruction to enhance learning of mathematical terms (Herbal-Eisenmann, 2002; Monroe & Orme, 2002).

There are other specific vocabulary activities that are effective in helping students learn content area vocabulary, many of which reflect good literacy practices (e.g., Jackson & Ray, 1983). We provide more detailed descriptions of several strategies later in this chapter.

Teaching Word-Learning Strategies

The ultimate goal in any vocabulary instructional program is to equip students with strategies that enable them to become independent word learners, strategies that are useful for reading like a scientist, historian, or mathematician. Such strategy instruction would need to include context clues, morphemic and structural analysis, word origins, and references such as dictionaries and glossaries in textbooks. Content area instruction in word-learning strategies is especially important for struggling learners—students learning English as a second language, minority and economically disadvantaged students with limited exposure to content area concepts, students with learning disabilities, and students who have fallen behind their peers for whatever reason.

Context clues, while not always explicitly helpful, can provide enough hints to help students infer possible word meanings. In many of today's content area textbooks, publishers have inserted definitions in the body of texts either in the form of appositives or as complete sentences following the use of a term in an effort to offer more considerate texts to students. For example, a high school U.S. history text currently in use included an explanation of *deism* in its description of the rise of evangelicalism through this sentence: "As deism—the belief in a God who expressed himself through natural laws accessible to human reason—declined in popularity in the early to mid-nineteenth century, Catholic immigration increased..." (Divine, Breen, Fredrickson, & Williams, 2003, p. 310). However, just because the meaning of a term may be apparent to us, that does not necessarily mean that students, especially struggling readers, are aware of the connection between the term and the brief meaning given nearby. Many students may require explicit instruction in how authors provide clues to word meanings through extending phrasing and sentences.

Instruction about the morphemic elements and structural components of a word can also strengthen students' independent word learning abilities with content area texts. This is a valuable strategy for content area reading given the high percentage of content words containing common affixes and roots (Milligan & Ruff, 1990). Studies also support the importance of teaching morphemic analysis. For example, using social studies textbook lessons with eight fifth-grade classes, Baumann, Edwards, Boland, Olejnik, and Kame'enui (2003) compared the effects of two types of instruction: (1) morphemic and contextual analysis instruction and (2) textbook vocabulary instruction. They found that students learned what they were taught with both groups obtaining similar scores on social studies content assessment. Students who were taught with the textbook vocabulary instruction learned the textbook vocabulary; students who were taught with the morphemic and contextual analysis instruction were able to infer word meanings of new words more readily. This study supports direct instruction of specific vocabulary as well as morphemic and contextual analysis instruction.

In addition, based upon her research findings in an inner city middle school in England, Robinson (2005) argued that English as an additional language (EAL) students need more than semantic knowledge about content vocabulary in science and geography. She argued that EAL students also need explicit instruction in both syntactical and morphological word knowledge to participate in class discussions that enable students to construct even deeper conceptual understandings. Passive listening to teacher explanations does not promote deeper cognitive processing for greater understanding. Students need the appropriate linguistic tools that will enable them to participate in the negotiation and construction of meanings during class discussions.

Along another line, Rubenstein (2000) presented a convincing argument for teaching word origins in mathematics classrooms. She noted several benefits: mathematical terms are typically very precise and clearly related to their roots; verbal connections help many learners; and EAL students have the added benefit of making connections with cognates from their first language.

Promoting Word Consciousness

Scott and Nagy (2004) define word consciousness as "an interest in and awareness of words" (p. 202). Their description of word consciousness involves several types of knowledge and skills, including a metalinguistic knowledge of words (i.e., having semantic and syntactic awareness of words) and an understanding that word knowledge goes beyond a definitional level, occurs incrementally, and requires different strategies for different words. We believe that teachers should talk to students about word learning in this manner so that they understand what it means to actually learn new words. Too often students assume that memorizing a definition is all they need to do to understand a concept with little regard to the limitations of most definitions.

Fostering word consciousness can play a very useful role in content area learning for several reasons. First, developing an interest in content area words, both technical and nontechnical, enables students to become more adept at using the language of science, social studies, and mathematics to communicate in both speaking and writing. Second, word consciousness raises students' awareness of polysemous words that appear frequently in various content areas. Students can be on the lookout for these words and can assess how the meanings differ across the subject matter disciplines. Finally, a raised level of word consciousness is motivating, especially when teachers incorporate word play activities for review, reinforcement, and even fun. For example, puns can heighten word consciousness and engage students in higher level thinking as they consider what the author means, as in this example (Cleary, 2006) of a geography pun:

> We went out to the racetrack,
>
> **Kenya** tell why I'm upset?
>
> I picked out all the winners,
>
> but my dad's too cheap **Tibet**! (p. 45)

Connecting Research to Practice

In our recent book, *Instructional Strategies for Teaching Content Vocabulary* (Harmon, Wood, & Hedrick, 2006), we emphasized the need for teachers to consider many factors when deciding how to focus on vocabulary development in the content areas, including the specific nature of selected terms and the situated context of the terms as well as student learning ability. Through our research in this area, we identified five specific features that represent the vocabulary instructional demands for the content areas: *integration, clarification, identification, linguistic attention,* and *metacognition*. In this section, we describe these five features and give instructional suggestions related to each category.

Integration

Integrating, categorizing, and making connections between words and concepts are essential in deepening and strengthening students' understanding of any content area. Teaching words in semantically related groups enables learners to build upon their prior knowledge and relate this knowledge to the new information in the text. Similarly, showing the relationship between words through visual displays, such as graphic organizers and semantic maps, has long been established as effective means of teaching and reinforcing content information (Johnson & Pearson, 1984; Merkley & Jeffries, 2000/2001). Two strategies that accomplish the task of integration—list-group-label and write and concept circles—are described next.

List-group-label and write. This categorization strategy (Wood & Taylor, 2005, adapted from Taba, 1967) can be used to integrate vocabulary into the content areas in a meaningful way. In this activity, the teacher identifies a broad topic of the text and leads students in brainstorming group related words or subtopics. Students then label or categorize groups of words. Next, students read the selected topic. After reading, students identify the previously identified vocabulary contained in the text and group and classify the categories with justification as needed. Finally, students can work in pairs or individually to write a paragraph by using a category of terms. Figure 7.1 illustrates the list-group-label and write strategy used with a middle school lesson on Feudalism.

Concept circles. As another categorization strategy, concept circles (Vacca & Vacca, 2005) provides a means to help students get a sense of the conceptual relationships among vocabulary terms. First, the teacher demonstrates four related words by putting a related text word in each quadrant of a circle and then has the students name the concept relationship among them. For variation, the teacher can put each of three related words in one quadrant of the circle and leave one quadrant empty. Students put a word that relates to the others in the empty quadrant and then identify the overall concept that the circle represents.

Clarification

Clarification is one necessary component of vocabulary instruction because many words in content reading are polysemous and can be puzzling for students. Students may understand the meaning of the word *foot* to be twelve inches in math or an anatomical part of the body while reading a health text, but they may not understand the word *foot* as in a base of a hill from a social studies' lesson. These multiple definitions can be tenuous for many students. In addition, students can be confused with procedural phrases that are found in context areas, such as

Figure 7.1. List-group-label and write sample lesson

Topic: Middle Ages: feudalism
Brainstorming (whole class)

feudalism	chivalry	knights
manor	religion	royalty
lord	serf	Middle Ages
kingdom		

Grouping and labeling (small groups)

Concepts and ideas	Places	People	Time periods
feudalism	castle	lord	Middle Ages
chivalry	kingdom	kings	
religion		knights	
royalty			

Postreading: Adding new terms (whole class or small groups)

secular	vassal	manor
peasants	fief	clergy
serfs	tithe	

Grouping and labeling new terms with old terms (small groups)

Concepts and systems	Places	People/roles	Time periods	Things "given"
feudalism	castle	lord and vassal	Middle Ages	tithe
chivalry	kingdom	kings		fief
religion	manor	knights		
royalty		serfs		
secular		clergy		
		peasants		

Writing exercise (pairs or individuals)
The structure of feudalism is like a pyramid of distinct roles and classes. At the top of the pyramid, with the most power, is the king. Next there are the wealthy lords or landowners and high-ranking clergy such as bishops. At the next level of power are the knights. Knights are warriors on horseback who defend their lords' land in exchange for fiefs or land. At the bottom of the pyramid are the landless peasants or serfs who work the land for their lords.

Note. From Harmon, J.M., Wood, K.D., & Hedrick, W.B. (2006). *Instructional strategies for teaching content vocabulary: Grades 4–12.* Columbus, OH: National Middle School Association. Reprinted with permission from National Middle School Association.

composed primarily of and *be adjacent to*. Examples such as these can create uncertainty and anxiety with text comprehension, particularly among ELLs. Then too, other students find difficulty with intentional words and phrases that indicate unique relationships found in text, such as cause and effect, sequence, and problem solution. Next we provide some examples of instructional strategies that help students clarify word meanings through context analysis and that strengthen their understanding of multiple words and functions found in content reading: contextual redefinition, coding polysemous words, and signal words.

Contextual redefinition. This clarification strategy (Tierney & Readence, 2000) offers students specific steps for determining the meaning of unknown words in a reading passage by using context clues from the text. This strategy encourages students to concentrate on what is clear in a reading passage, state the meaning as much as possible, and use the context to interpret unclear terms. First, the teacher selects several words that have multiple meanings or unclear words for students and writes the words on the board. Then, students are asked to suggest definitions for the words before reading the selection while the teacher records all definitions on the board. The students then read the text selection and note specific sentences where the words can be found. Finally, the students revisit their original definitions but now share their new thoughts about the meaning of the words. We recommend filling out a chart while reading a passage, which might look like that shown in Figure 7.2 from a science lesson on seismology.

Coding polysemous words. This word-coding strategy (Paivio, 1990; Strong, Silver, Perini, & Tuculescu, 2002) instructs students to understand that many words have multiple meanings. First, the teacher peruses a reading passage and selects any polysemous words that students will encounter while reading. Then, the teacher discusses the general meaning of each word and particular context meanings. Students then

Figure 7.2. Contextual redefinition chart example

Word	Word-level clues	Context clues	Predicted word meaning	Actual word meaning
Seismology	Clues—ology means "study of" Guess—study of something in science	Clues—earthquakes; learning more about earthquakes	Study of earthquakes	Study of earthquakes, including the effects, location, and timing

Note. From Harmon, J.M., Wood, K.D., & Hedrick, W.B. (2006). *Instructional strategies for teaching content vocabulary: Grades 4–12.* Columbus, OH: National Middle School Association. Reprinted with permission from National Middle School Association.

Figure 7.3. Sample vocabulary coding chart for music

Word: *scale*	
Common meaning: device for measuring weight	
Content meaning: series of musical steps	
Code	**Task**
Visual code	Draw a musical scale.
Kinesthetic code	Play a musical scale on an instrument.
Social code	Play a musical scale with a partner.
Linguistic code	Write your own description of a musical scale.

Note. From Harmon, J.M., Wood, K.D., & Hedrick, W.B. (2006). *Instructional strategies for teaching content vocabulary: Grades 4–12*. Columbus, OH: National Middle School Association. Reprinted with permission from National Middle School Association.

pair-up and complete a coding chart. When each pair is finished, the whole class meets to share how they coded the words by meaning. The coding chart in Figure 7.3 helps students distinguish between the many meanings of the word *scale* and helps solidify their understanding of the term as used in music.

Signal words. Signal words are words or phrases that cue the reader about an organizational pattern in the text or show a link or transition between ideas, such as cause and effect, problem solution, comparison–contrast, and sequence. Comprehension is enhanced as students learn to make the connections between reading and writing tasks in subject-related texts. Before students read, the teacher provides students with different examples of signal words and related text organizational patterns. Then, the teacher selects a passage and tells the students that as the passage is read aloud, they are to identify and highlight the signal words. Next, the teacher provides students other text examples taken from their textbooks and then asks students to complete a chart by recording the signal words with the related text structure heading.

Identification

Middle school learners encounter a multiplicity of content area terms daily in school. Many of the terms are familiar; yet many more may be unknown, complex, and abstract. To identify a concept, a student must be able to recognize the concept to which he or she was previously exposed and then make connections and see relationships between the items of information to apply their prior knowledge to new and more difficult concepts. In this section, we describe a visualization tactic and mnemonic device that help students formulate concepts and generalizations.

Link, imagine, note, construct, self-interest (LINCS). The LINCS strategy (Ellis, 1992; Foil & Alber, 2002) is a way for students to learn the meaning of new words through powerful memory techniques. The strategy teaches students to use keyword mnemonics to create associations among the elements of a concept, visual images, and prior knowledge. The teacher begins by asking students to write the vocabulary words on index cards and write the essential definitions on the back. Then, with each word, the students are required to visualize the word and describe the word to a partner. Next, the teacher tells the students to think of a similar word or a word that sounds the same and write this word on the bottom of the card. Finally, the students create a story or write sentences about the meaning of the word, including the reminding word. Students then recall their words from memory (see Figure 7.4 for an example).

Figure 7.4. LINCS sample lesson of Spanish vocabulary

Word	L	I	N	C	S Did you get it right?
el/la amigo(a)	friend	a high school age girl	Amelia—my best friend	Amelia is my amiga.	+
el arbol	tree	The big tree in my backyard	Arbor Day	I looked at el arbol at the Arbor Day Festival.	+
la boca	mouth	a big smile	Boca Burgers	You eat Boca Burgers with la boca.	—
la carta	letter	a stamped addressed envelope	card	My birthday card is la carta I got in the mail!	+
la madre	mother	my mom	mad	La madre is always mad!	+

Note. From Harmon, J.M., Wood, K.D., & Hedrick, W.B. (2006). *Instructional strategies for teaching content vocabulary: Grades 4–12.* Columbus, OH: National Middle School Association. Reprinted with permission from National Middle School Association.

Linguistic Attention

Middle school students encounter a high percentage of words in content reading that have easily identifiable morphological structure, meaningful word parts that readers can identify and put together to determine the meaning of an unfamiliar word. Knowledge of word structures, such as affixes and roots, plays a valuable role in learning words from context because readers can use such knowledge to examine unfamiliar words and figure out their meanings. To be most effective, word-part instruction should teach students the meanings of particular word parts as well as a strategy for when and why to use them. Next we describe two strategies helpful for understanding the role of word structure in understanding; these strategies are useful and applicable to all content areas.

Incidental morpheme analysis. This method (Manzo & Manzo, 1990) is an effective approach to understanding unfamiliar words when reading content-specific materials. Students use their prior knowledge of word roots and affixes to decipher new words and to determine their meanings. First, the teacher identifies unknown words and determines any unknown word parts the students might not know and displays the words on the chalkboard, breaking the words into meaningful smaller parts. Then the teacher says each word aloud, pointing to the word part and asking students to repeat the words orally and to determine the possible meanings. The teacher writes the student-contributed correct meaning on the board and provides clues as needed if students are uncertain about the meanings. To support learning, the teacher can tell students the meaning of the root word and affix and, from there, students can then use their new knowledge to predict the meaning of the word. (See also Chapter 4, this volume, for more detail on this strategy.)

Morpheme circles. Similar to the concept circles mentioned previously, morpheme circles (Vacca & Vacca, 2005) encourage students to think conceptually about various words that have similar morphemes. The teacher determines words that students need to know that have common morphemes. Then the words are presented visually in a circle format with students filling in additional words in each of the quadrants. Then they are asked to explain how the words are related. The example shown in Figure 7.5 illustrates a completed morpheme circle for the root "graph."

Metacognition

Having metacognitive ability means the learner can think and make conscious decisions about the learning process. Metacognition applies to

Figure 7.5. Sample morpheme circle

Complete the following morpheme circle with other words containing the root *graph*. Then below the circle, explain how the word meanings are related.

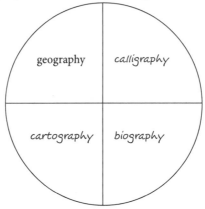

All four words have something to do with writing or describing.

Note. From Harmon, J.M., Wood, K.D., & Hedrick, W.B. (2006). *Instructional strategies for teaching content vocabulary: Grades 4–12.* Columbus, OH: National Middle School Association. Reprinted with permission from National Middle School Association.

learning content area vocabulary because metacognitive students understand how to select and use a particular strategy and then monitor their use of that strategy as they interact with new words. Students should be explicitly taught that once they have selected and begun to use the specific strategies, they need to periodically check whether or not those strategies are effective and being used as intended for vocabulary learning. A metacognitive strategy that will enable students to take ownership of their vocabulary development in the content areas is described next.

Vocabulary overview guide. The vocabulary overview guide (Carr, 1985) places the responsibility of learning new content area words on students. It allows students to make a connection with new terms that draws upon their previous knowledge or experiences. Students self-select words they deem to be important and then determine their word meanings from the context. Students may also use glossaries or dictionaries to check their definitions. To begin the strategy, the teacher distributes a blank vocabulary overview guide and discusses the main topic to be studied with the class. The teacher models how to preview the text, noting important vocabulary words on a sticky note. The students are then instructed to read the text and identify words that have some connection to the topic. Then they are asked to determine a category for each word, as listed across the top of the guide. The teacher instructs students to list the words under the categories, followed by definitions for each word. In the last step, the students are to brainstorm clues that will assist them in learning and remembering each new word. (Figure 7.6 shows an example of a vocabulary overview guide.)

Figure 7.6. Vocabulary overview guide example

Topic: Geography of the Americas

Category—Landforms	Category—People	Category—Resources	Category—Economy
Word—tundra Clue—No trees Meaning—rolling plain without trees found in Arctic	Word—bilingual Clue—Canadians who speak French and English Meaning—referring to two languages	Word—wood pulp Clue—paper Meaning—wet, ground-up chips of wood	Word—inflation Clue—Buy less with your money Meaning—a decrease in the value of money as prices for goods and services increase
Word—prairie Clue—Wheat grows there Meaning—rolling land with tall grasses and fertile soil	Word—immigrant Clue—most Americans Meaning—person who moves to one country from another country to live permanently	Word—renewable resource Clue—trees Meaning—resources that can be replaced after being used	Word—capital Clue—poor countries have little money Meaning—money needed for a country to develop
Word—coastal plain Clue—harbors and shipping Meaning—flat land bordering a coast	Word—Hispanic Clue—My friend Juan Meaning—American ethnic group that speaks Spanish		Word—regional specialization Clue—fishing in New England Meaning—a special activity of a region that helps the economy
	Word—Mestizo Clue—people in north and central Mexico Meaning—person whose ancestors are both European and American Indian		

Note. From Harmon, J.M., Wood, K.D., & Hedrick, W.B. (2006). *Instructional strategies for teaching content vocabulary: Grades 4–12.* Columbus, OH: National Middle School Association. Reprinted with permission from National Middle School Association.

Conclusions

We have addressed many critical topics about content vocabulary teaching and learning in this chapter—topics that we hope resonate with content area teachers. We began by positioning vocabulary acquisition within the greater context of conceptual teaching and learning in content area classrooms. From this broad position, we can understand how vocabulary permeates background knowledge and conceptual understanding, both necessary aspects of content area learning. We further posited the need for functioning communication abilities in reading and writing using organizational structures found in informational texts as well as the specialized grammar found in content reading. Such skills enable learners to read, write, speak, and listen like mathematicians, scientists, and historians. We then zoomed in on the distinctive features of content vocabulary across the domains of mathematics, science, and social studies and provided specific instructional examples to support vocabulary learning. These instructional strategies represent a few ways in which we can help students build essential content vocabularies—vocabulary knowledge needed for success in content area learning.

Questions for Discussion

1. Examine the teacher's manual for the textbook you use in your classroom. What vocabulary instructional strategies do the publishers recommend for supporting vocabulary learning? How do these strategies compare with the essential features for effective vocabulary learning and teaching? What words are recommended for instruction? Are there other terms and phrases that you consider to be important? How would you teach these terms?

2. As an experienced content teacher, you are asked to be a mentor for a newly hired, first-year teacher. One critical aspect of the mentoring is to support this teacher's vocabulary instructional program. Outline the key points about effective vocabulary teaching and learning that you would share with the novice teacher. Provide concrete instructional suggestions for each key point.

3. Many research studies have been reviewed and cited in this chapter. With the recent emphasis on research-based instruction, imagine that you have been asked to share what the research says about content area vocabulary instruction with your faculty. What are some of the major findings you would choose to share? Present

your summary in the form of a PowerPoint presentation that would be of interest to your colleagues.

4. Reread the portion of this chapter on integration, clarification, identification, linguistic attention, and metacognition in content area vocabulary instruction. Then using a chapter from your own content area textbook, choose some important words you want your students to know that will strengthen their understanding of the content. Decide which features best represent your selected words and describe instructional activities for each feature. You may use the suggested activities we have described and/or think of other vocabulary strategies you have seen that address the same feature.

REFERENCES

Baumann, J.F., Edwards, E.C., Boland, E.M., Olejnik, S., & Kame'enui, E.J. (2003). Vocabulary tricks: Effects of instruction in morphology and context on fifth-grade students' ability to derive and infer word meanings. *American Educational Research Journal, 40*(2), 447–494.

Baumann, J.F., Kame'enui, E.J., & Ash, G.E. (2003). Research on vocabulary instruction: Voltaire redux. In J. Flood, D. Lapp, J.R. Squire, & J.M. Jensen (Eds.), *Handbook of research on teaching the English language arts* (2nd ed., pp. 752–785). Mahwah, NJ: Erlbaum.

Beck, I.L., McKeown, M.G., Hamilton, R.L., & Kucan, L. (1997). *Questioning the author: An approach for enhancing student engagement with text.* Newark, DE: International Reading Association.

Beck, I.L., McKeown, M.G., & Kucan, L. (2002). *Bringing words to life: Robust vocabulary instruction.* New York: Guilford.

Blachowicz, C.L.Z., Fisher, P., Ogle, D., & Watts-Taffe, S.M. (2006). Vocabulary: Questions from the classroom. *Reading Research Quarterly, 41*(4), 524–539.

Borasi, R., Siegal, M., Fonzi, J., & Smith, C.F. (1998). Using transactional reading strategies to support sense-making and discussion in mathematics classrooms: An exploratory study. *Journal for Research in Mathematics Education, 29*(3), 275–305.

Cardinale, L.A. (1991). *The facilitation of vocabulary acquisition by embedding explication in expository text.* Washington, DC: Educational Resources Information Center. (ERIC Document Reproduction Service No. ED334978)

Carlisle, J.F., Fleming, J.E., & Gudbrandsen, B. (2000). Incidental word learning in science classes. *Contemporary Educational Psychology, 25*(2), 184–211.

Carney, J.J., Anderson, D., Blackburn, C., & Blessing, D. (1984). Preteaching vocabulary and the comprehension of social studies materials by elementary school children. *Special Education, 48*(3), 195–196.

Carr, E.M. (1985). The vocabulary overview guide: A metacognitive strategy to improve vocabulary comprehension and retention. *Journal of Reading, 28*(8), 684–689.

Cloer, T. (1981, December). *Factors affecting comprehension of math word problems: A review of the research.* Paper presented at the annual meeting of the American Reading Forum, Sarasota, FL. (ERIC Document Reproduction Service No. ED209655)

Divine, R.A., Breen, T.H., Fredrickson, G.M., & Williams, R.H. (2003). *America past and present: Advanced placement edition* (6th ed.). New York: Longman.

Durkin, D. (1978/1979). What classroom observations reveal about reading comprehension instruction. *Reading Research Quarterly, 14*(4), 481–533.

Durkin, K., & Shire, B. (1991). Primary school children's interpretations of lexical ambiguity in mathematical descriptions. *Journal of Research in Reading, 14*(1), 46–55.

Ellis, E. (1992). *LINCS: A strategy for vocabulary learning.* Lawrence, KS: Edge.

Fang, Z. (2006). The language demands of science reading in middle school. *International Journal of Science Education, 28*(5), 491–520.

Foil, C.R., & Alber, S.R. (2002). Fun and effective ways to build your students' vocabulary. *Intervention in School & Clinic, 37*(3), 131–139.

Fry, E.B. (2004). *The vocabulary teachers' book of lists.* San Francisco: Jossey-Bass.

Gomez, K., & Madda, C. (2005). Vocabulary instruction for ELL Latino students in the middle school science classroom. *Voices From the Middle, 13*(1), 42–47.

Gordon, J., Schumm, J.S., Coffland, C., & Doucette, M. (1992). Effects of inconsiderate versus considerate text on elementary students' vocabulary learning. *Reading Psychology, 13*(2), 157–169.

Graves, M.F. (2000). A vocabulary program to complement and bolster a middle-grade comprehension program. In B.M. Taylor, M.F. Graves, & P.W. van den Broek (Eds.), *Reading for meaning: Fostering comprehension in the middle grades* (pp. 116–135). Newark, DE: International Reading Association.

Graves, M.F. (2006). *The vocabulary book: Learning and instruction.* Newark, DE: International Reading Association.

Groves, F.H. (1995). Science vocabulary load of selected secondary science textbooks. *School Science and Mathematics, 95*(5), 231–235.

Grubaugh, S.J., & Metzer, D.J. (1986). Increasing comprehension. *Special Education, 50*(7), 543–544.

Gullatt, D.E. (1987). How to help students in reading mathematics. *The Education Digest, 52*(5), 40–41.

Harmon, J.M., Hedrick, W.B., & Wood, K.D. (2005). Research on vocabulary instruction in the content areas: Implications for struggling readers. *Reading & Writing Quarterly, 21*(3), 261–280.

Harmon, J.M., Wood, K.D., & Hedrick, W.B. (2006). *Instructional strategies for teaching vocabulary in the content areas: Grades 4–12.* Columbus, OH: National Middle School Association.

Hedrick, W.B., Harmon, J.M., & Linerode, P.M. (2004). Teachers' beliefs and practices of vocabulary instruction with social studies textbooks. *Reading Horizons, 45*(2), 103–125.

Herbal-Eisenmann, B.A. (2002). Using student contributions and multiple representations to develop mathematical language. *Mathematics Teaching in the Middle School, 8*(2), 100–105.

International Reading Association & National Council of Teachers of English. (1996). *Standards for the English language arts.* Newark, DE; Urbana, IL: Authors.

Itza-Ortiz, S.F., Robello, N.S., & Zollman, D.A. (2003, March). *The vocabulary of physics and its impact on student learning.* Paper presented at the National Association for Research in Science Teaching, Philadelphia, PA.

Jackson, M.B., & Ray, P.E. (1983). Vocabulary instruction in ratio and proportion for seventh graders. *Journal for Research in Mathematics Education, 14*(5), 337–343.

Jenkins, J.R., & Dixon, R.J. (1983). Vocabulary learning. *Contemporary Educational Psychology, 8*(3), 237–260.

Jetton, T.L., & Alexander, P.A. (2004). Domains, teaching, and literacy. In T.L. Jetton & J.A. Dole (Eds.), *Adolescent literacy research and practice* (pp. 15–39). New York: Guilford.

Johnson, D.D., & Pearson, P.D. (1984). *Teaching reading vocabulary* (2nd ed.). New York: Holt, Rinehart and Winston.

King-Sears, M.E., Mercer, C.D., & Sindelar, P.T. (1992). Toward independence with keyword mnemonics: A strategy for science vocabulary instruction. *Remedial and Special Education, 13*(5), 22–33.

Konopak, B.C. (1988). Eighth graders' vocabulary learning from inconsiderate to considerate text. *Reading Research and Instruction, 27*(4), 1–14.

Konopak, B.C., & Williams, N.L. (1994). Elementary teachers' beliefs and decisions about vocabulary learning and instruction. In C.K. Kinzer & D.J. Leu (Eds.), *Multidimensonal aspect of literacy research, theory, and practice* (43rd yearbook of the National Reading Conference, pp. 485–495). Chicago, IL: National Reading Conference.

Krussel, L. (1998). Teaching the language of mathematics. *The Mathematics Teacher, 91*(5), 436–441.

Lloyd, C.V., & Contreras, N.J. (1985, December). *The role of experience in learning science vocabulary.* Paper presented at the 35th annual meeting of the National Reading Conference, San Diego, CA.

MacGregor, M., & Price, E. (1999). An exploration of aspects of language proficiency and algebra learning. *Journal for Research in Mathematics Education, 30*(4), 449–467.

Manzo, A.V., & Manzo, U.C. (1990). *Content area reading: A heuristic approach.* Columbus, OH: Merrill.

Marco, M.J., & Luzon, M.J. (1999). Procedural vocabulary: Lexical signaling of conceptual relations in discourse. *Applied Linguistics, 20*(1), 1–21.

McKeown, M.G., Beck, I.L., Omanson, R.C., & Pople, M.T. (1985). Some effects of the nature and frequency of vocabulary instruction on the knowledge and use of words. *Reading Research Quarterly, 20*(5), 522–535.

Merkley, D.M., & Jefferies, D. (2000/2001). Guidelines for implementing a graphic organizer. *The Reading Teacher, 54*(4), 350–357.

Miller, J.S. (2005). The language of science in daily conversation. *Science Activities, 42*(2), 3–4.

Miller, L.D. (1993). Making the connection with language. *The Arithmetic Teacher, 40*(6), 311–316.

Milligan, J.L., & Ruff, T.P. (1990). A linguistic approach to social studies vocabulary development. *Social Studies (Maynooth, Ireland), 81*(5), 218–220.

Monroe, E.E., & Orme, M.P. (2002). Developing mathematical vocabulary. *Preventing School Failure, 46*(3), 139–142.

Monroe, E.E., & Panchyshyn, R. (1995). Vocabulary considerations for teaching mathematics. *Childhood Education, 72*(2), 80–83.

Monroe, E.E., & Pendergrass, M.R. (1997). Effects of mathematical vocabulary instruction on fourth grade students. *Reading Improvement, 34*(3), 120–132.

Moran, M.Q. (1990). *Improving science vocabulary of sixth grade migrant students through a program of intensive direct vocabulary instruction.* M.S. Practicum, Nova University. (ERIC Document Reproduction Service No. ED325301)

Nagy, W.E. (1988). *Teaching vocabulary to improve reading comprehension.* Newark, DE: International Reading Association.

Nagy, W.E., Anderson, R.C., & Herman, P.A. (1987). Learning word meanings from context during normal reading. *American Educational Research Journal, 24*(2), 237–270.

Nagy, W.E., Herman, P.A., & Anderson, R.C. (1985). Learning words from context. *Reading Research Quarterly, 20*(2), 233–253.

Paivio, A. (1990). *Mental representations: A dual coding approach.* New York: Oxford University Press.

Robinson, P.J. (2005). Teaching key vocabulary in geography and science classrooms: An analysis of teachers' practice with particular reference to EAL pupils' learning. *Language and Education, 19*(5), 428–445.

Rubenstein, R.N. (2000). Word origins: Building communication connections. *Mathematics Teaching in the Middle School, 5*(8), 493–498.

Rubenstein, R.N., & Thompson, D.R. (2002). Understanding and supporting children's mathematical vocabulary development. *Teaching Children Mathematics, 9*(2), 107–112.

Salsbury, D.E. (2006). Comparing teacher-directed and computer-assisted instruction of elementary geographic place vocabulary. *The Journal of Geography, 105*(4), 147–154.

Scott, J.A., Jamieson-Noel, D., & Asselin, M. (2003). Vocabulary instruction throughout the day in twenty-three Canadian upper-elementary classrooms. *The Elementary School Journal, 103*(3), 269–286.

Scott, J.A., & Nagy, W.E. (2004). Developing word consciousness. In J.F. Baumann & E.J. Kame'enui (Eds.), *Vocabulary instruction: Research to practice* (pp. 201–217). New York: Guilford.

Seaver, J. (1991). *The effect of pre-reading vocabulary development strategies on sixth grade science text results.* Master's thesis, Kean College. (ERIC Document Reproduction Service No. ED329952)

Short, D. (1995, February). *The academic language of social studies: A bridge to an all-English classroom.* Paper presented at the National Association for Bilingual Education, Phoenix, AZ. (ERIC Document Reproduction Service No. ED378835)

Smith, B., & Larkins, A.G. (1990). Should place vocabulary be central to primary social studies? *Social Studies (Maynooth, Ireland), 81*(5), 221–226.

Snouffer, N.K., & Thistlethwaite, L.L. (1979, November). *The effects of the structured overview and vocabulary pre-teaching upon comprehension levels of college freshmen reading physical science and history materials.* Paper presented at the National Reading Conference, San Antonio, TX.

Stahl, S.A., & Clark, C.H. (1987). The effects of participatory expectations in classroom discussion on the learning of science vocabulary. *American Educational Research Journal, 24*(4), 541–555.

Stahl, S.A., & Kapinus, B.A. (1991). Possible sentences: Predicting word meanings to teach content area vocabulary. *The Reading Teacher, 45*(1), 36–43.

Steele, D.F. (1999). Learning mathematical language in the zone of proximal development. *Teaching Children Mathematics, 6*(1), 38–42.

Strong, R.W., Silver, H.F., Perini, M.J., & Tuculescu, G.M. (2002). *Reading for academic success: Powerful strategies for struggling, average, and advanced readers, grades 7–12.* Thousand Oaks, CA: Corwin.

Swanborn, M.S.L., & de Glopper, K. (1999). Incidental word learning while reading: A meta-analysis. *Review of Educational Research, 69*(3), 261–285.

Taba, H. (1967). *Teacher's handbook for elementary social studies.* Reading, MA: Addison Wesley.

Thompson, D.R., & Rubenstein, R.N. (2000). Learning mathematics vocabulary: Potential pitfalls and instructional strategies. *Mathematics Teacher, 93*(7), 568–574.

Tierney, R.J., & Readence, J.E. (2000). *Reading strategies and practices: A compendium* (5th ed.). Boston: Allyn & Bacon.

Tracy, D.M. (1994). Using mathematical language to enhance mathematical conceptualization. *Childhood Education, 70*(4), 221–224.

Vacca, R.T. (2002). Making a difference in adolescents' school lives: Visible and invisible aspects of content area reading. In A.E. Farstrup & S.J. Samuels (Eds.), *What research has to say about reading instruction* (3rd ed., pp. 184–204). Newark, DE: International Reading Association.

Vacca, R.T., & Vacca, J.L. (2005). *Content area reading: Literacy and learning across the curriculum* (8th ed.). Boston: Pearson Education.

Vygotsky, L.S. (1986). *Thought and language* (A. Kozulin, Trans.). Cambridge, MA: MIT Press. (Original work published 1934)

Watts, S. (1995). Vocabulary instruction during reading lessons in six classrooms. *Journal of Reading Behavior, 27*(3), 399–424.

Wood, K.D., & Taylor, D.B. (2005). *Literacy strategies across the subject areas.* Boston: Allyn & Bacon.

LITERATURE CITED

Cleary, B.P. (2006). *Rhyme and punishment: Adventures in wordplay.* Minneapolis, MN: Millbrook.

Chapter 8

More Than Merely Words: Redefining Vocabulary Learning in a Culturally and Linguistically Diverse Society

Judith A. Scott, William E. Nagy, and Susan Leigh Flinspach

Imagine this scenario: Huron, a sixth grader, sits down to work on his vocabulary assignment. On the worksheet in front of him are 15 words: *parcel, monstrous, brood, anxiety, defense, vacant, thorough, observations, leisure, remedy, cunning, numerous, lecture, tart,* and *gloomy.* His task is to identify synonyms for these words and to match them to appropriate sentences. He sighs, picks up his pencil, and starts guessing. He only recognizes one of the words from the 10-minute discussion about the words given at the beginning of the week.

Huron is unlikely to develop a good understanding of the meanings of the assigned words from this exercise. He may be able to recognize the words or identify their definitions on the Friday quiz, but he probably won't use them in his writing or understand texts containing them any better. Vocabulary tasks like Huron's are pervasive in North American schools. Words are introduced with little or no context and with no apparent connection to one another. It is assumed that students will be able to draw on their background knowledge or on brief word introductions by teachers to complete the task. Recently, there has been an outpouring of material on vocabulary learning, too much of which re-creates the scenario above for students across many different grade levels in many different schools.

Vocabulary researchers have attempted to identify the attributes of vocabulary instruction that produce reliable gains in the comprehension of text containing instructed words through meta-analysis (Stahl & Fairbanks, 1986), narrative reviews of the literature on vocabulary instruction (e.g., Graves, 1986; Mezynski, 1983), and studies contrasting specific types of instruction (e.g., McKeown, Beck, Omanson, & Pople, 1985). More recently, the National Reading Panel (National Institute of Child Health and Human Development [NICHD], 2000) singled out the following best practices:

What Research Has to Say About Vocabulary Instruction, edited by Alan E. Farstrup and S. Jay Samuels. © 2008 by the International Reading Association.

- Vocabulary should be taught both directly and indirectly.
- Multiple exposures to vocabulary items are important.
- Learning in rich contexts is valuable for vocabulary learning.
- Vocabulary tasks should be restructured when necessary.
- Vocabulary learning should entail engagement in learning tasks.
- Computer technology can be used to help teach vocabulary.
- Vocabulary can be acquired through incidental learning.
- How vocabulary is assessed and evaluated can have differential effects on instruction.
- Dependence on a single vocabulary instruction method will not result in optimal learning.

These are valuable guidelines. However, we consider them to be only a partial characterization of what is needed for effective vocabulary instruction.

Most vocabulary instruction and research have been informed by cognitive linguistics and psychology with little regard for the social or cultural aspects of the learning environment. Cognitivists focus on word learning at the level of the individual learner, studying whether particular strategies or factors help students learn a particular set of words. Sociocultural theorists, on the other hand, tend to investigate language learning in a community, looking primarily at social interactions, context, and power relationships that influence learning and use. Like Pearson (2004), we prefer a balanced approach to literacy, which calls for multiplicity and complementarity in research and in instructional methods. As he says, "The problems we face are too vexing to limit ourselves to a single methodology or epistemology" (p. 244). We believe that a blended perspective that considers both cognitive and social aspects of learning can enhance vocabulary instruction in schools. Indeed, we believe that such multiplicity is necessary as teachers deal with the complexity of teaching students who come to us from culturally and linguistically diverse backgrounds.

Our chapter draws on both sociocultural theory and on cognitive and linguistic ideas about vocabulary instruction. The sociocultural perspective on literacy learning emerges from Vygotskian theory (Vygotsky, 1978, 1934/1986; Wertsch, 1991), which sees language as a tool of the mind, working in a milieu in which action is mediated by others, inseparable from sociocultural factors. In this sense, word learning or vocabulary acquisition in academic settings is a socially negotiated phenomenon; it is part of learning a new Discourse for many students such as Huron. Gee (1996) identifies Discourses, with an uppercase *D*, as ways of being in the world that "integrate words, acts, values, beliefs, attitudes, and social identities, as well as gestures, glances, body positions, and clothes" (p. 127). From a sociocultural perspective, promoting vocabulary growth in schools is a matter of encouraging students to become part of the Discourse of the classroom community, embracing its academic words and language without rejecting the linguistic and cultural identities they bring with them from home. From the viewpoint of functional linguists and psychologists, teachers also need to recognize that word learning is a complex cognitive task and that metalinguistic attention to elements of the task is necessary (Carlisle, 2003; Halliday, 1987, 1989, 2004; Nagy & Scott, 2000; Schleppegrell, 2004). We maintain that both the sociocultural and the cognitive perspectives are necessary to facilitate academic success for students who are traditionally underserved by schools.

The divide between these theoretical frameworks and disciplinary priorities is wide, and so we narrow our discussion in this chapter to just two strands from a much larger web of ideas about effective vocabulary instruction: (1) metalinguistic awareness, that is, explicit and purposeful reflection on elements of academic language, and (2) the development of a literate identity that values academic language. We do not consider either of these strands to be novel, or even controversial. In other literacy domains, they have been discussed, examined, and implemented extensively, yet applying either of them in any depth to vocabulary instruction would result in a substantial shift from conventional practice. We intend to show how the research behind these strands can be seen as complementary and how, when they are combined, they provide a more balanced approach to vocabulary instruction. As we begin to sketch out how these two theoretical strands come into play when teaching vocabulary, we will reflect on how teachers might use this knowledge to help students like Huron.

Academic Language

A balanced approach to vocabulary instruction rests with how teachers teach academic language—the dominant Discourse in schools. Academic language draws on "a different constellation of linguistic resources from what is typical or expected in everyday conversation" (Schleppegrell, 2004, p. 9). It is a register of English that has distinctive lexical, morphological, syntactic, and stylistic features. Although people sometimes speak it in educational or other prestigious contexts, academic language is most often written. Learning to use academic language is one of the greatest challenges of schooling.

The academic register is not just talk written down. Developing mastery of academic forms of writing and speaking involves movement away from narrative forms of writing and speaking. Horowitz and Samuels (1987), for example, identify the hedges, vagueness, and redundancies typically found in conversation as defining characteristics of weak writing. An adult familiar with the academic genre of science texts may combine six propositions into one sentence containing a single clause (e.g., "Aluminum, an abundant metal with many uses, comes from bauxite, a clay-like ore" [Hunt, 1977, p. 95].). A fourth grader, on the other hand, using language more typical of a conversational register, might express the same content using several sentences (e.g., "Aluminum is metal, and it is abundant. It has many uses, and it comes from bauxite. Bauxite is an ore and looks like clay" [Hunt, 1977, p. 95].). Learning to write and read successfully in the academic register requires an understanding of how information can be packed into each clause, how logical relationships are presented, and how to use an expanded vocabulary to convey meaning (Fang, 2008). Although academic language can easily become unnecessarily obscure, at its best it allows for a compact expression of complex ideas.

Word choice is a critical element of academic language. Success in conversation depends heavily on attention to nonlinguistic clues—not just intonation, gesture, and facial expression, but even more on sensitivity to what one knows about the attitudes, beliefs, and purposes of one's interlocutors. In school texts, on the other hand, the nonlinguistic clues available in conversation are absent, and the reader is reliant on the language of the text itself. In written language, and in academic and literate language in particular, word choice plays a far more important role than it does in conversation. Precise choice of words is perhaps the single most powerful tool available to the writer. For students to be motivated to learn vocabulary in school, they need to have some sense of the power that precise word choice offers.

In academic circles, including classrooms, academic language has higher status than other English registers. Yet treating the distinction between academic language and other registers primarily as a matter of power and prestige is missing an important dimension. A conversational register and the academic register differ in the functions for which they are suited. A form of conversational English is better suited for carrying on conversations, and academic language is better suited for communicating certain types of information to a nonpresent audience or, as in lectures, to audiences where opportunity for immediate feedback is limited. Thus academic language is not a substitute for other varieties of English; academic language is a form that needs to be added to students' already formidable linguistic repertoires.

The Metalinguistic Nature of Learning Academic Language

Metalinguistic awareness is the ability to reflect on and manipulate features of language (Tunmer, Nesdale, & Wright, 1987). Although some word learning, especially in early childhood, may occur without reflection, word learning in school is fundamentally a metalinguistic task, requiring students to reflect on various aspects of language and text (Nagy, 2007; Nagy & Scott, 2000).

Metalinguistic awareness is a central component of word consciousness, and researchers generally agree that word consciousness is key to promoting students' vocabulary growth (Anderson & Nagy, 1992; Blachowicz & Fisher, 2006; Graves &Watts-Taffe, 2002; Johnson, von Hoff Johnson, & Schlichting, 2004). Word consciousness is an interest in and awareness of words. Graves and Watts-Taffe (2002) explain:

> Students who are word conscious are aware of the words around them— those they read and hear and those they write and speak. This awareness involves an appreciation of the power of words, an understanding of why certain words are used instead of others, a sense of the words that could be used in place of those selected by a writer or speaker, and cognizance of first encounters with new words. It involves an interest in learning and using new words and becoming more skillful and precise in word usage. (p. 144)

One of the ways that word consciousness contributes to vocabulary learning is by helping students pay attention to words they encounter within the community of the classroom and during their independent reading. Though vocabulary instruction is important, much vocabulary growth occurs as students gradually gain more information about words through repeatedly encountering them in context (Sternberg, 1987).

One way of fostering word consciousness is calling students' attention to specific instances of the effective use of language. Because words are around us all the time, asking students to look closely at words is akin to asking a fish to examine water. Stepping back from the flow of language to look closely at words is a foreign concept to many students. The practice of noticing allows students to become aware of words in their environment on a different level. Scott, Skobel, and Wells (2008) compared this type of word awareness to music or art appreciation. For example, it is easy to enjoy good music without metacognitive reflection on the elements involved. However, when listeners have knowledge about how the elements have been combined by the musician to create a song, they develop a deeper understanding and appreciation of the composition. An awareness of talk and of text that enables a parallel deeper understanding and appreciation of words is central to word consciousness.

Teachers help students become aware of what is worth noticing about words. They can guide students' exploration of how published authors use words effectively to convey their ideas or visual images. In particular, teachers can make a practice of noting and expressing their appreciation of well-crafted sentences or phrases when reading to and with students. Johnston (2004) quoted a teacher who asked students to "write down a line you wish you had written" (p. 16). Scott et al. (2008) called attention to Gifts of Words, phrases that express an idea exquisitely. They also suggested that students catch words (or record them) in a word-catcher mitt, share the words with one another, and make the words available to scaffold each other's writing.

Providing opportunities to focus on word choice within social situations where there is an authentic task, such as writing for a real audience or giving directions, helps students see the value of using precise language. One of us observed a teacher who asked her first-grade students to write down all the rules and equipment necessary to play their favorite playground games, for example, foursquare. She warned them that when they got to the playground, they would be held to what they had written: "If you don't write down that we should bring a ball, you won't get to use a ball." The intent was to help the students understand the need to be explicit—one of the key ways that academic language can differ from conversation. Students benefit from authentic tasks that help them hone their metalinguistic awareness.

To successfully read academic texts, students also need to have strategies for dealing with new words—and for dealing with familiar words used in unfamiliar ways. No matter how large their reading vocabularies, students will routinely encounter words that they have never seen before in print. Even the most conservative estimates of students' word knowledge suggest that average students add at least 1,000 words per year to their reading vocabularies (Anglin, 2000; Goulden, Nation, & Read, 1990). Students starting with smaller-than-average vocabularies need to learn words at an even greater rate to catch up with their peers.

One important goal of vocabulary instruction, therefore, must be to increase students' rate of vocabulary growth. For instruction in word strategies to be as effective as possible, two kinds of reflectiveness must be cultivated in students. First, students must reflect on the language of the text—with more intensity and in more detail than usual. Second, they must reflect on the process of word learning, which requires the flexible orchestration of information from multiple sources (Berninger & Nagy, 2008). To put it in slightly different terms, both strategic knowledge (What do I do when I come across a word I don't know, and how do I integrate the various types of information that may be available?) and metalinguistic awareness (What aspects of language and text structure do I need to be aware of to learn what this word means?) are fundamental aspects of word learning. We'll look next at some specific types of metalinguistic awareness that contribute to independent word learning, and what it means for students to be able to apply this awareness strategically.

Metalinguistic Word-Learning Strategies

Morphological awareness. Morphological awareness is the ability to reflect on and manipulate meaningful subparts of words. Although young children can manipulate some aspects of the morphological structure of words, for example, creating novel compounds and suffixed words (Clark, 1982), much of children's knowledge of morphology develops in the mid-elementary grades and later (Anglin, 2000; Bear, Invernizzi, Templeton, & Johnston, 2008; Nunes, Bryant, & Bindman, 1997) as they come into contact with the increasingly complex language of school texts. There are substantial individual differences in students' abilities to use such information (Carlisle, 2000, 2003; Freyd & Baron, 1982; Tyler & Nagy, 1989, 1990), and morphological awareness has been found to be highly correlated with both vocabulary knowledge and with reading comprehension (Nagy, Berninger, & Abbott, 2006; Nagy, Berninger, Abbott, Vaughan, & Vermeulen, 2003).

The majority of new words that students encounter can be broken into meaningful subparts (prefixes, roots, and suffixes) that give information about the meaning of the word (Nagy & Anderson, 1984). However there

are also countless examples of cases in which word parts are uninforma-
tive and even misleading—for example, *casualty* has nothing to do with
being casual. Thousands of websites repeat the question "Why do we
drive on a parkway and park on a driveway?" Students need to recognize
that word parts are usually helpful, but not universally so.

In many cases, the connection between the word parts and the meaning of the whole word may be clear enough once it has been explained,
but it might not be helpful to a person encountering a word for the first
time. Knowing that the Latin root *struct* means "to build" is unlikely to
help a reader unfamiliar with the word *obstruct* infer its meaning; but if
one is told that the Latin parts of the word mean "to build against," this
might serve as a helpful mnemonic.

There are numerous resources providing detailed information about
teaching word parts (e.g., Bear et al., 2008; Henry, 2003; Nunes & Bryant,
2006). We recommend that instruction in word parts include two facets
that cannot always be done at the same time: first, modeling and applying the use of word parts as a strategy while reading, and second, gaining a better understanding of how word parts work. The first type of
instruction would be most likely to take place in the context of reading
a text, where the main purpose is comprehension and learning about
word parts is a secondary goal. The other type of instruction would be
more likely to take place apart from reading a specific text, when there
was time to explore the creative potential of word parts (How many
words can you make by adding prefixes and suffixes to the word *act*?),
to compare and contrast different possible meanings of word parts (*un-
happy* versus *untie*), and to consider multiple examples of a word part
(How many words can you think of that end in -*ness*? What do they have
in common?).

Context and syntactic awareness. If, as is widely believed, much of students' vocabulary growth comes from encountering words repeatedly in
context while reading, it would follow that improving their ability to use
context could produce gains in vocabulary. Though long-term effects of
instruction in using context have not been demonstrated, a number of
studies have shown that students can be taught to be more effective in
using context (Fukkink & de Glopper, 1998).

Numerous studies have shown that the ability to infer the meanings of
words from context is highly related to reading ability (McKeown, 1985;
Sternberg & Powell, 1983; van Daalen-Kapteijns & Elshout Mohr, 1981).
To some extent, the effect of reading ability can be traced to the fact that

when trying to infer the meaning of a new word, less-able readers are less likely to know the meanings of the other words that occur in the context (Shefelbine, 1990). However there are also great individual differences in students' understanding of how the context constrains the meaning of a new word (McKeown, 1985; Goerss, Beck, & McKeown, 1999).

The metalinguistic skill most directly related to effective use of context is syntactic awareness, the ability to reflect on the structure of sentences. Syntactic awareness is not formal knowledge of grammar, but rather sensitivity to how words are combined. It includes knowing that a particular word is, for instance, a noun or a verb by its position within a sentence. Performance on cloze tasks—trying to decide what word would fit in a blank replacing the word originally in the text—depends on syntactic awareness (Lesaux, Rupp, & Siegel, 2007).

As with morphological awareness, there are two different instructional situations in which students could be helped to develop the sensitivity to sentence structure necessary to make effective use of context. Obviously it is essential that teachers model the use of context for students and give students scaffolded experiences in using context while reading texts. However research indicates that some students would benefit from more intensive and specific attention to how a text constrains the possible meanings of new words through the use of activities specifically tailored to this goal (Goerss et al., 1999). Modeling and discussing hypotheses for words in cloze tasks can help students reflect on the use of context to constrain their guesses.

Dictionary use. The dictionary is a traditional tool for learning new words. Teachers often teach alphabetization and use of guidewords to locate a definition in a dictionary. Aside from the question of whether these skills are still necessary in light of the availability of electronic dictionaries, it is important to recognize that these skills are insufficient for effective dictionary use. It is when the student has located the definition of a word that the hardest work begins—integrating the information in the definition with the information in the text containing the word in question.

This task is not an easy one for upper elementary-grade students (Scott & Nagy, 1997). The metalinguistic demands of using a dictionary are considerable. The learner must have a concept of what constitutes a possible word meaning (Nagy & Scott, 1990). The learner must also have some familiarity with the conventions of dictionaries—knowledge that is still developing in elementary school (Watson, 1985; Watson & Olson,

1987) and beyond. In addition, the working memory demands of the task are enough to make it challenging (Miller & Gildea, 1987). Students must hold in mind both the definition of the new word and the context in which it occurs, and if multiple definitions are offered, as is often the case, their work is even more complicated. To integrate the information provided by a definition with the text in which the new word occurs, the learner must also have the metalinguistic abilities associated with effective use of context.

It is likely that both the importance and difficulties of dictionary use are widely underestimated. The advent of online dictionaries may reduce or remove the need to learn some of the mechanics of dictionary use, but the difficulty of taking the information provided to construct a meaning for the text containing the new word still remains. We believe that the use of definitions as a tool for understanding text containing unfamiliar words should be treated as an essential but difficult cognitive strategy. It is important, therefore, that teachers apply what is known about effective strategy instruction to the teaching of dictionary use—a point we will return to shortly.

Learning about polysemy. For most commonly used words, polysemy (multiple meanings) is the norm. Examination of any dictionary of substantial size reveals that words with just one meaning, though plentiful, are almost always low-frequency technical terms or words derived from more familiar words by affixes or compounding. Since the most common words in the language are those with the greatest number of meanings, most students already have, in principle, the tacit ability to cope with polysemous words. Nevertheless multiple meanings can pose a serious problem for learners.

Given their pervasiveness, multiple meanings, figurative language, and idioms are essential to developing the metalinguistic foundations necessary for proficient word learning and reading. Perhaps the most fundamental instructional step for developing students' ability to cope with multiple meanings is calling their attention to words used with figurative or otherwise nonprimary meanings.

Carlo et al. (2004) included work on polysemy in their vocabulary intervention that was found to have a variety of benefits both for English learners and for students who spoke only English. Although the design of the study did not make it possible to determine the effectiveness of teaching about polysemy, their intervention offers an example of how polysemy can be addressed as one component of a multifaceted approach to promoting vocabulary growth.

Strategic Application of Metalinguistic Awareness

Word-learning strategies, in addition to being important for students to learn, also pose some serious metacognitive difficulties. Morphological awareness can be deceptive; *shiftless* does not mean "unchangeable" or "having an automatic transmission." Context and syntactic structure do not always supply helpful information about the meaning of a new word (Beck, McKeown, & McCaslin, 1983). Learners must simultaneously generate hypotheses about the possible meanings of new words based on the word-learning strategies they know and evaluate the plausibility of these hypotheses.

Because of the limitations of each potential source of information about a new word, learners must be able to apply word-learning strategies in combination. The meaning a student derives from word parts must be tested against context. Likewise if a dictionary supplies multiple definitions for a word—as is usually the case—the learner must decide on the basis of context which of these meanings fits. Skills related to polysemy are also required in using word parts because in many cases the addition of a prefix or suffix requires students to focus on a specific meaning of a word, often a less frequent one. For example, *divisive* builds on the nonmathematical, rather than the mathematical, sense of *divide*; *considerate* focuses on a very specific sense of *consider*.

Because word-learning strategies supply partial information about the meaning of a new word, students must learn to be flexible and reflective in their use. When students encounter an unfamiliar word in a text, the question is not whether they can come up with a definition for that word, but whether they know enough to continue reading with an adequate level of comprehension. Thus word-learning strategies must be coordinated with a sophisticated level of comprehension monitoring.

Therefore, word-learning strategies cannot be treated as simple, mechanical skills (e.g., when you come to an unfamiliar word, reread the sentence and see if you can find a context clue, or if you come across a new word, see if it contains any familiar parts that might give a clue to its meaning). Such skills are part of what a proficient word learner knows, but proficient word learning requires far more: the integration of multiple sources of information, the evaluation of their plausibility, and the orchestration of word-learning strategies with comprehension monitoring and other higher level skills required to construct a coherent meaning from a text. In other words, word learning needs to be taught as a set of complex metacognitive and metalinguistic strategies, not as a set of skills.

A good deal is already known about what kind of instruction is necessary to foster the development of metacognitive strategies—explicit explanation of why, when, and how to use a strategy; modeling of the strategy; gradual transfer of responsibility to students; and prompting and encouraging application of the strategy across the curriculum (Pearson & Gallagher, 1983). Word-learning strategies are in fact complex and demanding cognitive strategies. Teaching them well means that teachers apply the principles of effective strategy instruction thoroughly.

A crucial component of strategy instruction is the gradual transfer of responsibility for using the strategy to the students. We would like to emphasize the importance of the word *gradual*, which implies that substantial scaffolding be available and not be removed too quickly. In the teaching of any word-learning strategy, whether it involves the use of dictionaries, context, or word parts, there should be opportunities for scaffolded practice in which students have opportunities to receive support from one another and from the teacher. Working together may help students deal with the complexity of integrating, evaluating, and orchestrating the information at hand to develop plausible hypotheses for new words. Through careful instruction about word-learning strategies and the cultivation of students' word consciousness, teachers can guide students toward the challenging goal of becoming strategic, independent word learners.

The Social Nature of Learning Academic Language

Teaching the metalinguistic knowledge and skills needed to master academic language is one strand of successful vocabulary instruction, but one that unfolds in the sociocultural environment of classrooms and schools. All teaching and most learning are social activities set in particular cultural contexts. We contend that vocabulary instruction should teach metalinguistic strategies for learning words in contexts that build on the social and cultural lives of students.

Language Acquisition Through Social Relationships

Verbal activities, including word learning, are socially organized and embedded within cultural systems of meaning. Words are not learned in isolation but in the process of acquiring knowledge of the language practices within particular sociolinguistic environments (Schieffelin & Ochs, 1986). In general, "children come to share the world view [and social practices] of their community through the arrangements and interactions in which they are involved, whether or not such arrangements and interactions are intended to instruct them" (Rogoff, 1990, p. 98).

Much of children's initial language learning evolves from the caregivers in their society, most often their mothers, during interactions in which children develop an understanding of the communities of practice in which they live. However, the normative style of mother–child conversations varies across sociocultural groups and from situation to situation (Heath, 1983; Hoff-Ginsberg, 1991; Schieffelin & Ochs, 1986). In these conversations, social cues and social intent have been found to influence word learning in young children (Bloom, 2000; Tomasello & Farrar, 1986). Tomasello and his colleagues (Tomasello & Farrar, 1986; Tomasello & Todd, 1983) provided some of the first indications that the way mothers interacted with their young children influenced vocabulary growth. When mothers' conversations with their children followed and extended the child's interest and attention, there was a positive effect on vocabulary growth. When mothers took a more directive approach, without consideration of the child's focus of attention, word learning suffered (Tomasello & Farrar, 1986). Not surprisingly, the type of social situation in which conversations occur influences both the type and form of conversations (Fivush, Haden, & Reese, 2006; Hoff-Ginsberg, 1991). Mothers tend to keep to a minimum the variety of words used as a child gets dressed, to use mostly directive statements during toy play, and to talk more with their children using a variety of words with extended discourse when they read together (Hoff-Ginsberg, 1991).

The function of interpersonal communication with children is tied to particular intents or purposes within particular sociocultural frameworks. For instance, during mealtime conversations, the frequency, length, and kind of narratives and explanations found among families vary across cultures, across language groups, and as a function of social class (Snow & Beals, 2006). While narratives told at American dinner tables recount events that are out of the ordinary (e.g., Josh threw up today), narratives in Norwegian homes report everyday events (e.g., Sara wore a blue sweater). Israeli conversations often feature reminiscing, while Americans tend toward explanations of events. What warrants the conversational floor is specific to each culture (Snow & Beals, 2006).

Extending this to classrooms, Wilkinson and Silliman (2000) state, "to a great extent, the language used by teachers and students in classrooms determines what is learned and how learning takes place" (p. 337). What counts as knowledge and appropriate discourse in any classroom is shaped, to a great extent, by the questions teachers ask, their response to students, and the type of dialogue allowed within the class (Applebee, 1996; Nystrand, 2006). However, within the discourse frame of classrooms, students rarely engage in the activities that could improve vocabulary learning (Scott, Jamieson-Noel, & Asselin, 2003; Watts-Taffe, 1995). Scott et al. (2003) found that, on average, 6% of school time was devoted to the development of vocabulary knowledge in sixth-grade classrooms, with only 1.4% devoted to vocabulary development in subjects (math, science, art, music, social studies) other than language arts. In their observation of 61 preschool teachers for over 500 minutes, Dickinson, McCabe, and Clark-Chiarelli (2004) found that intentional talk about words never occurred in 90% of the classrooms.

All language learning—including mastery of academic language—is situational and interpersonal. To learn vocabulary, students must have opportunities to read it, hear it, and use it to communicate with others. Context and communicative intent play a central role in vocabulary instruction.

Identity and Academic Language

Students quickly become aware of the differences between academic language and other language registers with which they are likely to be far more familiar. Their motivation to learn the vocabulary of academic English depends, in part, on their home literacy practices, their introduction to academic language at school, and the attitude they have toward these differences. This section discusses the literature that lays the foundation for two conclusions about students who want to learn the words of academic English. First, students who feel that the literate identities they are already forming in their homes and communities are respected and reinforced at school are ready to expand on those identities; and second, students need to see themselves as full participants in the classroom community in which academic language functions as a powerful tool (Dutro, Kazemi, & Balf, 2005; Gee, 2004).

Students' identities as readers or as word learners depend on the literacy practices of the communities with which they identify. Gee argued that the more aligned a child's home literacy experiences are with school experiences (teacher-type questioning and social interactions about texts, familiarity with academic language, similar literacy events), the easier it is for the child to maintain and nurture a literate identity at school.

Thus white, middle class children, many of whom have alignment in their home-school language and literacy experiences, tend to enter the classroom with an advantage (Gee 2001, 2004). There is ample evidence that the benefits of this alignment extend to familiarity with words found in an academic environment (Chall, Jacobs, & Baldwin, 1990; Hart & Risley, 1995; White, Graves, & Slater, 1990).

What teachers believe and do when their students lack the benefits of this alignment is critical to their students' mastery of vocabulary and of all elements of academic language. The literature on the social foundations of education documents a long and continuing history of educators whose view of students as having deficits in academic English leads to instruction that devalues, rather than maintains and builds on, the students' language and literacy practices from home and community (see Erickson, 1987; Heath, 1983; and Michaels & Collins, 1984, for early examples, and Davidson, 1996; Hermes & Uran, 2006; Lee & Oxelson, 2006; and Valdés, 1998, for more recent discussions). Literacy scholars from Heath (1983) to Gee (2004) have underscored that students who enter school with little knowledge of academic language are still likely to have a literate identity forged at home and that it discriminates against the child when teachers fail to respect this identity. Purcell-Gates, Jacobson, and Degener (2004) noted that literacy instruction that honors and builds on the student's existing literacy experiences is more successful:

> There is no reason to continue to believe that all children or adult literacy learners will enter the classroom door with the same notions of what literacy is, what and who it is for, who engages with it, where, and when. What little data we have to date suggest that print literacy instruction that builds on the literacy worlds and practices of the learners stands a much better chance of succeeding than that which does not. (p. 163)

Multicultural approaches enable teachers to address home and community literacy practices in ways that can enrich traditional teaching or even disrupt the hegemony of academic language in classrooms (Banks, 2001; Sleeter & Grant, 2007). In one multicultural approach, funds of knowledge (González, Moll, & Amanti, 2005; Moll, Amanti, Neff, & González, 1992), teachers assume the role of researcher to learn about students' literacy worlds firsthand. Following a series of home research visits, for instance, one elementary teacher designed an interdisciplinary unit around candy that included candy labels in Spanish and in English as texts and drew on the candy-making expertise of one mother (Moll et al., 1992). Because students begin to form literate identities in the home and community, incorporating vocabulary, texts, and interlocutors from those domains into the classroom reinforces students' literate selves. Teachers who recognize and value students' exposure to diverse literacy experiences draw on such resources to assist students with the acquisition of academic language and literacy.

Even for many white, middle class children, schooling presents a situation in which they must master new forms of language, new types of texts, and new types of interactions around disciplinary knowledge. Sociocultural theorists regard academic language as a resource residing in the academic or classroom community rather than being the property of individual learners (Barton & Hamilton, 2000; Gee, 2001). Students who want to identify as members of the academic community learn academic language to communicate with other community members. They learn the vocabulary, along with the grammar and stylistic elements of the academic register, through social interactions, that is, through oral and written communication with others (Purcell-Gates, Duke, & Martineau, 2007; Purcell-Gates et al., 2004). Students who do not identify with the classroom and its society (Gallas, 1992), or who find that academic language does not serve their communicative needs (Au, 1993, 1998; McCarthey, 2001) have little reason to become proficient in academic language.

Literacy is a social practice, so students learn academic vocabulary through social interactions as members of a learning community. Teachers who develop a community of learners that is inclusive and that regularly engages students in conversations and written exchanges about new words and texts help students' literate identities expand. They facilitate students' socialization into academic language learning (Gee, 2001). To do this, they embrace students' home speech and literacy practices, de-center their own role, and rely on pair or small-group activities, peer-led discussions, and literature circles to create social interactions around texts and words. Gallas (1992) presents a powerful example of an entire class that, over the course of a year of sharing stories, became a learning community that was appreciative of multiple literacies. A key figure in Gallas's account was an African American girl, Jiana, whose academic identity and enthusiasm for narratives fluctuated with her alignment with the classroom community. After four months of sharing haltingly about small objects and reacting to other students' stories, Jiana's level of learning and sense of belonging led her to begin relating personal narratives to the class. She then introduced fictional storytelling at sharing time but was rebuked by the teacher for her inappropriate story. The next month, following a public apology by the teacher and a class decision to include fictional stories in sharing time, Jiana took the lead in developing fantasy narratives that used multiple dramatic techniques and continually reinforced community bonds by incorporating other students, with their permission, as characters in her stories. Through sharing time structured this way, Jiana gained greater narrative fluency, exercised her growing vocabulary, and built a respected place in the classroom community. Like Jiana, students' desire to belong to a classroom community of learners can support their identification with academic language and literacy.

These types of literacy practices can heighten student motivation, participation rates, and academic achievement (Nieto, 2002; Rueda & Moll, 1994). Teachers who foster an inclusive academic word-learning community in their classrooms and who incorporate language and literacy practices from the home and community into literacy instruction are changing norms and reallocating power to reaffirm underserved students' literate identities.

Teaching Academic Language Through a Blended Approach

What would practice that blends the cognitive or metalinguistic and the sociocultural strands of learning academic vocabulary look like? How can teachers develop instruction that draws on both? We begin this discussion by reconceptualizing Huron's experience in the classroom:

> Huron, a sixth grader, takes out his writing assignment. As he begins to write a narrative about his cousin arriving from Mexico, he pulls out his word catcher booklet, where he has stored words and phrases that help him express his ideas. When he finishes his first draft, he goes with a friend to a "shades of meaning" tree on a bulletin board to look for more powerful language for their stories. Together they find the word *monstrous* on a leaf with other words for *BIG* and they find *gloomy* for *SAD*. They discuss whether or not these words would fit into the narrative and whether *monstrous* is related to *el monstruo* in Spanish. When he completes his narrative, Huron reads it aloud to the class, and his classmates ask questions about both his cousin and his writing.

Huron's vocabulary learning in this scenario differs radically from his experience at the start of the chapter. In this scenario, Huron sees himself as a writer who has something interesting to say; he has confidence that other classmates will help him prepare his piece and will want to hear what he has to say. The assignment has personal meaning for him; he does not perceive it as busywork. He is engaged and excited. He is word conscious and understands that word choice is a tool to communicate ideas. He has sources of support for making more sophisticated word choices in his writing: the word catcher, the shades of meaning tree, and the discussions with his classmate (Scott et al., 2008). The words he is learning are in context, and he is being asked to draw on his personal background knowledge to complete the task.

Huron's teacher uses complementary epistemologies to engage students in activities that foster their identities as authors, their familiarity with academic language, their metalinguistic awareness, and their explicit and purposeful attention to words. These types of activities are not mutually exclusive. The work of Beck and her colleagues (e.g., Beck, Perfetti, & McKeown, 1982; McKeown et al., 1985) and the meta-analysis of vocabulary instructional studies by Stahl and Fairbanks (1986) show that teaching children the definitions of words is not enough.

To have an impact on reading comprehension, vocabulary instruction must include (among other things) tasks that cause depth of processing—mental effort and creativity and the establishment of connections between new and familiar information (Stahl, 1986; Stahl & Fairbanks, 1986). This depth of processing is most likely to be achieved in tasks that students experience as authentic. And researchers as diverse as Delpit (1995) and the New London Group (1996) agree that authenticity—actual reading and writing for real audiences and real purposes—is critical.

The results of a recent study by Purcell-Gates, Duke, and Martineau (2007) empirically support the theoretical claim that language forms are best learned in the context of authentic use. They identified authentic reading and writing activities along a continuum according to the purpose or function of the literacy activity and the nature of the text being read or written. An authentic purpose or function was defined as one that serves a social communicative purpose, such as reading for information that one wants or needs to know or writing to provide information for others. This was contrasted with school-only tasks such as completing worksheets, spelling lists, or lists of sentences to punctuate, which are used primarily for the purpose of learning or improving reading and writing skills. They found that students in classrooms that contained both a high degree of authenticity and a high degree of explicit instruction grew in their ability to comprehend and write science texts at a faster rate than students in other classrooms. When students were exposed to highly explicit instruction without a context of authenticity, they learned at a much slower rate (Purcell-Gates, Duke, & Martineau, 2007). Although this study did not look specifically at vocabulary learning, we believe that it adds to a growing understanding regarding the importance of authenticity in considering the type of tasks we give students in schools.

Knowledge about academic vocabulary is likely to remain inert unless a student adopts a literate identity in which academic vocabulary is an essential aspect of the community of practice in the classroom. Classroom activities that draw on students' experiences and culture, such as writing personal narratives, giving directions for a heritage game, or creating a report that will be put in the classroom library, are not new or unusual. However, such activities can help children embrace academic literacy and acquire fluency in the language of schooling. In the process of acquiring a literate identity inclusive of academic language, we think it is important to help students learn and understand some of the forms and functions of the academic register. Helping students become conscious of words through discussion and scaffolding will expand students' ability to use academic discourse on their own.

Activities such as the creation of "where I'm from" poems (Christensen, 1998) ask students to share elements of their lives (e.g., their favorite food, what they see outside their window) and to describe them using rich and vivid language. These are then formatted into poetic images such as the one that follows, created by a sixth grader:

> I am from cartoons on the T.V.
> rap music on the radio
> lamps hanging by chains
> and the soft brown couch in the living room.
> I am from a bike with no wheels in the backyard,
> The climbing tree reaching up to the sky,
> Beautiful red flowers
> And a park filled with graffiti.
> I am from spicy tacos,
> A sandía with chile and limón
> From tortas with jamón, queso, and jalapeños.

I am from the black shoe box in the closet where
I keep my money and old pictures of me.

—Julio (Scott et al., 2008, p. 125)

Johnston (2004) gives examples of teacher talk that support students' expansion of literate identities into the academic world. Using phrases like "What a talented poet you are," "What are you doing as a writer today?" and "As scientists, how do you think we should handle this?" help to frame students' identities, at least temporarily, as poets, writers, and scientists. It helps them assume the role and try on the mantle.

We have described a number of reasons why students need to be reflective about word learning, about language, and about linguistic differences. We want students to construct a literate identity that will facilitate their understanding of how words have power and can be used for their own communication. Talking about language is itself a means of promoting vocabulary growth (Dickinson & Smith, 1994). Beyond that, however, we must add that reflection on language is an intrinsically valuable activity. Understanding how language is used to create and convey meaning is essential for appreciation of literature, for critical reading, and for resistance to manipulative language.

Learning to pay attention to the metalinguistic demands of academic language is not simple and can be in conflict with a student's other identities. Conversations that reflect on language variation in the classroom—that talk openly about differences between the dialects, registers, and languages that students know—can help students come to regard the acquisition of academic language as an important tool that they add to their linguistic competencies without compromising their home languages and conversational registers. Likewise, playful use of language—one aspect of being reflective about language—makes it easier to deal with linguistic phenomena that are often emotionally loaded.

Reflection on language differences offers other benefits as well. Bilingualism is often associated with higher levels of metalinguistic awareness (Bialystok, 1988; Ransdell, Barbier, & Niit, 2006), which is in turn associated with an advantage in the acquisition of literacy (Bialystok, 2007). Being bilingual may not guarantee heightened metalinguistic awareness, but appropriate classroom discussion of linguistic differences is likely to increase the cognitive and metalinguistic advantages associated with bilingualism.

One specific type of metalinguistic awareness associated with bilingualism is cognate awareness. Students whose first language is Spanish have a powerful resource for vocabulary learning to the extent that they are aware of the relationships between everyday Spanish words and academic English vocabulary. Again the advantages of bilingualism (or bidialectalism) may depend, not just on awareness of differences, but also on attitudes toward these differences. Jiménez, García, and Pearson (1996), examining the reading strategies of more successful and less successful bilingual readers, found that the more successful readers saw their two languages as related. These students also made use of comprehension strategies such as translation that are uniquely available to bilinguals.

Teachers who blend metalinguistic awareness, word consciousness, and word-learning strategies with the development of students' identities are facilitating their students' abilities to negotiate the complex world of academic language. While this type of teaching is important for all students, it is particularly important for students who are traditionally underserved by schools. This type of teaching may be a radical shift from traditional vocabulary instruction, but we feel it holds promise for the students from culturally and linguistically diverse backgrounds that populate our schools.

Conclusions

In this chapter, we have tried to cover some areas of research that are not typically included in discussions concerning vocabulary learning. Traditional vocabulary instruction does not take the identities of students or metalinguistic factors into account. Issues of why anyone would want to know these words, how you could use them appropriately to communicate, or how an academic register is different from other types of communication are often ignored. The integration of these perspectives offers teachers a more balanced approach to vocabulary instruction.

Our basic premise is that words are tools for communication. The value of having a large vocabulary comes, in part, from the ability to communicate across different discourse communities, both understanding what people are trying to communicate and being able to express yourself.

Imagine students completing a unit on hammers in which they learn the name for parts of hammers and learn to distinguish between different kinds of hammers. They even draw pictures of hammers and learn to sing hammer songs, accompanied with hammer-like hand motions. But, what happens if they are asked to actually use a hammer? They may be able to identify and distinguish a ball pein hammer from a sledgehammer on a test, but would they be comfortable using a ball pein hammer to shape metal?

Becoming a carpenter who can distinguish when, where, and why to use particular tools effectively usually occurs in an apprenticeship setting. More experienced others scaffold the use of the tools with an authentic goal in mind. We think this is a good model for word learning. Children become members of an academic Discourse community by expanding their literate identities to include academic language and appropriate word use through scaffolded apprenticeships in classrooms. When we encourage students to learn academic vocabulary, we are asking many of them to master a new form of language. Presenting words alone, without having nurtured a classroom of students who want to learn to use them, is unlikely to produce much vocabulary growth. There are different levels of knowledge and awareness in all fields. Attention to both individual and interpersonal dimensions of vocabulary learning can help students learn to use academic language to communicate within and across Discourse communities.

Questions for Discussion

1. Arrange to observe a vocabulary lesson in a local school and classroom. Note the type of activities that are used to develop vocabulary knowledge. Is there a metalinguistic or metacognitive focus to learning about words? What is the teacher doing to foster students' identities as people who are interested in and aware of the academic register? Should or could this instruction change to implement the ideas in this chapter?

2. Look at textbooks or basals used in local schools or classrooms. Examine the way that new vocabulary words are introduced in these materials. Critique two lessons in terms of the arguments presented in this chapter. Is word learning considered a complex cognitive strategy? Is word consciousness being developed? Will students' identities as people who are interested in and aware of the academic register be developed as a result of these lessons?

3. Think about students you are teaching or have taught in the past. Identify someone who shows evidence of either accepting or rejecting an identity as someone who values the academic register

as a form of communication. Describe the characteristics that lead you to believe that they are accepting or rejecting that identity. Brainstorm ways to encourage the development of an identity that values word learning in your classroom.

4. Develop a plan to implement at least one idea from this chapter into your own teaching. Identify authentic activities you will introduce to promote vocabulary learning or word consciousness, or to foster your students' development of identities that value the type of word learning found in schools. Explain how this plan fits in with the rest of your language arts program. Explain how this plan helps develop word learning across the curriculum.

NOTE

This paper was funded, in part, by IES Reading/Writing Education Research Grant #R305G060140 (U.S. Dept. of Ed.), FY2006–2009. This paper is the sole responsibility of the authors and does not necessarily reflect the opinions of the U.S. Dept. of Education. However, we gratefully acknowledge their support. We would like to thank Brad Olsen for his insightful and helpful comments as he read drafts of this paper.

REFERENCES

Anderson, R.C., & Nagy, W.E. (1992). The vocabulary conundrum. *American Educator, 16*(4), 14–18, 44–47.

Anglin, J.M. (2000). *Vocabulary development: A morphological analysis.* Boston: Blackwell. (Original work published in 1993)

Applebee, A. (1996). *Curriculum as conversation: Transforming traditions of teaching and learning.* Chicago: University of Chicago Press.

Au, K.H. (1993). *Literacy instruction in multicultural settings.* Fort Worth, TX: Harcourt Brace.

Au, K.H. (1998). Social constructionism and the school literacy learning of students of diverse backgrounds. *Journal of Literacy Research, 30*(2), 297–319.

Banks, J.A. (2001). Multicultural education: Historical development, dimensions, and practice. In J.A. Banks & C.A.M. Banks (Eds.), *Handbook of research on multicultural education* (pp. 3–24). San Francisco: Jossey-Bass.

Barton, D., & Hamilton, M. (2000). Literacy practices. In D. Barton, M. Hamilton, & R. Ivanic (Eds.), *Situated literacies: Reading and writing in context* (pp. 7–15). London: Routledge.

Bear, D.R., Invernizzi, M., Templeton, S., & Johnston, F. (2008). *Words their way: Word study for phonics, vocabulary, and spelling instruction* (4th ed.). Upper Saddle River, NJ: Merrill.

Beck, I.L., McKeown, M.G., & McCaslin, E.S. (1983). Vocabulary development: All contexts are not created equal. *The Elementary School Journal, 83*(3), 177–181.

Beck, I.L., Perfetti, C.A., & McKeown, M.G. (1982). Effects of long-term vocabulary instruction on lexical access and reading comprehension. *Journal of Educational Psychology, 74*(4), 506–521.

Berninger, V.W., & Nagy, W.E. (2008). Flexibility in word reading: Multiple levels of representations, complex mappings, partial similarities, and cross-modality connections. In K. Cartwright (Ed.), *Flexibility in literacy processes and instructional practice: Implications of developing representational ability for literacy teaching and learning* (pp. 114–141). New York: Guilford.

Bialystok, E. (1988). Levels of bilingualism and levels of linguistic awareness. *Developmental Psychology, 24*(4), 560–567.

Bialystok, E. (2007). Acquisition of literacy in bilingual children: A framework for research. *Language Learning, 57*(1), 45–77.

Blachowicz, C.L.Z., & Fisher, P. (2006). *Teaching vocabulary in all classrooms* (3rd ed.). Columbus, OH: Allyn & Bacon/Merrill.

Bloom, P. (2000). *How children learn the meanings of words.* Cambridge, MA: MIT Press.

Carlisle, J.F. (2000). Awareness of the structure and meaning of morphologically complex words: Impact on reading. *Reading and Writing. An Interdisciplinary Journal, 12*(3–4), 169–190.

Carlisle, J.F. (2003). Morphology matters in learning to read: A commentary. *Reading Psychology, 24*(3–4), 291–322.

Carlo, M.S., August, D., McLaughlin, B., Snow, C.E., Dressler, C., Lippman, D., et al. (2004). Closing the gap: Addressing the vocabulary needs of English-language learners in bilingual and mainstream classrooms. *Reading Research Quarterly, 39*(2), 188–215.

Chall, J.S., Jacobs, V.A., & Baldwin, L.E. (1990). *The reading crisis: Why poor children fall behind.* Cambridge, MA: Harvard University Press.

Christensen, L. (1998). Inviting student lives into the classroom: Where I'm from. *Rethinking Schools, 12*(2), 22–23.

Clark, E.V. (1982). The young word maker: A case study of innovation in the child's lexicon. In E. Wanner & L.R. Gleitman (Eds.), *Language acquisition: The state of the art* (pp. 390–425). Cambridge, UK: Cambridge University Press.

Davidson, A.L. (1996). *Making and molding identity in schools: Student narratives on race, gender, and academic engagement.* Albany: State University of New York Press.

Delpit, L. (1995). *Other people's children: Cultural conflict in the classroom.* New York: The New Press.

Dickinson, D.K., McCabe, A., & Clark-Chiarelli, N. (2004). Preschool-based prevention of reading disability: Realities versus possibilities. In C.A. Stone, E. Silliman, B. Ehren, & K. Apel (Eds.), *Handbook of language and literacy* (pp. 209–227). New York: Guilford.

Dickinson, D.K., & Smith, M.W. (1994). Long-term effects of preschool teachers' book readings on low-income children's vocabulary and story comprehension. *Reading Research Quarterly, 29*(2), 104–122.

Dutro, E., Kazemi, E., & Balf, R. (2005). The aftermath of "You're only half": Multiracial identities in the literacy classroom. *Language Arts, 83*(2), 96–106.

Erickson, F. (1987). Transformation and school success: The politics and culture of educational achievement. *Anthropology & Education Quarterly, 18*(4), 335–356.

Fang, Z. (2008). Going beyond the Fab Five: Helping students cope with the unique linguistic challenges of expository reading in intermediate grades. *Journal of Adolescent & Adult Literacy, 51*(6), 476–487.

Fivush, R., Haden, C., & Reese, E. (2006). Elaborating on elaborations: Role of maternal reminiscing style in cognitive and socioemotional development. *Child Development, 77*(6), 1568–1588.

Freyd, P., & Baron, J. (1982). Individual differences in acquisition of derivational morphology. *Journal of Verbal Learning and Verbal Behavior, 21*(3), 282–295.

Fukkink, R.G., & de Glopper, K. (1998). Effects of instruction in deriving word meaning from context: A meta-analysis. *Review of Educational Research, 68*(4), 450–469.

Gallas, K. (1992). When the children take the chair: A study of sharing time in a primary classroom. *Language Arts, 69*(3), 172–182.

Gee, J.P. (1996). *Social linguistics and literacies: Ideology in Discourses* (2nd ed.). London: Taylor & Francis.

Gee, J.P. (2000). The new literacy studies: From "socially situated" to the work of the social. In D. Barton, M. Hamilton, & R. Ivanič (Eds.), *Situated literacies: Reading and writing in context* (pp. 180–196). London: Routledge.

Gee, J.P. (2001). Reading as situated language: A sociocognitive perspective. *Journal of Adolescent & Adult Literacy, 44*(8), 714–725.

Gee, J.P. (2004). *Situated language and learning: A critique of traditional schooling.* New York: Routledge.

Goerss, B.L., Beck, I.L., McKeown, M.G. (1999). Increasing remedial students' ability to derive word meaning from context. *Reading Psychology, 20*(2), 151–175.

González, N., Moll, L.C., & Amanti, C. (Eds.). (2005). *Funds of knowledge: Theorizing practices in households, communities, and classrooms.* Mahwah, NJ: Erlbaum.

Goulden, R., Nation, P., & Read, J. (1990). How large can a receptive vocabulary be? *Applied Linguistics, 11*(4), 341–363.

Graves, M.F. (1986). Vocabulary learning and instruction. In E.Z. Rothkopf & L.C. Ehri (Eds.), *Review of research in education* (Vol. 13, pp. 49–89). Washington, DC: American Educational Research Association.

Graves, M.F., & Watts-Taffe, S.M. (2002). The place of word consciousness in a research-based vocabulary program. In A.E. Farstrup & S.J. Samuels (Eds.), *What research has to say about reading instruction* (3rd ed., pp. 140–165). Newark, DE: International Reading Association.

Halliday, M.A.K. (1987). Spoken and written modes of meaning. In R. Horowitz & S.J. Samuels (Eds.), *Comprehending oral and written language* (pp. 55–82). San Diego: Academic.

Halliday, M.A.K. (1989). *Spoken and written language.* Oxford, UK: Oxford University Press.

Halliday, M.A.K. (2004). The place of dialogue in children's construction of meaning. In R.B. Ruddell & N.J. Unrau (Eds.), *Theoretical models and processes of reading* (5th ed., pp. 133–145). Newark, DE: International Reading Association.

Hart, B., & Risley, T. (1995). *Meaningful differences in the everyday experience of young American children.* Baltimore: Paul H. Brookes.

Heath, S.B. (1983). *Ways with words: Language, life, and work in communities and class-rooms.* Cambridge, UK: Cambridge University Press.

Henry, M.K. (2003). *Unlocking literacy: Effective decoding and spelling instruction.* Baltimore: Paul H. Brookes.

Hermes, M., & Uran, C. (2006). Treaties that dominate and literacy that empowers? I wish it was all in Ojibwemowin. *Anthropology & Education Quarterly, 37*(4), 393–398.

Hoff-Ginsberg, E. (1991). Mother–child conversation in different social classes and communicative settings. *Child Development, 62*(4), 782–796.

Horowitz, R., & Samuels, S.J. (1987). Comprehending oral and written language: Critical contrasts for literacy and schooling. In R. Horowitz & S.J. Samuels (Eds.), *Comprehending oral and written language* (pp. 1–52). San Diego, CA: Academic.

Hunt, K.W. (1977). Early blooming and late blooming syntactic structures. In C.R. Cooper & L. Odell (Eds.), *Evaluating writing: Describing, measuring, judging* (pp. 91–106). Buffalo, NY: National Council of Teachers of English.

Jiménez, R.T., García, G.E., & Pearson, P.D. (1996). The reading strategies of bilingual Latina/o students who are successful English readers: Opportunities and obstacles. *Reading Research Quarterly, 31*(1), 90–112.

Johnston, P. (2004). *Choice words: How our language affects children's learning.* Portland, ME: Stenhouse.

Johnson, D.D., von Hoff Johnson, B., & Schlichting, K. (2004). Logology: Word and language play. In J.F. Baumann & E.J. Kame'enui (Eds.), *Vocabulary instruction: Research to practice* (pp. 179–200). New York: Guilford.

Lee, J.S., & Oxelson, E. (2006). "It's not my job": K–12 teacher attitudes toward students' heritage language maintenance. *Bilingual Research Journal, 30*(2), 453–477.

Lesaux, N.K., Rupp, A.A., & Siegel, L.S. (2007). Growth in reading skills of children from diverse linguistic backgrounds: Findings from a 5-year longitudinal study. *Journal of Educational Psychology, 99*(4), 831–834.

McCarthey, S.J. (2001). Identity construction in elementary readers and writers. *Reading Research Quarterly, 36*(2), 122–151.

McKeown, M.G. (1985). The acquisition of word meaning from context by children of high and low ability. *Reading Research Quarterly, 20*(4), 482–496.

McKeown, M.G., Beck, I.L., Omanson, R.C., & Pople, M.T. (1985). Some effects of the nature and frequency of vocabulary instruction on the knowledge and use of words. *Reading Research Quarterly, 20*(5), 522–535.

Mezynski, K. (1983). Issues concerning the acquisitions of knowledge: Effects of vocabulary training on reading comprehension. *Review of Educational Research, 53*(2), 253–279.

Michaels, S., & Collins, J. (1984). Oral discourse styles: Classroom interaction and the acquisition of literacy. In D. Tannen (Ed.), *Coherence in spoken and written discourse* (pp. 219–230). Norwood, NJ: Ablex.

Miller, G.A., & Gildea, P. (1987). How children learn words. *Scientific American, 257*(3), 94–99.

Moll, L.C., Amanti, C., Neff, D., & González, N. (1992). Funds of knowledge for teaching: Using a qualitative approach to connect homes and classrooms. *Theory Into Practice, 31*(2), 132–141.

Nagy, W.E. (2007). Metalinguistic awareness and the vocabulary–comprehension connection. In R.K. Wagner, A. Muse, & K. Tannenbaum (Eds.), *Vocabulary acquisition: Implications for reading comprehension* (pp. 52–77). New York: Guilford.

Nagy, W.E., & Anderson, R.C. (1984). The number of words in printed school English. *Reading Research Quarterly, 19*(3), 304–330.

Nagy, W.E., Berninger, V.W., & Abbott, R. (2006). Contributions of morphology beyond phonology to literacy outcomes of upper elementary and middle school students. *Journal of Educational Psychology, 98*(1), 134–147.

Nagy, W.E., Berninger, V.W., Abbott, R., Vaughan, K., & Vermeulen, K. (2003). Relationship of morphology and other language skills to literacy skills in at-risk second grade readers and at-risk fourth grade writers. *Journal of Educational Psychology, 95*(4), 730–742.

Nagy, W.E., & Scott, J.A. (1990). Word schemas: Expectations about the form and meaning of new words. *Cognition and Instruction, 7*(2), 105–127.

Nagy, W.E., & Scott, J.A. (2000). Vocabulary processes. In M.L. Kamil, P.B. Mosenthal, P.D. Pearson, & R. Barr (Eds.), *Handbook of reading research* (Vol. 3, pp. 269–284). Mahwah, NJ: Erlbaum.

National Institute of Child Health and Human Development. (2000). *Report of the National Reading Panel. Teaching children to read: An evidence-based assessment of the scientific research literature on reading and its implications for reading instruction* (NIH Publication No. 00-4769). Washington, DC: U.S. Government Printing Office.

New London Group. (1996). A pedagogy of multiliteracies: Designing social futures. *Harvard Educational Review, 66*(1), 60–92.

Nieto, S. (2002). *Language, culture, and teaching: Critical perspectives for a new century*. Mahwah, NJ: Erlbaum.

Nunes, T., & Bryant, P. (2006). *Improving literacy by teaching morphemes*. New York: Routledge.

Nunes, T., Bryant, P., & Bindman, M. (1997). Morphological spelling strategies: Developmental stages and processes. *Developmental Psychology, 33*(4), 637–649.

Nystrand, M. (2006). Research on the role of classroom discourse as it affects reading comprehension. *Research in the Teaching of English, 40*(4), 392–412.

Pearson, P.D. (2004). The reading wars. *Educational Policy, 18*(1), 216–252.

Pearson, P.D., & Gallagher, M.C. (1983). The instruction of reading comprehension. *Contemporary Educational Psychology, 8*(3), 317–344.

Purcell-Gates, V., Duke, N.K., & Martineau, J.A. (2007). Learning to read and write genre-specific text: Roles of authentic experience and explicit teaching. *Reading Research Quarterly, 42*(1), 8–45.

Purcell-Gates, V., Jacobson, E., & Degener, S. (2004). *Print literacy development: Uniting cognitive and social practice theories*. Cambridge, MA: Harvard University Press.

Ransdell, S., Barbier, M.L., & Niit, T. (2006). Metacognitions about language skill and working memory among monolingual and bilingual college students: When does multilingualism matter? *International Journal of Bilingual Education and Bilingualism, 9*(6), 728–741.

Rogoff, B. (1990). *Apprenticeship in thinking: Cognitive development in social context*. New York: Oxford University Press.

Rueda, R., & Moll, L.C. (1994). A sociocultural perspective on motivation. In H.F. O'Neil & M. Drilling (Eds.), *Motivation: Theory and research* (pp. 117–140). Mahwah, NJ: Erlbaum.

Schieffelin, B., & Ochs, E. (1986). Language socialization. *Annual Review of Anthropology, 15*(25), 163–191.

Schleppegrell, M. (2004). *The language of schooling: A functional linguistics perspective.* Mahwah, NJ: Erlbaum.

Scott, J., Skobel, B., & Wells, J. (2008). *The word conscious classroom: Building the vocabulary readers and writers need* (Theory Into Practice series). New York: Scholastic.

Scott, J.A., Jamieson-Noel, D., & Asselin, M. (2003). Vocabulary instruction throughout the day in twenty-three Canadian upper-elementary classrooms. *The Elementary School Journal, 103*(3), 269–286.

Scott, J.A., & Nagy, W.E. (1997). Understanding the definitions of unfamiliar verbs. *Reading Research Quarterly, 32*(2), 184–200.

Shefelbine, J. (1990). Student factors related to variability in learning word meanings from context. *Journal of Reading Behavior, 22*(1), 71–97.

Sleeter, C.E., & Grant, C.A. (2007). *Making choices for multicultural education: Five approaches to race, class, and gender* (5th ed.). Hoboken, NJ: John Wiley & Sons.

Snow, C.E., & Beals, D.E. (2006, Spring). Mealtime talk that supports literacy development. In R. Larson, A. Wiley, & K. Branscomb (Eds.), *Family mealtime as a context of development and socialization: New directions for child and adolescent development,* (pp. 51–66). San Francisco: Jossy-Bass.

Stahl, S. (1986). Three principles of effective vocabulary instruction. *Journal of Reading, 29*(7), 662–668.

Stahl, S., & Fairbanks, M. (1986). The effects of vocabulary instruction: A model-based meta-analysis. *Review of Educational Research, 56*(1), 72–110.

Sternberg, R. (1987). Most vocabulary is learned from context. In M.G. McKeown & M.E. Curtis (Eds.), *The nature of vocabulary acquisition* (pp. 89–105). Hillsdale, NJ: Erlbaum.

Sternberg, R.J., & Powell, J.S. (1983). Comprehending verbal comprehension. *American Psychologist, 38*(8), 878–893.

Tomasello, M., & Farrar, M. (1986). Joint attention and early language. *Child Development, 57*(6), 1454–1463.

Tomasello, M., & Todd, J. (1983). Joint attention and lexical acquisition style. *First Language, 4*(12), 197–212.

Tunmer, W.E., Nesdale, A.R., & Wright, A. (1987). Syntactic awareness and reading acquisition. *The British Journal of Developmental Psychology, 5*(1), 25–34.

Tyler, A., & Nagy, W.E. (1989). The acquisition of English derivational morphology. *Journal of Memory and Language, 28*(6), 649–667.

Tyler, A., & Nagy, W.E. (1990). Use of derivational morphology during reading. *Cognition, 36*(1), 17–34.

Valdés, G. (1998). The world outside and inside schools: Language and immigrant children. *Educational Researcher, 27*(6), 4–18.

van Daalen-Kapteijns, M.M., & Elshout-Mohr, M. (1981). The acquisition of word meanings as a cognitive learning process. *Journal of Verbal Learning and Verbal Behavior, 20*(4), 386–399.

Vygotsky, L.S. (1978). *Mind in society: The development of higher psychological processes* (M. Cole, V. John-Steiner, S. Scribner, & E. Souberman, Eds. & Trans.). Cambridge, MA: Harvard University Press.

Vygotsky, L.S. (1986). *Thought and language* (A. Kozulin, Trans.). Cambridge, MA: MIT Press. (Original work published 1934)

Watson, R. (1985). Towards a theory of definition. *Journal of Child Language, 12*(1), 181–197.

Watson, R., & Olson, D.R. (1987). From meaning to definition: A literate bias on the structure of word meaning. In R. Horowitz & S.J. Samuels (Eds.), *Comprehending oral and written language* (pp. 329–353). New York: Academic.

Watts-Taffe, S.M. (1995). Vocabulary instruction during reading lessons in six classrooms. *Journal of Reading Behavior, 27*(3), 399–424.

Wertsch, J.V. (1991). *Voices of the mind: A sociocultural approach to mediated action.* Cambridge, MA: Harvard University Press.

White, T.G., Graves, M.F., & Slater, W.H. (1990). Growth of reading vocabulary in diverse elementary schools: Decoding and world meaning. *Journal of Educational Psychology, 82*(2), 281–290.

Wilkinson, L.C., & Silliman, E.R. (2000). Classroom language and literacy learning. In M.L. Kamil, P.B. Mosenthal, P.D. Pearson, & R. Barr (Eds.), *Handbook of reading research* (Vol. 3, pp. 337–360). Mahwah, NJ: Erlbaum.

Chapter 9

English Words Needed: Creating Research-Based Vocabulary Instruction for English Learners

Lori Helman

Knowing words in a language is a key component to understanding text and being able to produce it—reading and writing. Many students in the United States come to school with an oral language other than English, and an important charge of the school is to help them become literate in English. To fully carry out this responsibility, educators need to help English learners develop a deep and broad repertoire of basic and academic vocabulary words to use in their reading and writing. As one second-grade teacher shared, "What is one of the biggest challenges for my [English-language learning] students in becoming proficient readers and writers in English? Building up vocabulary and content related to what they're reading." To help with this goal, this chapter provides teachers with the research base on vocabulary learning and instruction with English learners at the elementary grades and suggests effective teaching practices that follow from this literature.

Recent demographic data showed that 9.9 million children in the United States ages 5–17 speak a language other than English at home; of this group, 2.8 million children speak English with difficulty (National Center for Education Statistics, NCES, 2006). Both of these figures represent more than double the number from 1979. Of the students who spoke English with difficulty, approximately 76% spoke Spanish as a home language. To serve all students in schools, it is imperative that educators become knowledgeable about vocabulary instruction for the sizable group of students learning English. While it is important to consider the needs of students from many language backgrounds, it is also clear that instructional strategies aimed at supporting the learning of Spanish speakers are especially relevant.

What Research Has to Say About Vocabulary Instruction, edited by Alan E. Farstrup and S. Jay Samuels.
© 2008 by the International Reading Association.

English-language learning (ELL) students are at increased risk of experiencing reading difficulty (Snow, Burns, & Griffin, 1998). In fact, the National Assessment of Educational Progress reports a persistent gap in performance on its reading measure between ELL and non-ELL students at the fourth-, eighth-, and twelfth-grade levels (NCES, 2005). An important factor in the reading achievement gap is likely the limited vocabulary knowledge of ELL students (August & Hakuta, 1997; August & Shanahan, 2006; Calderón et al., 2005).

A substantial body of research points to the importance of vocabulary knowledge for adequate reading comprehension in all students (McGregor, 2004; Nagy & Scott, 2000; National Institute of Child Health and Human Development, 2000). Reading comprehension is highly dependent on understanding spoken words (Rayner, Foorman, Perfetti, Pesetsky, & Seidenberg, 2001). Vocabulary knowledge in the early grades is a significant predictor of reading comprehension in middle and high school (Cunningham & Stanovich, 1997). There is also evidence that learning vocabulary has a positive influence on reading comprehension (Beck, Perfetti, & McKeown, 1982). With the understanding that vocabulary knowledge has been shown to play such a powerful role in reading comprehension for native English speakers, it is time to turn to the vocabulary research with English learners. Does vocabulary play an equally important role with nonnative speakers? If so, what does the research say about how to most effectively teach vocabulary to English learners?

Vocabulary Research With English Learners

An overview of research findings with English learners described the important role of oral English in the success of students in school. As English learners' oral proficiency grew, so did their abilities to use more complex language learning strategies, which led to greater use of academic language and a better grasp of word meanings (Genesee, Lindholm-Leary, Saunders, & Christian, 2005). The report of the National Literacy Panel on Language Minority Children and Youth found that students learning English did not perform as well on measures of reading comprehension as their native-speaking peers, and that oral language proficiency in English and English reading comprehension are positively correlated (August & Shanahan, 2006). A variety of research studies point to the importance of vocabulary knowledge for English learners—the positive effects of more developed vocabularies and the negative effects of low vocabulary knowledge. García (1991) found that students learning English often did not have the knowledge of keywords in English needed to comprehend their texts. Other researchers have echoed the finding that poor reading comprehension for English learners is often related to low vocabulary knowledge (Jiménez, García, & Pearson, 1996; Nagy, 1997; Verhoeven, 1990). In addition, vocabulary knowledge was found to be an important foundation for reading comprehension with English learners (Calderón et al., 2005) and a significant predictor of writing skills in English (Dufra & Voeten, 1999). In a review of the research, Cheung and Slavin (2005) concluded that the evidence supported the extensive use of vocabulary instruction as a key component of an effective reading program.

Despite the importance of vocabulary knowledge for English learners' proficient reading and writing, a very limited number of studies have examined the instructional practices that may be effective for teaching vocabulary. The National Literacy Panel on Language-Minority Children and Youth found only three experimental studies that dealt with the topic (Shanahan & Beck, 2006). The first study compared vocabulary instruction for first-grade Spanish speakers that was presented in individual sentence contexts versus vocabulary instruction that involved meaning-centered instruction, including words used in longer narratives, picture support, and student-generated dictations. Students who received the more meaningful instruction learned more than double the number of focus words as compared with the control group (Vaughn-Shavuo, 1990).

The second study reviewed by Shanahan and Beck (2006) was conducted with 75 third-grade Mexican American students (Pérez, 1981). Students received packets of activities that helped them work with and understand complex language concepts such as idioms, analogies, compound words, synonyms, antonyms, and words with multiple meanings. Students worked on these activities 20 minutes a day for a 3-month period. Results showed that the treatment group made significantly more growth on a reading inventory than the control group.

The final study involved fifth-grade Spanish speakers who were taught 10–12 words per week over 15 weeks. The treatment had the following characteristics: It was thematic with academically useful words; it included homework and periodic assessments; the words were presented first in Spanish, then in English; students were taught strategies for using information from context, morphology, multiple meanings, and cognates; and it was implemented in a classroom with both ELL and non-ELL students (Carlo et al., 2004). English learners showed significant gains on the intervention, although their pre- and posttest scores were lower than the non-ELL students. Shanahan and Beck (2006) concluded that, while the three studies provided results that are consistent with vocabulary research for native English speakers, "There is a great need for more investigation into what constitutes sound and effective vocabulary instruction for English-language learners" (p. 431).

Several other studies and reflections by the researchers involved provide us with important information about what may lead to effective practices in vocabulary instruction for English learners. Cognates, or words that share related spellings and meanings across two languages (e.g., *pause/pausa*), have been shown to be a useful learning tool for Spanish-speaking students, but the ability to use cognates may require explicit scaffolding for students (Carlo et al., 2004; García, 1991; Jiménez et al., 1996; Nagy, García, Durgunoglu, & Hancin-Bhatt, 1993).

Calderón et al. (2005) implemented a year-long study with 293 Spanish-dominant third graders who were transitioning from Spanish to English instruction. Vocabulary instruction focused on the words both in the decodable texts students read and in grade-level literature. Vocabulary was previewed with technology; teachers also discussed words before, during, and after the story had been read. Students listened to and discussed 50 literature texts throughout the year, focusing on key vocabulary words within the story. Additional oral language activities to build vocabulary included listening for target words outside of class and investigating cognates, multiple-meaning words, and idioms. The authors concluded that carefully designed vocabulary instruction improves vocabulary knowledge in both Spanish and English and that vocabulary practices effective with native English speakers have also proved useful with English learners but must be adapted to their backgrounds. Teachers who participated in the study expressed how helpful it was for them to have the vocabulary words selected and the strategies prepared for them—a task that would have been overwhelming on their own (Calderón et al., 2005).

Biemiller and Boote (2006) reported on a series of vocabulary studies with primary-grade students in classrooms with approximately 50% English learners. The first study found that repeated readings of books lead to a 12% gain in word meanings and that adding explanations of words added 10% for a total gain of 22%. The second study tested a more intensive format for word instruction and transfer with additional words taught and multiple opportunities for review. A greater number of words were learned in the second format, and the authors attribute this to added reviews and the instruction of word meanings.

A recent study by Roberts (2008) found that a home reading program that included storybook reading in the child's first language was as effective as English picture book reading for developing second-language vocabulary. In addition, Beck and McKeown (2007) examined the potential for increasing young low-income children's vocabulary knowledge through rich and focused instruction. While this study was not done with English learners, there was a similar need to help the students increase their vocabulary repertoires to be successful in the school world of academic language. Rich instruction involved focused discussion of read-aloud texts and teaching and encouraging the use of selected sophisticated words. Results showed that the richer the vocabulary instruction, the greater the pre- to posttest gains (Beck & McKeown, 2007).

As researchers discussed why they believe their vocabulary interventions were successful, the following key ideas were expressed:

- Words were presented in meaningful contexts, such as in interesting texts.
- Lessons motivated students and encouraged participation.
- Interventions were in-depth and took place over time with repetition and review.
- Lessons involved discourse around text.
- Vocabulary study built on students' background language such as with previews in the home language and cognate identification.
- Students learned to apply strategies for word learning, such as morphemic analysis.
- Lessons involved scaffolding such as with simplified syntax, visual materials, or oral language practice activities.

Connections Among Vocabulary Research and Second-Language Teaching Principles

Teachers reading the list of key ideas presented above are likely to nod their heads and think, "That fits with what I know about teaching students in a new language. Of course it helps to provide concrete support and in-depth, engaging instruction." In fact, many of the instructional procedures represented in the vocabulary studies described in this chapter also reflect key ideas from effective second-language teaching. These key ideas fit into five principles, and I expand on them in the following segment of text. It is important to examine *why* the techniques in the research studies are likely to be effective, because knowing why provides important criteria for selecting effective vocabulary teaching practices for ongoing classroom use.

Instruction builds on what students already know. We saw in the vocabulary research that projects that provided support in the student's home language, such as preview/review, translation of words, and making connections to cognates in the home language, were successful in developing vocabulary in English. Understanding students' home languages and how they relate to English provides information for the teacher to help students transfer knowledge that is similar or clarifies misconceptions that may arise because of distinctive features across the languages. Research on second-language learning highlights the importance of an additive as opposed to a subtractive philosophy of language learning, connecting instruction to students' lives, as well as using culturally respectful teaching practices (Au, 2006; Center for Research on Education, Diversity & Excellence [CREDE], 2002; Peregoy & Boyle, 2001).

Instruction is tailored to the particular needs of students learning English. Scaffolding may include the use of visuals, hands-on activities, a developmental progression of words or sequenced readers, and simplified, student-friendly language. All of the successful studies referenced above used scaffolded techniques of various sorts to support student learning in vocabulary. Research on second-language learning has long highlighted the concept of sheltered instruction and provided examples of how to make instruction comprehensible to students learning English (Baker, Gersten, Haager, & Dingle, 2006; Cheung & Slavin, 2005; Fitzgerald & Graves, 2004; Peregoy & Boyle, 2001; Saunders & Goldenberg, 2001).

Vocabulary instruction is taught in meaningful contexts. The research studies that were presented showed that more vocabulary learning took place when words were taught in context and when there were multiple opportunities for application in and out of the classroom. This finding aligns with second-language learning research that supports the use of social interaction strategies such as group work and collaboration, as well as opportunities for guided application of new learning (CREDE, 2002; Baker et al., 2006; Peregoy & Boyle, 2001).

Instruction is in-depth and comprehensive. In the research studies presented, the curriculum went beyond surface-level definitions; it addressed a variety of vocabulary components including the multiple meanings of words, finding synonyms and antonyms, using the spelling-meaning connection, and engaging in higher order thinking tasks. Rich instruction proved more effective for English learners. The idea of complex and interesting curriculum to engage and motivate diverse learners is supported throughout the literature (Au, 2006; CREDE, 2002; Gersten & Jiménez, 1994).

Goals are challenging, but not impossible. A consistent thread in the reflections of the vocabulary researchers was the need to implement a cohesive program and make a long-term commitment to its implementation. Several studies addressed the extra attention needed as students in bilingual programs transition to English-only classrooms. The literature in the second-language field tells us that language learning takes time and, while students need high expectations, they also need consistency and support to become academically proficient in a new language (Cummins, 2003; Genesee et al., 2005; Peregoy & Boyle, 2001).

These key instructional principles give teachers an overarching perspective on what to look for when planning research-based vocabulary instruction for English learners. The remainder of this chapter presents concrete examples of teaching practices that put these principles into action.

Providing Research-Based Vocabulary Instruction With English Learners

Effective vocabulary instruction for English learners will reflect the research both in vocabulary learning and in second-language acquisition because students are learning to read and write in English at the same time they are learning to speak the language. Limitations on their vocabulary skills will hold students back from comprehending the grade-level materials they encounter in the classroom. For this reason, vocabulary instruction needs to be thought of not as a separate curriculum area but rather as an integrated part of every instructional activity for English learners. In a recent "Theory into Practice" article, Blachowicz, Fisher, Ogle, and Watts-Tafe (2006). outlined three characteristics of strong vocabulary instruction: (1) the need for language- and word-rich environments, (2) the intentional teaching of selected vocabulary, and (3) the developing of word-learning strategies (see Chapter 2, this volume, for similar work by Blachowicz and Fisher). These characteristics are equally, if not more, important for English learners as they develop oral language and literacy skills simultaneously.

The next section addresses many important topics relating to research-based vocabulary instruction with English learners:

- What words are most important for students to know?
- How can the research guide teachers to select effective vocabulary activities for English learners?
- How can vocabulary learning be integrated into all areas of the curriculum?
- How can teachers modify their instruction for students with various levels of English proficiency to build up all students' vocabularies?
- What materials will support vocabulary learning in the classroom?

What Words Are Most Important for English Learners to Know?

English learners enter elementary classrooms at all levels of English proficiency. Some students may be new to the country and speak little to no English. Others may have lived in the United States for an extended period of time, may have been in school for a number of years, and may be nearing oral proficiency. Scaffolding instruction so that students learn the academic vocabulary and complex language structures of English requires in-depth teacher professional knowledge (Dutro & Moran, 2003). An important first step is for teachers to have information about their students' oral language proficiency in English so they can match their instruction to what students need next.

When possible, teachers should review available language assessment data to better understand their students' oral proficiency levels. A student who has scored at a beginning level is learning individual words and using one- to two-word responses; in contrast, a student at the early advanced level understands more complex stories and speaks using consistent standard English forms (California Department of Education, 1999). The first student will need to develop a basic oral vocabulary while the latter will need to work on the vocabulary of academic study. Once the teacher has a general idea of a student's oral English proficiency, informal measures can be used to assess particular vocabulary needs. Teachers can talk with students, ask questions, listen to their stories and retellings of personal or academic information, and observe interactions with others. Depending on students' reading and writing skills, written assessments can also help teachers understand what words students know.

Several factors come into play when considering what words should be taught to English learners. Students new to the language should focus on essential survival vocabulary—basic communication phrases and labels for common objects and school-related terms. (I offer suggestions for helping students learn a basic oral vocabulary below.)

Many English learners in mainstream classrooms have mastered a basic oral vocabulary, but they still have significant gaps in their knowledge of words common in print. Graves (2006) suggests that teachers need to provide explicit instruction in words that are highly frequent in texts but less common in oral language to ensure that English learners understand and learn to read the most frequent English words.

Once English learners get beyond the beginning level of proficiency, they will have mastered the majority of words in everyday speech. It is at this point that teachers often think that students are "fluent," or can be instructed without special consideration. Unfortunately most English learners do not have the depth of vocabulary knowledge needed to effectively understand the academic language of print without additional support. In discussing what words are most important to be taught, Kamil and Hiebert (2005) propose several guiding factors. Words may be selected because they are high frequency in print, they are important and useful, they relate to classroom instructional topics, or they foster important conceptual learning. While some vocabulary researchers suggest that teaching the most frequent words is unnecessary and recommend concentrating on the words used by mature language users, other researchers familiar with English learners see the need to include high-frequency words in print in the vocabulary curriculum of their students (Bear, Helman, Templeton, Invernizzi, & Johnston, 2007; Biemiller, 2004; Calderón et al., 2005; Graves, 2006).

In summary, the words that are most important to teach depend first on the English proficiency level of students, and next on the frequency, utility, and instructional potential of the words. The following segments describe some ways to help students develop a basic oral vocabulary when they are beginning to learn English and give some suggestions for the kinds of words to teach students as they become more orally proficient and grow in their ability to read and write in English.

Developing a basic oral vocabulary. When students are beginning to learn a new language, they need clear, comprehensible instruction that is offered in short chunks but is repeated over time. Students can only handle so much input before they tire and need to let the new words sink in. While it is important to provide opportunities for students to use language with others, teachers must be aware that beginners often do not have the words in English to express themselves fluently. Teachers can support English learners by creating simplified questions for students to show what they know, providing them with visuals or manipulatives to use as props, or finding ways for students to share what they know in their home languages.

An essential first step in developing a basic oral vocabulary is to help students learn the labels for common items in and outside of the classroom. Provide time for a "language buddy" to practice naming common words with the focus student using a photo library or other visual materials. A language buddy can be an educational assistant, a classroom volunteer, an older student, or a more-fluent classmate. These tutoring and practice sessions should be short but take place on a daily basis, if possible. In addition to learning the names of common terms, consider supporting beginning English speakers by

- Finding fellow students and community volunteers who can help translate important vocabulary for the student
- Providing student-friendly reference materials such as picture dictionaries, classroom charts and labels, and agendas of the day's schedule
- Embedding language development activities within content area study such as taking the time to clearly define key terms and processes, using visuals and gestures
- Providing breaks for students new to English to process their learning, such as by reviewing the material with others who speak their home language

Selecting words for intentional vocabulary instruction. There simply isn't enough time in the academic schedule for teachers to spend extended class time on every important and useful word in the English language. Focus words should help students to better understand grade-level material and extend their current knowledge. The kinds of words featured will depend on the following:

- The thematic studies that take place in the classroom—For example, a class that studies electricity will need to work in depth with words in that topic area such as *current* and *charge*.

- Words that describe important conceptual processes at each grade level—For example, words like *construct, separate, contrast,* and *summarize* represent essential activities that students will need to enact as they participate in classroom activities across the elementary grades.
- The reading texts used in the class—For example, a class listening to a read-aloud about the Wright Brothers will need to understand words such as *aerodynamic, invention,* and *biplane.*
- The word-study level of the class—As students develop reading skills, they examine deeper levels of the English orthography. Whether students are learning sound–symbol relationships, vowel patterns or connections between spelling and meaning, selecting vocabulary words that support their studies reinforces and extends this learning. In contrast to native speakers, English learners need explicit instruction in the meaning of some of the words that are used in their word-study lessons and need opportunities to extend their repertoire of available words that represent specific orthographic features. Table 9.1 outlines the kinds of words studied at various levels of orthographic development (cf. Bear, Invernizzi, Templeton, & Johnston, 2008; Henderson, 1981) and example vocabulary words that support students' learning.

Words selected for intentional focus in the classroom must be connected with other classroom learning and should be useful and relevant enough to merit the allocation of precious instructional time.

How Can the Research Guide Teachers to Select Effective Vocabulary Activities for English Learners?

Earlier in this chapter, I presented key ideas gleaned from the vocabulary research with English learners. The research literature suggested that techniques found to be effective in vocabulary instruction for native speakers would likely be effective with English learners as well, but that tailoring instruction to students' multilingual capabilities is important. Effective procedures include scaffolding, presenting words in meaningful contexts, motivating students and connecting to their background knowledge and languages, including opportunities for discourse, and focusing on strategies for word learning. A number of vocabulary activities fit with one or more of these guiding ideas. In this section, I share several example instructional ideas for students at the early grades, the

Table 9.1. Levels of orthographic development and word-study focus

Level of orthographic development	Word-study focus and sample words	Focus for English learners
Emergent: Students begin to learn about print, develop phonological awareness and make initial sound–symbol connections.	ABCs (*alligator, zebra*) rhyming words (*snug, bug, rug*) beginning sounds (/b/ for *ball, bounce,* and *bottle*)	Learn words that are common in alphabet books. Learn simple rhymes with natural language patterns.
Alphabetic: Students study letter–sound correspondences and short-vowel word families.	Less-common short-vowel words (*peg, mug, jab*) Words with blends (*clip, strand*) Words with digraphs (*chat, dash*)	Make sure that words used in phonics studies are comprehended.
Within-word pattern: Students study more complex vowel patterns. They begin to examine multiple meaning words and homophones.	Homophones (*meat, meet*) Words with multiple meanings (*lean, safe*) Idioms (*"lend an ear"*)	Continue to clarify unfamiliar vocabulary in reading materials and word study. Explicit focus on how spelling influences word meaning.
Syllables and affixes: Students study multisyllable words; base words and affixes; and interrelate spelling, meaning, and grammatical use.	Inflected endings (*glances, glanced, glancing*) Compound words (*backfire, eyewitness*) Affixes (**pre**paid, power**ful**) Two-syllable homophones and homographs (bury/berry, record/record)	Build vocabulary interest by investigating spelling–meaning connections. Look for cognates in grammatical affixes across languages (e.g., **pre**suppose/**pre**suponer, eat**ing**/comiendo).
Derivational relations: Students study morphology and word etymology, especially Latin and Greek roots, related words across languages and sound alternations across derivations.	Latin roots (*rupt* = to break: *disrupt, rupture, interrupt*) Greek roots (*bio* = life: *biology, biopsy, biography*) Cognates (*transparency/transparencia*) Sound changes in related words (*revise/revision*)	Use cognates to access academic vocabulary. Teach students to analyze word parts to delve into meaning.

transitional grades, and the upper grades of the elementary school that align with the research base on vocabulary instruction with English learners. The research has also told us that effective interventions take place over time with opportunities to practice and review. Any of the strategies selected should be implemented intentionally and consistently.

The early grades. Students in kindergarten, first grade, and early second grade are learning about print and interacting with simple beginning reading materials (Bear & Helman, 2004). While it is important to make sure students understand the words in the texts they are reading, these materials may not be a rich source of words to extend students' academic vocabularies. Read-aloud materials, however, provide fertile ground to engage students in inquiring about, defining, practicing, and discussing interesting and useful words. Interactive oral reading has been supported in the vocabulary research literature relating to both native speakers and English learners (Biemiller, 2004; Calderón et al., 2005; Nagy & Scott, 2000). Graves (2006) outlines the characteristics of interactive oral reading and describes four research-based instructional programs in use. Classroom teachers use this procedure as they share an interesting book with students, focusing explicitly on a few select words, expanding on the text and asking questions, eliciting students' background knowledge about the words, and providing clarifying examples. With English learners, interactive oral reading may also involve translating the focus words into students' home languages and making the content more comprehensible through visuals and demonstrations. For instance, an oral reading of *The Wolf's Chicken Stew* (Kasza, 1987) invites a focus on the word *prey.* The teacher might share that an animal's prey is what it hunts and eats; probe students' understanding of which animals are prey for others; and give translations of the word, such as *presa* in Spanish. The teacher might help students to act out an animal hunting for food or model an oral language pattern such as "A (animal) is prey for a (animal)" for students to create their own statements. If students bring up the meaning of the homophone *pray,* the teacher is presented with a wonderful opportunity to talk about how words that sound the same sometimes have different meanings. Depending on the literacy level of the students, the spelling of both words can be compared and discussed.

Another idea for vocabulary instruction with emergent and beginning readers who are learning English is concept sorts (Bear et al., 2007). Concept sorts involve taking a set of pictures or small objects and having students divide them into related groups. For instance, a set of animal pictures can be sorted by those with hair or without hair; those that swim, walk, or fly; big animals or small animals; or any other number of features. Students do not need to know the English vocabulary to be able to sort their pictures, but working with the visuals provides a rich opportunity for them to express the English words they know and ask language mentors for the labels they do not. When teachers listen to students describe their sorts, teachers have the opportunity to assess each student's vocabulary needs. Concept sorts encourage participation and sharing, build on student background knowledge, and provide scaffolding in the form of visual support. They can be used with students learning English at the upper grades as well, and the thematic topics can be adjusted to grade-level content.

The transitional grades. As students become better readers, their reading texts at the second- and third-grade level contain more challenging words. The vocabulary activities suggested for early grade students are still effective at this level, but a new opportunity now arises to help students learn vocabulary through their own reading materials. For transitional readers—no longer word-by-word beginning readers, but still not yet completely independent—I discuss two instructional activities that reflect effective principles from the vocabulary research: building vocabulary within book discussion groups and word study examining early spelling–meaning connections.

When students read books in small groups or book clubs (cf. McMahon & Raphael, 1997), words can be examined in meaningful and interesting contexts. After students read a section of their book, they meet to share thoughts and questions about the content and to address related class assignments. As part of the book club or reading group, teachers can ask students to keep track of words that they think are tricky or assign an individual student to lead the group in focusing on specific vocabulary words. For instance, a student reading *The Polar Express* (Van Allsburg, 1985) may draw attention to the interesting words *nougat, barren*, and *Great Polar Ice Cap*. Teachers can also add important conceptual words to the group's discussion to ensure that all students have the language to engage with the book's theme.

As described in Table 9.1, students at the transitional stage of reading are working with word-pattern spellings, such as those of long vowel words. This is an excellent time to provide focused instruction on the different meanings and spellings of homophones such as *meat/meet* or *tide/tied*. In word study-groups, students can match homophone pairs and share the words' distinct meanings by using them in sentences or illustrating them, while at the same time investigating and sorting the words by vowel patterns. For instance, homophones could be sorted by spelling pattern as in

- Vowel-consonant-*e* as in *male, bare,* and *tide* as compared with vowel-vowel-consonant as in *mail, bear,* and *tied*
- Spelling patterns for a specific long vowel, such as *ea* as in *cheap, dear, jeans, meat,* and *heal,* compared with *ee* as in *wee, deer, meet, heel* or the spelling of *genes* or *we*

For additional visual support, homophone pairs can be noted on charts and lists in the classroom and in students' personal picture dictionaries. These lists will aid students as they expand their writing vocabulary. It is hoped that students' beginning explorations of the spelling–meaning connection will infuse the classroom with a contagious excitement about word learning that may expand into studying synonyms, antonyms, and idioms at this stage as well.

Upper elementary grades. As English learners become intermediate readers, the academic vocabulary demands of their texts will likely be the greatest obstacles to their proficient reading. A teacher's scaffolding of important content area vocabulary is essential to comprehension. In their book on scaffolded reading experiences, Fitzgerald and Graves (2004) outline in detail procedures for supporting English learners before, during, and after text reading. The upper grades are also an important time to give students tools to take words apart by their meaningful chunks—morphemic analysis—and to provide students with explicit support in connecting cognates in their home language to English words, as described below.

Provide opportunities for students to identify and work with base words, word roots, and affixes. Start with simple prefixes or suffixes such as *un-, re-,* or *-ful.* Discuss what the word part means and help students create new words with it. For example, the suffix *-ful* means "an amount that fills." Guide students to create words using this suffix such as *hopeful, painful,* or *mouthful,* and discuss how the suffix changes the meaning of the word. Continue introducing and analyzing common affixes and helping students to build as many words as they can come up with. Have students work together to brainstorm, keep ongoing lists in their notebooks, and post charts in the classroom. Provide simple dictionaries and reference books that give students access to the meanings of word parts. After students are successful at coming up with sample words, guide them to use their skills to take apart words. For example, show students the word *replace*. Can they find two meaningful parts in that word? (*re-* and *place*). What can they predict about the meaning of the word? What about the word *replacement*? How does adding *-ment* to the end change the word's meaning? Helping students to build and take apart words containing multiple morphemes is an excellent strategy to extend word learning in their independent reading.

Several of the research studies noted in this chapter support explicit instruction with Spanish speakers on identifying cognates. For example, students can be asked to review a section of their content area reading text and note words that they think have cognates. A passage on nutrition, for example, may spark associations with the following cognates for Spanish speakers: *calorie/caloria, carbohydrate/carbohidrato, nutrient/ nutriente,* and *vitamin/vitamina.* Discussions of these cognate pairs help students apply knowledge in their home language to the work of comprehending English texts. Keep track of cognates from important content material on charts in the classroom or in the students' notebooks. Connect cognate study to learning about the Latin and Greek roots of words. For example, students with Latinate home languages such as Spanish will be able to contribute information about vocabulary words such as *arboretum* by connecting the Spanish word *árbol,* related to the Latin word *arbor.* Extensive lists of cognates exist in published sources such as NTC's *Dictionary of Spanish Cognates* (Nash, 1997). These reference materials are invaluable for helping students to apply the important background knowledge they have to their academic reading in English. (See also Chapter 5, this volume, for further discussion of using cognates in vocabulary instruction.)

How Can Vocabulary Learning Be Integrated Into All Areas of the Curriculum?

An effective vocabulary program extends beyond the instructional time in which a set of words is explicitly taught. An atmosphere of interest and engagement with words, a "word consciousness," must be cultivated so that students are motivated to learn words outside of directed lessons (Graves, 2006; Scott & Nagy, 2004). The tone of a classroom, the ways of interacting within its community of learners, and the way the physical environment supports an interest in learning about words are all key aspects of developing language and vocabulary. The following is a list of suggestions for encouraging English learners to reflect upon, engage with, and appreciate words throughout the curriculum and the school day.

Focus on meaning. Do students comprehend the content of the instruction, whether that be a read-aloud story, a textbook chapter, or the words in their spelling program? How can you tell? Check for understanding in numerous ways throughout the day. Don't ever abandon meaning to simply teach a skill. Students can easily get into the habit of going through the motions—for example reading a passage quickly without understanding it—if they don't think that comprehension is being valued. Provide ways for students to let you know if they don't understand what they are hearing or reading without feeling singled out. Once you get to know the language proficiency levels of your students, take the time to preteach and discuss words that you suspect will be critical to their understanding.

Create safe environments for students to talk and use their growing English. As students interact, they cement their vocabulary and other language capabilities. Some students are not as verbal as others. Encourage all students to add their voices in class whether through partner sharing, small-group interactions, games, creative dramatics, or dictating or reading their personal stories. Listen to what students say to informally assess their vocabulary needs in specific content areas.

Provide a word-rich physical environment for students to learn new vocabulary. Label important objects in the classroom such as tools used in science studies. Post charts with important words and directions for student reference. Display content area words with matching visuals in word banks. Supply easy reference materials such as picture dictionaries, rhyming dictionaries, cognate lists, bilingual dictionaries, and thematically organized encyclopedias so that students have access to words, meanings and spellings. Organize classroom library materials so that students can easily access thematic books and literary genres.

Model an excitement and curiosity about words. Think out loud about interesting or unknown words. Show students how you use reference materials to find out more about a word. Make connections to how words are used across curricular areas. Have students look for examples of the words they are studying outside the classroom. Play games and make simple jokes involving word plays. Help English learners understand idioms and the multiple meanings of words that inspire this humor. Notice and appreciate when students use delightful vocabulary in their speech or writing.

How Can Teachers Modify Their Instruction for Students With Various Levels of English Proficiency to Build Up All Students' Vocabularies?

English learners enter elementary school classrooms with a wide range of oral proficiency in English. What is comprehensible to an early advanced student of English will likely be beyond the understanding of a beginning level English learner. How then might teachers accommodate their vocabulary instruction to students of various levels—challenging all but not overwhelming any? Key ideas of effective vocabulary instruction discussed throughout this chapter include meaningful contexts, in-depth instruction, student participation and discourse, scaffolding content, and teaching word-learning strategies. These ideas once again serve as useful guidelines to assist teachers in differentiating vocabulary instruction for English learners.

Begin at the beginning. Newcomers or other students at the beginning level of proficiency in English need particular instruction focusing on basic vocabulary and survival English. These students will profit from shorter lessons focusing on fewer words at a time with plenty of repetition and review. Efforts should be made to preview, review, and possibly translate key vocabulary from content area lessons for beginning speakers. When possible, partner newcomers with a language buddy who can discuss the content in the student's home language. In other words, provide as many life rings as possible so the student doesn't sink.

Become a sheltered-instruction teacher. The more you scaffold your teaching, the more likely your instruction will be understandable to students at a variety of oral proficiency levels. Sheltered strategies include speaking with clear, easy-to-understand language and using visuals, manipulatives, or physical actions to make your content more comprehensible. Sheltered instruction also involves organizing the content in thematic or other meaningful ways, designing group work, and creating opportunities for social interaction among students (Echevarria, Vogt, & Short, 2000; Genesee et al., 2005; Peregoy & Boyle, 2001). Consider making a list of sheltered strategies and keeping track of how many you will use as you plan and implement vocabulary and literacy lessons. Sheltered instruction supports all students' learning, and it is an absolutely essential practice to provide English learners with access to the curriculum.

Foster a community of language learners. An excellent way to provide differentiated vocabulary instruction is to enlist the resources of all members of your classroom and school community. Create an atmosphere in class in which students feel included and expected to excel. Make the classroom a safe place to experiment and grow with language without fear of being laughed at. Help all students become mentors—those who speak more English serve as supports to beginning speakers and all students' home languages become resources to share with the group. As the classroom leader, show students how to support the learning of their peers without doing their work for them. Demonstrate that you value their role as co-teachers. When you are not familiar with the home languages of your students, bring in family members or community members to talk about their languages and cultures. Ask community members to share stories and vocabulary related to current units of study in the classroom. Take the concept of word consciousness and transform it into "language consciousness"—an interest and motivation to learn about words in many languages and get to know the people who speak them.

Be aware of overload. An important aspect of delivering effective instruction is knowing how much is enough. Differentiating vocabulary instruction for English learners may not only mean providing more scaffolding, it may also mean controlling the number of words or the length of time of each lesson for specific students. While you teach, notice when English learners seem to fill up with new words or content. For instance, beginning English speakers may do well to focus on about three new words at a time, whereas intermediate speakers may be fine with 5–7, and advanced speakers with 7–10 (Helman & Burns, in press). If you can provide small-group instruction for students at similar proficiency levels, you can adjust the length of lessons accordingly. If you are presenting lessons with heterogeneous groups of English learners, find ways to accommodate students' language levels in your expectations, perhaps giving beginners a reduced list of focus vocabulary words. Provide many opportunities within the lesson for students to process the information with peers or apply their learning independently.

Reach for the stars, but prioritize. The research tells us that high expectations and in-depth content instruction are critical to the academic success of linguistically diverse students (Au, 2006; CREDE, 2002; Echevarria, Short, & Powers, 2006; Genesee et al., 2005). In your classroom, work diligently to help all students meet high standards, and positively communicate your vision of their coming success. At the same time you hold high aspirations for English-learning students, know that not all standards are "created equal." Assess your students informally to understand their language and literacy strengths and compare these with your grade-level goals. What skills and strategies will give students the most power to be successful in many aspects of their academic work? A priority area could be a specific reading skill such as more automatic recognition of high frequency words, knowledge of key vocabulary words in a math or science unit, or learning how to extract important information from non-fiction texts. Discuss your priorities with colleagues, students, and their family members and see what they have to add. Find ways for students to monitor and demonstrate progress, such as through graphs, portfolios, and personal checklists. Share accomplishments in the classroom and in communications with families. Help students know that you believe in them, and that you will do whatever you can to help them succeed.

What Materials Will Support Vocabulary Learning in the Classroom?

A word-rich physical environment can heighten vocabulary learning for students and serve as an extra pair of hands for the teacher. Print in the form of labels, word cards, posters and charts, reference books, and so on are often so well-used in the classroom that they wear out and need to be periodically replaced. The following is a suggested shopping list of possible print materials that your English learners will find extremely helpful. The particular materials you need vary depending on the developmental level and English proficiency of your students:

- Desktop reference materials for students such as picture alphabets and letter–sound charts
- Visual reference materials such as illustrated encyclopedias and picture dictionaries
- Small picture cards to use in concept sorts (see Bear et al., 2007, for examples)
- Pocket charts and photograph libraries to display and label items relating to thematic studies and new vocabulary words

- Illustrated word books that show photographs and labels around thematic topics (see *My Big Animal Book*, Priddy, 2002, as an example)
- Charts or posters illustrating and labeling thematic topics such as parts of the body or the solar system
- Manipulatives for storytelling such as flannel board pieces, props, or small plastic objects
- Puzzles with pieces that connect a picture and the object's name
- Bilingual puzzles connecting words in students' home languages and English
- Picture books from students' home languages so students can identify vocabulary words
- Longer texts in students' home languages for their independent reading
- Magazines with interesting pictures to prompt storytelling
- Nonfiction books on the topics the class is studying that are easier to read and contain more visuals than typical materials for that grade level
- Picture books that expand students' understanding of words, such as *Many Luscious Lollipops* (Heller, 1998)
- Cognate dictionaries for your students' home languages and English
- Bilingual dictionaries for the languages your students speak
- Cards, posters, or books with Latin and Greek roots and their meanings
- References for word derivations and etymologies such as *The Concise Oxford Dictionary of English Etymology* (Hoad, 2003)
- Lists of useful website addresses for research or word study (for home or school use)
- Technology support such as a projector to display the computer screen
- Computer programs for word learning and matching
- Composition books for students to use as word study or vocabulary notebooks to record their word lists of all kinds

The items listed above serve both as reference materials for students and as discussion starters. Students will use them to help explain things for which they don't yet have the words and, as a teacher, you will find them indispensable for clarifying what you are communicating to students.

Conclusions

Developing a broad and deep vocabulary repertoire in English is critical to the academic success of English learners in U.S. schools. While there is extensive research on effective vocabulary instruction for native speakers of English, the research base with English learners is much smaller. Many instructional strategies used with native speakers are likely to be effective with English learners as well, but will need to be adapted to accommodate students' specific strengths and background knowledge.

In the vocabulary research reviewed in this chapter, effective programs used instructional procedures such as choosing useful and interesting words presented in meaningful contexts, providing in-depth instruction over time with repetition and application tasks outside of the classroom, scaffolding instruction through sheltered techniques, building on students' background languages and finding cognates, encouraging participation and interactions with fellow students, and teaching strategies for word learning like structural analysis. These key procedures help teachers select and plan effective vocabulary instruction in their own classrooms.

The chapter answered some specific questions about how to help English learners acquire basic and academic vocabulary words both in and out of their literacy instruction, such as how to select important words for vocabulary study, depending on students' levels of English proficiency. I also provided example activities at the early, transitional, and upper elementary grades that reflected key ideas from the research base. I encouraged teachers to integrate vocabulary learning into all areas of the curriculum focusing on meaning, providing a safe environment for students to talk, providing a word-rich environment, and modeling an excitement and curiosity about interesting words.

In the final sections, I gave examples of how teachers can modify their instruction for students at various English proficiency levels by following research-based instructional principles. Teachers provide extra support to beginning English learners by adjusting the quantity and focusing on priority vocabulary words. Sheltered instructional techniques are used to make the instruction more comprehensible. A community of word learners is fostered that relies on all students' participation and high expectations. I ended with a suggested list of materials teachers might obtain to support oral and written vocabulary teaching in their elementary-grade classrooms.

As English learners become a larger percentage of students in elementary classrooms across the country, it is critical to build on the small research base relating to what vocabulary instruction works best for them. The field needs research that explores the specifics of effective vocabulary instruction as it relates to students at each level of reading and oral proficiency development. For instance, at what reading and language proficiency level is instruction in cognates most effective? How can early grade teachers best support the academic vocabulary learning needs that students will confront in the upper elementary grades? How can teachers at many grade levels, not just the early grades, learn how to best work with students who enter class with limited formal schooling and beginning-level skills in English?

This chapter has outlined many issues in vocabulary instruction with elementary-age English learners. It provides teachers with ideas for planning classroom instructional programs that incorporate research-based principles of effective vocabulary instruction. I encourage you to enjoy the journey as you lead students to learning about words and languages through systematic, meaningful, research-based vocabulary instruction in your teaching.

Questions for Discussion

1. Think about a time you tried to learn words in a new language, perhaps when you visited another country. What techniques did you find helpful for remembering new vocabulary? What, if any, of these techniques might be applicable to support English learners' vocabulary development in your classroom?

2. Find a paragraph of text in Spanish, either from the Internet or a book or periodical. Read through the words looking for cognates. When you see a possible cognate write it down along with your prediction about its meaning. Discuss your list of possible cognates with a partner.

3. Take a reading or writing lesson plan from a teacher's manual at your students' grade level. Highlight vocabulary words that you think would be challenging for students learning English. Now list four ways that you could scaffold the lesson to make it more comprehensible to your students.

4. Consider the word-study or spelling program used at your students' grade level. Make a list of words that English learners may find difficult to understand. How could you supplement the word study with rich instruction or print materials to support your students' learning?

REFERENCES

Au, K.H. (2006). *Multicultural issues and literacy achievement.* Mahwah, NJ: Erlbaum.

August, D., & Hakuta, K. (1997). *Improving schooling for language-minority children: A research agenda.* Washington, DC: National Academy Press.

August, D., & Shanahan, T. (Eds.). (2006). *Developing literacy in second-language learners: Report of the National Literacy Panel on Language Minority Children and Youth.* Mahwah, NJ: Erlbaum.

Baker, S.K., Gersten, R., Haager, D., & Dingle, M. (2006). Teaching practice and the reading growth of first-grade English learners: Validation of an observation instrument. *The Elementary School Journal, 107*(2), 199–219.

Bear, D.R., & Helman, L. (2004). Word study for vocabulary development in the early stages of literacy learning: Ecological perspectives and learning English. In J.F. Baumann & E.J. Kame'enui (Eds.), *Vocabulary instruction: Research to practice* (pp. 139–158). New York: Guilford.

Bear, D.R., Helman, L., Templeton, S., Invernizzi, M., & Johnston, F. (2007). *Words their way with English learners: Word study for phonics, vocabulary, and spelling instruction.* Upper Saddle River, NJ: Pearson Prentice Hall.

Bear, D.R., Invernizzi, M., Templeton, S., & Johnston, F. (2008). *Words their way: Word study for phonics, vocabulary, and spelling instruction* (4th ed.). Upper Saddle River, NJ: Prentice Hall.

Beck, I.L., & McKeown, M.G. (2007). Increasing young low-income children's oral vocabulary repertoires through rich and focused instruction. *The Elementary School Journal, 107*(3), 251–271.

Beck, I.L., Perfetti, C.A., & McKeown, M.G. (1982). The effects of long-term vocabulary instruction on lexical access and reading comprehension. *Journal of Educational Psychology, 74*(4), 506–521.

Biemiller, A. (2004). Teaching vocabulary in the primary grades: Vocabulary instruction needed. In J.F. Baumann & E.J. Kame'enui (Eds.), *Vocabulary instruction: Research to practice* (pp. 28–40). New York: Guilford.

Biemiller, A., & Boote, C. (2006). An effective method for building meaning vocabulary in primary grades. *Journal of Educational Psychology, 98*(1), 44–62.

Blachowicz, C.L.Z., Fisher, P.J., Ogle, D., & Watts-Taffe, S.M. (2006). Vocabulary: Questions from the classroom. *Reading Research Quarterly, 41*(4), 524–539.

Calderón, M., August, D., Slavin, R.E., Duran, D., Madden, N., & Cheung, A. (2005). Bringing words to life in classrooms with English-language learners. In E.H. Hiebert & M.L. Kamil (Eds.), *Teaching and learning vocabulary: Bringing research to practice* (pp. 115–136). Mahwah, NJ: Erlbaum.

California Department of Education. (1999). Content standards: English language development, English version. Retrieved April 15, 2007, from www.cde.ca.gov/be/st/ss

Carlo, M.S., August, D., McLaughlin, B., Snow, C.E., Dressler, C., Lippman, D.N., et al. (2004). Closing the gap: Addressing the vocabulary needs of English-language learners in bilingual and mainstream classrooms. *Reading Research Quarterly, 39*(2), 188–215.

Center for Research on Education, Diversity & Excellence (CREDE). (2002). *Research evidence: Five standards for effective pedagogy and student outcomes* (Technical Report No. G1). Santa Cruz: University of California.

Cheung, A., & Slavin, R.E. (2005). Effective reading programs for English language learners and other language-minority students. *Bilingual Research Journal, 29*(2), 241–267.

Cummins, J. (2003). Reading and the bilingual student: Fact and friction. In G.G. García (Ed.), *English learners: Reaching the highest level of English literacy* (pp. 2–33). Newark, DE: International Reading Association.

Cunningham, A.E., & Stanovich, K.E. (1997). Early reading acquisition and its relationship to reading experience and ability 10 years later. *Developmental Psychology, 33*(6), 934–935.

Dutro, S., & Moran, C. (2003). Rethinking English language instruction: An architectural approach. In G.G. García (Ed.), *English learners: Reaching the highest level of English literacy* (pp. 227–258). Newark, DE: International Reading Association.

Dufra, M., & Voeten, M.J.M. (1999). Native language literacy and phonological memory as prerequisites for learning English as a foreign language. *Applied Psycholinguistics, 20*(3), 329–348.

Echevarria, J., Short, D., & Powers, K. (2006). School reform and standards-based education: A model for English-language learners. *The Journal of Educational Research, 99*(4), 195–210.

Echevarria, J., Vogt, M.E., & Short, D.J. (2000). *Making content comprehensible for English language learners: The SIOP model.* Boston: Allyn & Bacon.

Fitzgerald, J., & Graves, M.F. (2004). *Scaffolding reading experiences for English-language learners.* Norwood, MA: Christopher-Gordon.

García, G.E. (1991). Factors influencing the English reading test performance of Spanish-speaking Hispanic children. *Reading Research Quarterly, 26*(4), 371–392.

Genesee, F., Lindholm-Leary, K., Saunders, W., & Christian, D. (2005). English language learners in U.S. schools: An overview of research findings. *Journal of Education for Students Placed at Risk, 10*(4), 363–385.

Gersten, R., & Jiménez, R.T. (1994). A delicate balance: Enhancing literature instruction for students of English as a second language. *The Reading Teacher, 47*(6), 438–449.

Graves, M.F. (2006). *The vocabulary book.* New York: Teachers College Press.

Helman, L.A., & Burns, M.S. (in press). What does oral language have to do with it? Helping young English-language learners acquire a sight word vocabulary. *The Reading Teacher, 62*(1).

Henderson, E.H. (1981). *Learning to read and spell: The child's knowledge of words.* DeKalb, IL: Northern Illinois Press.

Hoad, T.F. (2003). *The concise Oxford dictionary of English etymology.* Oxford: Oxford University Press.

Jiménez, R.T., García, G.E., & Pearson, P.D. (1996). The reading strategies of bilingual Latino/a students who are successful English readers: Opportunities and obstacles. *Reading Research Quarterly, 31*(1), 90–112.

Kamil, M.L., & Hiebert, E.H. (2005). Teaching and learning vocabulary: Perspectives and persistent issues. In E.H. Hiebert & M.L. Kamil (Eds.), *Teaching and learning vocabulary: Bringing research to practice* (pp. 1–23). Mahwah, NJ: Erlbaum.

McGregor, K.K. (2004). Developmental dependencies between lexical semantics and reading. In C.A. Stone, E.R. Silliman, B.J. Ehren, & K. Apel (Eds.), *Handbook of language and literacy: Development and disorders* (pp. 302–317). New York: Guilford.

McMahon, S.I., & Raphael, T. (1997). *The book club connection: Literacy learning and classroom talk*. New York: Teachers College Press.

Nagy, W.E. (1997). On the role of context in first- and second-language vocabulary learning. In N. Schmitt & M. McCarthy (Eds.), *Vocabulary: Description, acquisition and pedagogy* (pp. 64–83). Cambridge: Cambridge University Press.

Nagy, W.E., García, G.E., Durgunoglu, A.Y., & Hancin-Bhatt, B. (1993). Spanish-English bilingual students' use of cognates in English reading. *Journal of Reading Behavior, 25*(3), 241–259.

Nagy, W.E., & Scott, J.A. (2000). Vocabulary processes. In M.L. Kamil, P.B. Mosenthal, P.D. Pearson, & R. Barr (Eds.), *Handbook of reading research* (Vol. 3, pp. 269–284). Mahwah, NJ: Erlbaum.

Nash, R. (1997). *NTC's dictionary of Spanish cognates thematically organized*. Lincolnwood, IL: NTC Publishing Group.

National Center for Education Statistics. (2005). *Reading assessment*. Retrieved April 19, 2007, from nces.ed.gov/nationsreportcard/itemmaps/?year=2005&grade=4&subj=Reading.

National Center for Education Statistics. (2006). *The condition of education 2006*. NCES 2006-071. Washington, DC: U.S. Government Printing Office. Retrieved April 19, 2007, from nces.ed.gov/pubsearch/pubsinfo.asp?pubid=2006071.

National Institute of Child Health and Human Development. (2000). *Report of the National Reading Panel. Teaching children to read: An evidence-based assessment of the scientific research literature on reading and its implications for reading instruction* (NIH Publication No. 00-4769). Washington, DC: U.S. Government Printing Office.

Peregoy, S.F., & Boyle, O.F. (2001). *Reading, writing, and learning in ESL: A resource book for K–12 teachers*. New York: Longman.

Pérez, E. (1981). Oral language competence improves reading skills of Mexican American third graders. *The Reading Teacher, 35*(1), 24–27.

Rayner, K., Foorman, B.R., Perfetti, C.A., Pesetsky, D., & Seidenberg, M.S. (2001). How psychological science informs the teaching of reading. *Psychological Science in the Public Interest, 2*(2), 31–74.

Roberts, T.A. (2008). Home storybook reading in primary or second language with preschool children: Evidence of equal effectiveness for second-language vocabulary acquisition. *Reading Research Quarterly, 42*(2), 103–130.

Saunders, W., & Goldenberg, C. (2001). Strengthening the transition in transitional bilingual education. In D. Christian & F. Genesee (Eds.), *Bilingual education* (pp. 41–56). Alexandria, VA: Teachers of English to Speakers of Other Languages.

Scott, J.A., & Nagy, W.E. *(2004). Developing word consciousness*. In J.F. Baumann & E.J. Kame'enui (Eds.), *Vocabulary instruction: Research to practice* (pp. 201–217). New York: Guilford.

Shanahan, T., & Beck, I.L. (2006). Effective literacy teaching for English-language learners. In D. August & T. Shanahan (Eds.), *Developing literacy in second-language learners:*

Report of the National Literacy Panel on Language Minority Children and Youth (pp. 415–488). Mahwah, NJ: Erlbaum.

Snow, C.E., Burns, M.S., & Griffin, P. (Eds.). (1998). *Preventing reading difficulties in young children.* Washington, DC: National Academy Press.

Vaughn-Shavuo, F. (1990). *Using story grammar and language experience for improving recall and comprehension in the teaching of ESL to Spanish-dominant first-graders.* Unpublished doctoral dissertation, Hofstra University, New York.

Verhoeven, L.T. (1990). Acquisition of reading in a second language. *Reading Research Quarterly, 25*(2), 90–114.

LITERATURE CITED

Heller, R. (1998). *Many luscious lollipops: A book about adjectives.* New York: Putnam.

Kasza, K. (1987). *The wolf's chicken stew.* New York: Putnam.

Priddy, R. (2002). *My big animal book.* New York: St. Martin's.

Van Allsburg, C. (1985). *The polar express.* Boston: Houghton Mifflin.

Author Index

Subject Index

Page numbers followed by *f* indicate figures; those followed by *t* indicate tables.

I

IDENTIFICATION: and content area vocabulary, 171–172
IDENTITY: and academic language, 195–198
INCIDENTAL MORPHEME ANALYSIS, 97–99, 173
INCIDENTAL WORD LEARNING, 33; in content areas, 162
INDIVIDUAL ACTIVITIES: on word roots, 24–28
INDIVIDUAL WORDS, INSTRUCTION ON, 56–79; in content areas, 163–165; Questions for Discussion on, 74–75
INFORMAL WORD LEARNING, 32–55; definition of, 32–33
INFORMATIONAL TEXTS: content area vocabulary and, 152; and vocabulary learning, 153–154; for vocabulary visits, 40
INSTRUCTIONAL ACTIVITIES: for ELLs, 221–226; on word roots, 17–24
INTEGRATION: and content-area vocabulary instruction, 167–168
INTENTIONAL VOCABULARY INSTRUCTION: for ELLs, word selection for, 220–221
INTRODUCTORY VOCABULARY INSTRUCTION, 71–73; in content areas, 137
IQ: vocabulary and, 82

J

JOKES, 46–49
JUMBLES, 46

K

KEYWORD VOCABULARY, 95–96
KRAUSS, ROBERT, 93

L

LANGUAGE ACQUISITION: social relationships and, 193–198
LANGUAGE BUDDIES, 220
LANGUAGE CONSCIOUSNESS: for ELLs, 229
LANGUAGE EXPERIENCES: and content-area vocabulary instruction, 161–163
LATIN WORD ROOTS: prevalence of, 6; in science vocabulary, 159; and vocabulary instruction, 6–31
LEARNING STRATEGIES: definition of, 83; instruction in, vocabulary and, 82–85
LEVELING WORDS, 9
LINGUISTIC ATTENTION: and content area vocabulary, 172–173
LINGUISTIC DIVERSITY: Questions for Discussion on, 203–204; and vocabulary instruction, 182–210
LINK, IMAGINE, NOTE, CONSTRUCT, SELF-INTEREST (LINCS), 171–172, 172f
LIST: in vocabulary instruction, 89
LIST-GROUP-LABEL AND WRITE, 168, 169f
LITERACY: school, vocabulary for, 8–9, 106–129
LITERARY VOCABULARY, 108, 109t, 111
LOOK UP: in vocabulary instruction, 89

M

MATERIALS: for ELLs, 230–232
MATHEMATICS: vocabulary in, 157–158
METACOGNITION: and content area vocabulary, 173–175
METALINGUISTIC STRATEGIES: and academic vocabulary, 186–193, 201; application of, 192–193; concepts in, 16f; word play and, 43–44; and word roots, 11
MIDDLE GRADES: content-area vocabulary instruction in, 150–181; roots for, 15–16, 15t; word root instruction in, 6–31

MORPHEME CIRCLES, 173, 174*f*

MORPHEMES/MORPHOLOGY, 97–99; and academic vocabulary, 113–114; and academic vocabulary instruction, 116–119; and content-area vocabulary instruction, 160, 165–166; for diverse audiences, 188–189; importance of, 123–124

MOTIVATION: and vocabulary instruction, 32–55

MOTOR IMAGING, 93–95, 95*t*

MULTICULTURAL APPROACHES: to academic vocabulary instruction, 196–197

MULTIPLE-MEANING WORDS: clarification and, 168–171; coding, 170–171, 171*f*; in content areas, 133–134, 156; for diverse audiences, 191–192

N

NAME RIDDLES, 48

NEW WORDS: strategies for, 187–188

NO CHILD LEFT BEHIND ACT: on vocabulary, 56

NONFICTION TEXTS. *See* informational texts

O

ODD WORD OUT, 20–22, 21*f*

ORAL VOCABULARY: versus academic vocabulary, 106–107, 185; building, 62–65; for English-language learners, 219–220; growth of, 60

ORTHOGRAPHIC DEVELOPMENT: levels of, and word study focus, 222*t*

OVERLOAD: ELLs and, 229

P

PARTICIPATION: active, in read-alouds, 35–36

PEER TECHNIQUE, 36–37

PLANNING GUIDELINES: research-based, 9–10; for word root instruction, 10–12

PLAY. *See* word play

POETRY: "where I'm from," 200–201

POLYSEMOUS WORDS. *See* multiple-meaning words

POSSIBLE SENTENCES, 99–100; for content area vocabulary, 140

POVERTY, CHILDREN OF: building oral vocabularies of, 62–65. *See also* achievement gap

PRACTICE: in vocabulary instruction, 89

PRIMARY GRADES: ELL vocabulary instruction in, 223–224

PUNS, 46–49

PUZZLES, 46

Q

QUESTIONS: in text talk, 37–38

QUESTIONS FOR DISCUSSION, 4; on academic vocabulary, 125–126; on content area vocabulary, 145, 176–177; on diversity, 203–204; on ELLs, 233–234; on individual word instruction, 74–75; on read-alouds and word-play, 50; on vocabulary-learning strategies, 102; on word root instruction, 29–30

R

READ-ALOUDS, 34–43; active participation in, 35–36; for ELLs, 223; Questions for Discussion on, 50; resources on, 49

READING: dialogic, 36–37; and vocabulary acquisition, 60

RECIPROCAL QUESTIONING, 83

RESEARCH ON VOCABULARY INSTRUCTION, 56–58, 182–183; on content area vocabulary, 135–136, 139–140, 152–167; on English-language learners, 212–217; on keyword method, 96; on morphological awareness, 117; on read-alouds, 34–35; on strategy instruction, 84; on word play, 43–44; and word root instruction, 9–10; on word-learning strategies, 80–81